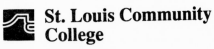

St. Louis Community College

Forest Park
Florissant Valley
Meramec

Instructional Resources
St. Louis, Missouri

Stunt Man

The future rodeo champion, top stunt man and leading action director
when he was still known as Enos Edward Canutt.

STUNT MAN

The autobiography of
Yakima Canutt

with
Oliver Drake

 WALKER AND COMPANY
NEW YORK

First published in the United States of America
in 1979 by the Walker Publishing Company, Inc.

Published simultaneously in Canada by Beaverbooks,
Limited, Pickering, Ontario.

ISBN: 0-8027-0613-4

Library of Congress Catalog Card Number: 78-58869

Designed by Irene Friedman

Printed in the United States of America

10   9   8   7   6   5   4   3   2   1

To my family . . .

Acknowledgment

The illustrations in *Stunt Man* are included by courtesy of Columbia Pictures, Inc., Metro-Goldwyn-Mayer Inc., TV Cinema Sales Corporation, United Artists Corporation, Universal Pictures, and Walt Disney Studios. Others are from the collection of Yakima Canutt.

Contents

Foreword

Though I didn't know it at the time I was always, like everyone else going to the movies in the Thirties and Forties, a fan of Yakima Canutt. Most of the heroics and hairbreadth escapes that filled the screen so richly then were performed by Yak, not by the actors whose exploits I thought I was watching.

By the time I came into films myself, Yak, having built the reputation he still holds as the best stunt man of them all, was building another career as a second unit director. His preeminence in this field, to no-one's surprise, is now as unchallengeable as is his record of falling off horses and wrecking stagecoaches. For twenty years and more, most of the action sequences in most of the pictures we remember for those sequences were directed by Yakima Canutt. I know; my films have profited as much as anyone's from his contributions.

I first met Yak on a chariot track outside Rome, some weeks before we began shooting on *Ben Hur*. I had asked for as much time as possible to learn to drive the chariot for the race sequence, a skill I had somehow failed to acquire in my youth. My first sight of Yak and the turmoil of his preparations for the race did little to improve my confidence. There was the practice track, churned to oatmeal by the Italian spring rains. Behind it was the track we'd actually use in filming, swarming with screaming Roman carpenters building the amphitheater. There were the hundred and more horses Yak had bought in Yugoslavia, still only sketchily broken to the four-abreast chariot harness he'd designed; there were the four drivers Yak had recruited in Italy, and the five he'd imported from the States. Among them was his younger son, Joe (who's since had enough hide skinned off doing hard falls for me to cover a dozen copies of this book). At that point he was spending all his time training four of the white horses used for Ben Hur's team to do the climactic shot in the race: jumping a wrecked chariot.

There, in the middle of all the Italian confusion, stood Yak, the classic figure of the laconic Westerner—cool and calm, watching the chariots skid through the turns. Of course he wore boots, jeans, and his thumb hooked in his back pockets, but he did NOT have a sombrero. Instead, he wore a black beret, the same one, as far as I know, he's worn on every film we've been on together. What's more, he was confident, not only about the race, but that I could learn to drive the bloody thing. When I expressed some misgivings about surviving the sequence, let alone triumphing in it, he reassured me. "Don't worry, Chuck," he said. "You just learn to drive the team. I guarantee you'll win the damn race."

We did. With patience, good humor, and amazing resourcefulness, he not only taught me to drive, but to enjoy it. Starting from the first uneasy ride with him at the reins, I progressed cautiously to some dual sessions with Yak standing behind, coaching me through the turns. I ended with an unaware solo in which I talked anxiously to him through the fastest lap I'd ever done, then, reassured by his silence, I thundered into the stretch only to see him standing, grinning at the first turn, where he'd stepped off just as I'd let the horses out.

He also kept the other drivers out of my somewhat erratic way (and me out of theirs) through three months of sweaty, dusty shooting on the scene and ended by giving me my win, just as he'd promised the first day. What's more, he created one of the finest action sequences ever filmed.

It is not only his work, but he, himself, who provides us all with a model of the finest kind of professional—the kind of man who always gives his best. In a time when, increasingly, nobody cares about excellence, Yak cares. A few years ago I was proud to present to him the Oscar that he surely earned if any man has. I'm proud to call him my friend.

Chuck Heston

ONE

The Race to Beat: BEN HUR

The lights went down, the room was quiet, and a line of mounted trumpeters dressed as ancient Romans sounded off on the silent screen.

I've been to the screenings of more films than I'd care to remember, but the circumstances of this particular showing were enough to keep me as alert as a pointer that's just spied game. Around me sat most of the M.G.M. studio brass. We were watching one segment of a silent film made in 1926 and everyone there was making notes in his head. I know that I was, even though I had already seen the entire film two or three times—the film was the M.G.M. spectacle, *Ben Hur*, and the segment that we were all focusing on was Breezy Eason's famous chariot race.

As a book written by General Lew Wallace and published in 1880, *Ben Hur* had broken all previous publishing sales records. As a play some twenty years later, it had been one of the most profitable productions in theatrical history, and as the earliest and most lavish of M.G.M.'s silent films (it had cost $5 million), it had become one of the studio's most popular and enduring films. In 1958 M.G.M. budgeted $15 million for its remake of this popular classic. It was going to be the most expensive film ever made until that time—they were planning to shoot in Italy, in color and Cinemascope. Charlton Heston was cast as the lead and an exciting newcomer, the late Stephen Boyd, would play Messala.

William Wyler, one of the industry's all-time greats, the Academy-award-winning director of *Mrs. Miniver* and *The Best Years of Our Lives*, was to direct the film.

Right up to his death in 1956, Eason had hoped to direct the chariot race himself. A shot in a film like this would be the opportunity of a lifetime and when Walter Strohm, the M.G.M. Production Chief, called me into his office to say that I was being considered to direct the chariot race, I was on cloud nine. By this time I had developed a reputation in the industry as a second unit director and had already worked for the producer, Sam Zimbalist, on *Mogambo*. I had just signed a short-term contract with M.G.M., but had never expected anything quite this big to land in my lap so soon. I was feeling pretty good when I dropped into the office of Henry Henixson, the General Manager of the picture, to discuss the overall details and make sure that the assignment went to me.

Henixson had just returned from Rome where he had arranged for space for the construction of the Colosseum and a training track and stables for the horses at the studio in Cinecitta. He was a dour, partially deaf man who, I found out, used his deafness to hear only what he wanted. Before coming to M.G.M., he had been General Manager for many years at Universal. Going over the details of the film with him soon brought me down to earth—this was one tough customer. He told me that he had already made all the arrangements to film the chariot race in Italy and that we could get what we needed there, including stunt drivers. Horses would be imported from Spain and Yugoslavia. Italy was short on good horses, I agreed, but I had grave doubts about trying to use Italian drivers.

I told him that I "filmed the second unit of *Helen of Troy* in Rome, and I used a number of two-horse chariots. In any complicated scenes I had to bring over English stunt men. The race in *Ben Hur* will have four horses to each chariot and the driving will be that much more hazardous. If we expect to get the thrilling effects we want, we'll need five or six key men from Hollywood, men who are not just good drivers but picturewise. To try a spectacular race with all Italian drivers would be disastrous. Believe me, Henry, I'd hate to be staging a wreck on the track and have ten Italian drivers coming at me!"

Henry gave me a patronizing look and turned his hearing aid down. "Don't worry about it, Yak," he replied, "I want to get things rolling as soon as possible. Listen, we're screening the race sequence out of the old *Ben Hur* this afternoon for some of the executives. Come look at it again. You may get some ideas."

That was the end of the interview. A few hours later I sat watching Eason's version with Henixson and the brass, my face screwed into a frown. I hadn't looked at this footage for a good twenty years, but this time around I was bringing to it the trained eye of an experienced action director. Eason's race was impressive, no doubt about it. In fact, I had worked with him on *Gone with the Wind, Man of Conquest* and countless Westerns and knew him to be a pro. Staging a chariot race involves some unique problems and I watched the film carefully, seeing how he designed his equipment, how he set up his wrecks, and where his stunt men and horses fell.

Breezy taught everyone who worked with him one very important lesson: it doesn't matter how great the stunt is, what matters is what gets on film. For the race in *Ben Hur*, he used eighteen cameras and forty-two cameramen and spent four months shooting over 200,000 feet of film. In the final version, the race scene uses only 750 feet of film. As I watched the film, I saw a lot of room for improvement. For one thing, he had taken too many unnecessary risks. There were safer and less expensive ways to stage the scene. I knew that I could stage a more spectacular race with a better safety factor. But I couldn't do it with Italian drivers.

The film ended, the lights came up and Ed Mannix, the Business Affairs Manager at the studio, looked at me with a questioning grin. "Well, Yak," he asked, "can you beat that race?" I returned his grin. "That's a straight question, so I'll answer it straight. Give me cooperation and the tools I need and I'll make that race look like Ned in a third-grade reader!"

Mannix shook his head. "You really think so?" I could feel Henixson glowering at me. "I mean exactly what I said." I had already come up with a list that I wanted to discuss with them but, before I could say anything else, Henixson said what I'm sure he thought was the last word. "I've already told Yak that we can get everything we need in Italy."

It's one thing to take orders, it's another to know what you need. I had made up my mind that if I couldn't do the race my way, I wasn't doing it at all—so far, my luck had been good in directing stunt sequences in other big pictures—I wasn't about to lead with my chin on this one.

"Henry, you'd better let me explain what we'll need," I said flatly. He was toying with his hearing aid, but I wasn't sure if he was turning it up or down. "I told you this morning that I've worked with men and chariots in Italy before. I can't film an exciting race with all Italian drivers. I want a few good men from here and I know who they are. I'll also need a good horse-trainer for the high-schooling of the *Ben Hur* team and for the horses that'll be rearing in full hook-up. We should have eighty good horses, two teams for each chariot. This way we can switch teams and bring in a good day's work without running them to death. All the chariots will have to be fitted with gooseneck tongues and low under-carriages so the horses can hug the end of the *spina* in fast, skidding turns. In the race you just saw all the turns were very wide with no real skids. There's a reason for that—when a horse makes a sharp turn he leans in and his legs hit the low tongue, so naturally he fights to make wider turns. These are the basic needs, the details I'll be happy to work out later."

There was a moment of silence, looks were exchanged, then the executives got to their feet and filed out, leaving me alone with Mannix and Henixson. "This is going to run into a lot of additional money," Mannix said. "I'll have to call a production meeting and see just how much your plans for the race will cost." He started away, then turned back. "Yak," he asked, "just what the hell is a *spina* and a gooseneck tongue?"

I chuckled and explained that a *spina* was the structure in the center of the Colosseum area that was twenty-five to thirty feet in width and extended to within one-hundred-and-fifty feet of either end of the arena. It was quite a striking piece of architecture, with giant Roman statuaries. A gooseneck tongue is just what it sounds like. The gooseneck is a kind of rod that connects the horses' harnesses to the chariot. It extends upwards from the front of the chariot for a few feet, then levels off so that the fore part swings above the horses' legs.

As we followed Mannix outside, Henixson dropped back to walk beside me. "Yak," he said irritably, "you certainly threw a wrench into the machine." "At least I didn't fall into it," I replied. "If I went over to Italy, did the race your way and it was a flop, who would get the blame? Not you!"

I still had a few weeks left on my contract, so the studio had me take the *Ben Hur* script and rewrite the race, adding additional thrills and wrecks. I designed a pattern for the harnesses that was a compromise between the collar type and breast-strap harness. I also lowered the under-carriages and gooseneck tongues of the chariots. These changes would create good skids without the danger of accidental pileups. While I was still at work on the script, the studio heads decided to postpone the picture until the following year. When my contract was up, I left the studio, more than a little disappointed at not being included in the project.

My agent had a call from the Walt Disney Studio. In 1956 I had directed the action in *Old Yeller*, a picture that has come to be a Disney classic. Disney was making the "Zorro" television series and Bill Anderson, Disney's top man, hired me to film second units for the two directors who were alternating on the series.

That fall news came that Mr. Zimbalist had engaged Andrew "Bunty" Marton to do the race in *Ben Hur*. I suspected that Henry Henixson blamed me for the picture being postponed, but I didn't think he would go that far. Any hope that I had in being recalled was now gone.

I was surprised to receive a call, a short time later, from M.G.M. with the message: Mr. Zimbalist would like to talk with you. He opened by explaining that he had hired Marton to oversee the race as an official second unit director. However, he would like to make a deal with me to take over the management of the race.

"In other words, a ramrod," I said.

He nodded. "Yes, that's the idea."

"Mr. Zimbalist," I said, "I've been directing for seven years now and have several spectacular jobs to my credit. You must know that two bosses on the same job just doesn't work. I have nothing against Marton. With the help of his special effects men, he's made some very good sea and war pictures. But from what I've seen and heard he knows nothing about horses. I also know that a ramrod takes orders which, in this case, I cannot accept. If I worked on the race at all, I would have to have full charge, pick my own drivers and shoot the race as I see it. I would only confer with Mr. Wyler. Also, I know that a ramrod gets less pay and I will not cut my salary."

Mr. Zimbalist insisted that I would be in full charge of the race, but I said that I didn't see how we could negotiate since I was still under a short-term contract to the Disney Studio. By the time it expired I did not see how I would have time to get the race properly set up for his shooting date.

"All I can say, Yak," Zimbalist replied, "is that we've already started putting your plan into action. Henixson has already sent the two men that you recommended to Yugoslavia to buy seventy horses—a Frenchman by the name of Nadal, and an Italian that worked with you on *Helen of Troy*. We're also sending the horse trainer you recommended, Glen Randall." He paused to let this sink in. "Can you get loose from your Disney deal?"

There is one rule that I never break: I never leave a job until it is either finished or I am released by the boss, and I told him as much. He said that he would call Disney and get back to me.

I left with somewhat mixed feelings. Doing the chariot race as a ramrod was to me like being given a new rifle and only being allowed to use it if someone else pulled the trigger. I went straight to my agent and told her what Zimbalist and I had discussed. I also told her what I wanted: my regular salary, a good expense account and my choice of drivers.

A day or two later Mr. Disney called me into his office and said he had received a call from M.G.M. I told him what it was all about, that it was very iffy, and that I would never leave the Disney studio without his okay.

"Yak," Mr. Disney said, "you continue working here. If you get a good deal with M.G.M., I'll release you."

Walt Disney was that kind of a man, always ready to do a favor. He believed in the old proverb, "Live and let live." His studio had the most congenial personnel in the industry. It was always a pleasure to work there.

A few days later I got a call from Mr. Zimbalist. He wanted to have a talk. I told him that I was sorry but I couldn't get away for a few days—was it anything that my agent could take care of?

"That's the trouble," he said. "I don't think your agent is handling things right for your own good." Mrs. Paul Small was my agent and, I might add, one of the best in the picture industry.

"What has she done wrong?" I asked.

"She wants a couple of clauses in the contract that the studio just won't accept."

"I'm sorry," I said. "I'm sure she hasn't asked for anything we didn't talk over, so I'll leave it up to her."

I was beginning to get disgusted with the whole deal. My agent finally called me.

"Yak," she said, "I have fought with M.G.M. for a week now. The money is all right but I don't believe they will go for a couple of clauses in the contract. They say that it would set a precedent for future contracts."

"Don't argue with them any longer," I said. "Just call and tell them if the contracts are not on your desk for me to sign tomorrow evening the deal is off and no maybe's." The next day she called. The contract was on her desk. That night I signed to do *Ben Hur*.

I left for Rome with an uneasy feeling. I knew that Henixson blamed me for the postponement of the picture and that the studio was unhappy with my contract. Never having worked with Marton, who would certainly be in a position to get into my hair, also worried me. Fortunately, throughout the filming of the race Marton stayed by the cameras and contented himself with hollering "action" and "cut." Of course, if we were shooting the principals, he naturally got involved. I found that my main interference was still Henry Henixson. He got into the act a couple of times. One of his decisions delayed the start of the race a couple of weeks and cost the studio several thousand dollars.

In Rome I stayed at the same hotel I had during the filming of *Helen of Troy*. I called the studio the next morning and Mr. Henixson asked me to join him at the Grand Hotel for dinner at eight. I met him in the lobby.

"Well, you got to them, didn't you?" he remarked coldly as we shook hands.

"That all depends on the way you look at it," I said. "I certainly got what I asked for."

We had dinner and he loosened up and seemed friendly. He told me seventy Lippizaner horses had arrived from Yugoslavia that morning and, according to Glen Randall, were in good shape.

At the studio the next day I looked them over and was pleased to find that all but eight or ten of them were Arabians. Some of them looked a little rough, but I knew that with good feed and care they would shape up in time for the race. I bought eight or ten more in Sicily and Italy. Glen Randall, the trainer, had the stables in order and had started high-schooling the whites for scenes with the first unit. When the training track was finished and three or four training chariots with harness were ready, I had my American drivers brought over from Hollywood. They were Ed Jauregua, Jerry Brown,

Cliff Lyons, Joe Yrigoyen and Joe Canutt, my youngest son who was to double Charlton Heston. Joe Yrigoyen was to double Stephen Boyd. Both Heston and Boyd put in what spare time they had, about three hours a day, learning how to drive the chariots.

Charlton Heston was one of the most cooperative men I have ever worked with. He was keen to learn and not afraid to work. From his second day in Rome, he came out to the training track every morning to practice. He loved horses and I knew immediately that we were going to hit it off. During the first three days we rode together and I taught him all the "dos" and "don'ts" of charioteering. It takes a good deal of courage to step into an open two-wheeled cab and try to control four horses that are running away from you. It taxes your body a lot more than driving a stagecoach where you're sitting down and you have the weight of the wagon to back you up. But Heston is a good athlete and he had a good feel for the horses. I couldn't have asked for better casting.

By the third day I was ready to just stand behind him as he went through a few figure eights, then a trot. As we neared the end of the track I told him to take it easy around the turn, then, as we came onto the straightaway, to put the team into a wide open run, skid around the far turn, and check them on the back straightaway. He nodded, set his jaw, rewrapped the reins around his hands and we were off. Just before he broke the team into a run I quietly stepped off the back of the chariot. The horses hit the far turn at full speed, the chariot went into a picture-perfect skid, Heston neatly pulled out of it and slowed down into a jog on the backstretch. His set face broke into astonishment when he saw me. He pulled the horses up short.

"What happened to you?" he cried.

"Chuck," I said smiling, "you've just soloed. From here on in, you're on your own." Few actors would have stood that test so well.

Stephen Boyd also came out to drive the teams. He got some blisters on his hands when he tried driving without gloves, but by the time we started shooting they were both good drivers. With cooperative principals like these, we could cut down on trick shots and get some great scenes when we hooked our camera cars to the chariots. In the film, you can see the principals themselves getting into wheel locks, skids, and even slamming their horses together. They made the job a pleasure and a real camaraderie developed among us.

William Wyler started shooting the first unit a few weeks ahead of us. Wyler is a director whom I've admired and always enjoyed working with. He expects his assistants to know what they're doing, but if they get into a tight spot, he's happy to help out. Wyler's involvement with *Ben Hur* dated back to the 1926 film—he was one of Eason's thirty assistants who helped direct the crowd reacting to the chariot race.

One day I was called into the studio to sit in on a meeting. The Colosseum was near completion and Henixson and Ed Carfagno, the art director, were going over how to build the race track. I had never been consulted on the track construction, but I certainly knew the kind of surface on which a horse could run best.

In the meeting they proposed taking the top soil off to a depth of three or four feet, then adding a layer of rocks and filling that with soil. This would create good drainage, they said, if we had any rainy weather. Finally, the track would be rolled well, then sand would be added to the surface.

I smelled disaster. I spoke up and said it would take more than a layer of rocks to create good drainage. Unless they put several feet of soil on top it could cause a shudder on the camera car which would hurt our travel shots. Then again, too much soil over the rocks would stop the drainage. I reminded them that I had worked in Rome this time of year and the rain was not as much a problem as the heat. I suggested Carfagno cultivate the surface, then level it, roll it, and top it with an inch of sand. Each evening after work the track should be dragged and sprinkled and a few loads of new sand should be moved in on call. I was sure the company would save time and money by doing it this way.

Nobody interrupted me while I was talking but when I finished, Zimbalist, the producer, said, "Yak, Henixson and Carfagno have had a lot of experience with this kind of work. I think they know what they're doing."

"Fine," I said, "I guess I can't be of any help here so if you will excuse me I'll get back to the training track."

Now don't get me wrong—Ed Carfagno is one of the top art directors in motion pictures and has many credits to prove it. It was Henixson's judgment and influence I questioned. I kept quiet but kept my eye on the track.

They dropped the rock drainage idea, plowed the track, dragged and rolled it, and covered it with an inch of sand. I figured they had decided to follow my plan until I saw workmen broadcasting what looked like cement over the surface. When that was finished they started sprinkling it with water. I went to Ed Carfagno and asked him if they were using cement on the track. He said they were. I told him that sprinkling it in the sand would turn the surface into solid cement. Ed only smiled and went on with his work. The next day they started hauling sand by the truck loads until it was several inches deep. No use complaining. We would have to try it out.

The training had gone fine. When we were ready for the race, Mr. Wyler brought out the principals. The first day was spent shooting the grand entrance of the charioteers, the grand march of the chariots, and teams around the track and up to the starting line. This was accomplished with a very simple trick. I had special effects take some small, flexible cable and make checks about three feet long and small metal snaps in each end. These were snapped on the bit of the outside horse of each team to the bit of the horse on the team next to it. This made the entire ten teams function as one team. The effect on the screen was great. Mr. Wyler finished all the shots up to the start of the race. These were mostly matte shots that left the upper part of the frame for the art director's ingenuity. The finished effects were magnificent. Ed Carfagno deserves a lot of credit. The second unit was to pick it up at the start of the race the following day.

The next morning we lined the teams up for the race. After several close cuts of horses rearing and drivers trying to control them, we finally gave the drivers the starting flag. Some got away easily but others were stymied by the deep sand. When they leaned on the turns, they would slip on the thin layer of cement under the sand. I had the drivers change teams a couple of times, but before noon the horses were practically dehydrated. I stopped work and told the wranglers to take the horses to the stables. I knew that if we kept on using the track as it was, we would lose a lot of horses. I sat down on the spina curb to thrash out the situation. I was upset and angry. I had tried to prevent just this kind of a situation from happening. Now we were in trouble, thanks to Henry Henixson! My first thought was to sack it, but I quickly decided against it. I decided to take this directly to Zimbalist. He was the boss and had put his okay on the plan. Just as I got up, a big limousine pulled alongside and stopped near the edge of the track. Sam Zimbalist got out and came over to me.

"Well, Yak," he asked, "how's the race going?"

I shrugged glumly. "Pretty bad, Mr. Zimbalist. Glad you showed up. I'd like to have you take a look at the horses. They're practically dehydrated from running on this track. I've worked all morning and haven't got a scene worth printing."

Zimbalist frowned. "What's the trouble?"

"The track is impossible. The chariot wheels sink in the deep sand and the teams can't get any speed on the turns. They skid on the thin layer of cement under the sand. If we go ahead with the shooting the way the track is, we'll injure a lot of horses and won't get a race worth a counterfeit dime!"

"Now is a great time to find out!" he barked. "Why wasn't I told of this earlier?"

"You *were* told about it earlier," I snapped, mad beyond caring about my job. "If you remember, I tried to tell you at the meeting a few weeks ago how the track should be built. You wouldn't listen to me."

Zimbalist stared at me silently for a moment, and I thought, "This is where I get fired from a job for the first time." Then he beckoned to his driver and ordered him to get Henixson and bring him to the track.

Henixson was in a black mood when he showed up. He must have learned what was up. As soon as he stepped out of the car, Zimbalist turned on him, "Yak says it's impossible to run horses on this track."

"There's nothing wrong with it," Henixson replied shortly, then whirled to glare at me. "I've talked with some of your drivers, and they say it's fine."

"Who've you talked to?"

"Jerry Brown for one . . ."

"I don't believe you!"

I turned to one of the men working on the track and asked him to get Jerry. When Jerry arrived I asked him bluntly: "Jerry, did you tell Henixson this track was good to work on?"

Jerry exploded with indignation. "I told him it was *no good* to work on," he said angrily, "and I'll say it again. The track is lousy!"

Henixson was shifting uneasily. He couldn't meet my eyes when I demanded to know the names of the other drivers who had told him that the track was okay.

"You say the horses slip on the cement," he growled. "Hell, I can stick my thumb through it."

I knelt down on the track and scraped away some sand, exposing the hard cement surface beneath it.

"Let me see you stick your thumb through this," I said.

With Sam Zimbalist silently looking on, Henixson had no choice but to try and bull it through. He poked his thumb hard against the cement. Not a dent. I raked the sand off another spot. He failed again. The scowl on his face grew as I turned to Jerry.

"Get Henixson a pick, Jerry," I said quietly.

Henixson started to bluster some more, but Zimbalist broke in coldly: "There's no use in arguing, Henry." Then he turned to me. "Yak, what can we do to make the track usable?"

"All the sand has to be removed," I answered, "and the cement taken out. Then it should be harrowed and rolled smooth. After that an inch of sand should be put back over the surface. If that's done, I guarantee you that I'll shoot one helluva race!"

The construction company took two weeks to do this and when they hauled the sand out and dumped it, it looked like the Sahara Desert.

Henry Henixson was what I would term a Jekyll-and-Hyde character. Being with him at a party or a dinner, he'd be full of fun and a real nice person to be around. He ignored our squabble over the track construction and was quite friendly during the rest of the shooting.

We shot the race without any further trouble. At this point Marton, the second unit director, was in Israel. He'd been sent there to shoot a prologue for the picture involving The Three Wise Men. When he returned, the footage was unusable and rejected. Zimbalist almost sent me to shoot the sequences over before it was decided to cut them. I couldn't see shooting in Israel, anyway. The horses and locations in Spanish Morocco were much better and closer. I was glad that I didn't have to get into another fight over that one.

When we were ready to start I had eleven drivers: five Americans and six Italians. All of them were fitted for contact lenses to keep the dust from their eyes, but once we started the race, I don't think that any of the drivers used them. I was very happy with my crew. We managed to stage many close misses, skids, wheel locks and three good wrecks without an injury to man or horse. Our only accident was when the Messala and the Ben Hur chariots were locked and Joe Yrigoyen's team knocked over a camera. Fortunately, nobody was hurt. Between scenes we dragged the track and sent a sprinkling tank around to keep it in shape. We also sprinkled it every night and morning to keep the dust and sand down.

The first wreck was to take place at the end of the spina, the spot where charioteers could skid their chariots dangerously close to the curb to gain a slight advantage. I had the special-effects man, Bob McDonald, set in a short, one-wheel ramp at the off corner of the turn, so that a driver, when hugging the turn, would hit this ramp with his inside wheel, and flip his chariot upside down. We also had a swivel connecting the gooseneck tongue to the chariot. This allowed the chariot to turn over and over without tangling the team and harness, so the horses could drag the wrecked chariot away, rolling and bouncing—a nice effect.

For all my comments about Italian stunt drivers I must say that they have courage. One driver in particular was very serious about his work. He had two brothers—one was in charge of the stables and worked with us as a horse wrangler, and the other was a lawyer. Knowing that their brother was going to do the first wreck, they were both on hand to wish him well and watch the event.

The spot for the wreck was well prepared with several inches of soft sand covering the track where the driver would land when thrown from the chariot. A thorough check had found everything in order. I looked over to see if the drivers were ready, and there, standing by the soon-to-be-wrecked chariot, were the three brothers with their heads bowed. They each made the sign of the cross, then the two gave their brother a big hug and kiss. He stepped into the chariot and waved that he was ready.

On the order of "action" the drivers got underway—this being the first turn after the start of the race, there were eleven chariots. (The story called for ten, but I slipped in the eleventh for this wreck. I did not want to cut the number too fast. This is a license often used in the name of showmanship.) The teams came racing around the end of the spina in a spectacular group—chariots skidding wildly with many near collisions, yet holding their given positions.

The driver who was doing the first wreck pulled his team in close to the curb, striking the ramp with the inside wheel, the chariot bounced into the air, flipped upside down and threw the driver end over end, right into the path of an oncoming team. The second driver swerved his chariot as planned, narrowly missing the downed man. Guards from the spina platform ran in, picked the driver up and carried him to safety. As we cut the scene, the driver's brothers and a few close friends ran to him, and for a minute or two it looked like the patch-up of a family feud—they kissed and hugged him and shook his hand.

Our second wreck was staged at the wall beneath the spectators' seats. Messala's chariot had steel blades projecting from the hubs of the heavy wheels. These blades not only looked vicious, they worked. We only used them in close shots, actually cutting the spokes from a chariot's wheels and causing a wreck. However, in all other scenes we used substitutes made of heavy rubber.

In this scene, Messala doubled by Joe Yrigoyen, slammed his powerful black horses against Ben Hur's white Arabian team, throwing them off stride. He then urged his team ahead so that the vicious wheel blades could try to cut the whites down. This forced Ben Hur's double to swing his team to the right to save them. But, in making this move, he crowded another chariot against the wall where we had hidden a one-wheel ramp. As the wheel struck the ramp and bounced the chariot into the air, a trick spring attached to the axle threw the wheel spinning against the wall ten or twelve feet above the ground. The team then dragged the tumbling chariot to the end of the track. The driver was tossed head over heels onto the track just to the rear of Ben Hur's chariot, which sped on in the race.

Our third pileup was a two-chariot wreck caused by teams jamming against each other while fighting for positions. Two ended up in a wheel lock, with one of the teams pinned against the spina wall. The driver on the outside swung his team hard to the right, trying to break out of the lock, but instead of freeing the wheel, the pressure broke the shaft loose from his own chariot, turning it end over end. The driver, who was being dragged by the running horses, freed himself from the runaway team, and rolled out of the way of a team following close behind him, only to end up squarely in front of another oncoming charioteer's team. Here I cut the cameras and substituted for the thrown driver a mechanical dummy. The team

Charlton Heston and Yakima Canutt on the *Ben Hur* location in Italy.
(Photo courtesy of MGM)

Heston learning to handle the chariot team for *Ben Hur*.
(From the MGM release *Ben Hur* © 1959)

Heston at the reins with Yak. The photo shows the rigging that
Can:tt, as second unit director, designed so the camera crew
could get the spectacular angle shots in the
climactic chariot race. (Photo courtesy of MGM)

Joe Canutt, Yak's stunt man son, doubling Charlton Heston
in a wreck during the *Ben Hur* chariot race.
(From the MGM release *Ben Hur* © 1959)

and chariot ran over the dummy which created the thrilling effect of the real driver being killed. The loose team then swung back to the left, collided with the inside team, and wrecked the chariot. Some of the horses fell, but regained their footing and raced away, with harness pieces flying in all directions. The two wrecked chariots were left at the spina wall.

We next rehearsed a bit of action that was to be one of the high spots of the race. We had seven chariots, seven teams, and seven men left. While the camera crews were making a final check of their equipment, and the chariots were racing around the track in a last rehearsal, I turned to look over the set.

The afternoon sun cast weird shadows from the columns of the Colosseum onto the thousands of extras in colorful wardrobe. It was like looking back in time, back to the days of the Caesars. Then I recalled seeing a picture, an artist's sketch, of a pileup during a chariot race on the track of the ancient Circus Maximus—a scary entanglement of smashed chariots, broken horses and men.

I looked over toward the group of chariots now ready and waiting for the call of "action." My eyes could only focus on one team—the white Arabians of Ben Hur's chariot. For the first time I realized how tricky this scene could be, and how dangerous if anything went wrong. Suddenly, my knees seemed weak and I could feel a slight twitching in my cheeks. It was a hot day, yet the sweat on my forehead was cold. I knew I was doing the one thing that a man in the action business should never do—let his imagination get the best of him. I tried to shake off the feeling, telling myself that everything would be okay, but this was a new kind of fear, strange, bewildering.

The driver of Ben Hur's chariot was my son Joe, who was doubling Heston, and was about to do the most hazardous stunt in the race. He was just twenty-one years old, a good-looking young man, tall (six-foot-four and a half, to be exact). He was loaded with ability and certainly didn't lack courage. He had also logged more hours driving chariots than most drivers do in a lifetime.

For a couple of months he had worked out three or four teams daily, putting the horses through their routines—he had mastered the walk, then the trot, then the gallop. He was able to execute figure eights both to the left and to the right, all at a full gallop! After a short rest, he would finish his work out with a couple of laps at a dead run. This not only conditioned the horses, but the driver, too.

Most stunt men, in the early years of their work, have a tendency to try out their own ideas when doing a stunt. Joe was no exception. He probably inherited this trait from the fellow who had made this business seem so attractive. I remember learning quite a number of stunts the hard way. It was only after getting out of the hospital that I figured out how to do them. In his four years in the business, Joe had already shown the same hard-headed ability to learn.

My nerves still played funny tricks on me, as I looked from the charioteers to the two wrecked chariots rigged for this scene by the spina wall. My face was clammy with sweat and I wondered if I had created a deathtrap for my own son.

I was just about ready to blow my top and change the stunt, when I heard my assistant's voice say, "We're all set and ready, Yak." I tried to keep my voice steady, as I told the camera crew, "Hold it, I want to run a last minute check."

I walked over to the chariots to refresh the drivers on the mechanics of the scene. In this scene they were to get their teams underway, skid around the end of the spina, and head down the straightaway with Ben Hur's team on the inside and Messala's team slightly to the outside, but running even with the Arabian whites. The two wrecked chariots were set about two thirds of the way down the spina, one against the spina wall and the other a few feet away, but not far enough to allow a team to pass between them. Messala sees the wrecked chariots and recognizes the opportunity to finish off Ben Hur, perhaps for good. He pulls hard on his left rein, slams his team against the smaller whites and crowds them against the spina, only allowing them enough room to run. They are headed straight for the wrecked chariots, which lie in the path of Ben Hur's chariot. Ben Hur then sees them and tries to set his team, slowing them enough to try to pull out behind Messala's chariot. But Messala prevents this by slowing his own team, holding Ben Hur in the trap. Ben Hur now realizes he is hopelessly penned in, and does the only thing he can. He forces his team into a full run. Messala does likewise, and they race neck and neck toward the wrecks.

The white team had been trained to jump in full hookup while pulling a specially-constructed chariot. The jumps used in the training were breakaways, but looked like the ones used in the picture. Special effects had camouflaged a wide ramp between the two wrecked vehicles. By using sand and angles, this ramp was not visible to the cameras. They put a heavy rubber bumper on the ridge of the ramp and earlier testing proved that this gimmick would bounce the chariot a good six feet into the air.

I checked Joe's chariot. I had tied the reins so that they could be dropped as the team made the jump, leaving him free to hang onto the rails. The front top of the left side had been wrapped with friction tape, as was the top of the back rail on the right side. This handhold was very important because without it, the driver ran the risk of being thrown in a somersault over the front of the chariot onto the team.

I noticed the right front rail was also taped, and I had a hunch that Joe was planning to use it instead of the back hold. I tried to impress upon him what could happen as a result of this. I explained to Joe that we had designed the undercarriage of these chariots with drop axles and wide iron tires on the wheels. This gave them a good stability for skids, but only about a nine or ten-inch underclearance—not room enough for a man to go under without getting chewed up.

Before heading back to the camera positions, I told Joe to let the whites out at a full run, then settle them down a little so that they could collect themselves for the jump. Then, just as they took off, to drop the reins and get his handholds, his left hand in front and his right to the rear.

"I think that will be more apt to double my knees and set me down on the floor of the chariot," he grinned, "instead of tossing me up in the air."

"Joe," I said, "if you take hold in front with both hands, you may end up on top of the horses . . . or under the chariot."

He took hold of the back rail, feeling it out and replied, "Okay," which made me think he had bought my idea.

I headed back to the cameras. We were ready, and over the loud speaker came the order, "action." The teams got underway. As they made the turn at the end of the spina, Messala's chariot swung wide and Joe, in the Ben Hur chariot, made a short, spectacular skid in the turn, which placed him on the inside and even with Messala. The seven teams were nicely grouped as they headed down the straightaway. Messala's black team and Ben Hur's whites were now neck and neck, heading straight for the trap. Instead of settling the white Arabians down a little, Joe was forcing them into a dead run right into the wrecked chariots.

I held my breath. If one of the whites was off stride at the jump, it could cause a pileup. However, they all took off together for the jump. Then my eyes caught sight of Joe's hands holding the front rail! I swallowed my Adam's apple. I knew this could mean a wreck on the main line. When the wheels hit the ramp, it looked like a bomb had gone off beneath the chariot. It went high into the air. Joe, hanging onto the top front rail, did a somersault over the front of the chariot at full arm's length. The reins were tied to the center of the top front rail, and Joe, being very strong, was able to hang onto the rail. He came down on the reins, which gave the horses a terrific jerk. Naturally, that slowed them down a bit. Joe grabbed the hitch rail, and turned a flip off to the side, hitting the spina wall. He was very lucky. He had a cut on his chin that needed a couple of stitches but he never figured out what caused it.

Fifteen minutes later, when he returned from First Aid ready to go back to work, he came over to where I was standing. Before I had a chance to say anything, he remarked sheepishly, "When the wheels hit that ramp, I felt like Mickey Mouse."

I told him he also looked like Mickey Mouse. He had certainly proved one thing to me, and that was that he could really think in a pinch. I have never seen anyone get out of a dangerous situation quicker.

As it turned out, we were able to shoot a close shot of Heston lying back down on the hitch bar, with the team running. He pulled himself up and, climbing back into the chariot, continued the race. When these two pieces of film were put together it made a more spectacular scene than we had originally planned.

During the filming of the race, I naturally conferred with William Wyler at times and, on a couple of occasions, he asked me if we were getting some good scenes. I told him that I thought the stuff looked good so far.

He said, "You know, Yak, you have a good reputation as an action man. Don't let the front office hurry you into spoiling it. I'll back you for anything you need, but I'll never settle for second best."

I had the feeling that someone had been giving him the

wrong information. It turned out that I was right. A young fellow that was working with the cutter had told him that we were not getting good material. I asked Mr. Wyler to come to the projection room and see some of the dailies. He declined, saying that he would wait until we finished, and the race was rough cut.

The one sequence in the race with which he was most concerned was the death of Messala. "I'm not going to tell you how to do it," he said, "that's your baby. But when the chariot is wrecked, I want it to drag on top of him. When it breaks loose, let the horses drag him and have one of the other teams trample him into the track."

We did that and more, but it took all the tricks of the trade. We hitched Ben Hur and Messala's horses together as one team, with my son, Joe, driving both teams. A well-made dummy (its face was molded from a cast of Boyd's face) was secured in a standing position in Messala's chariot, with the reins fastened to his hands. The chariot was rigged to lose a wheel in a lock with Ben Hur's chariot. A chain that would drag the chariot after it was wrecked was measured out so that the chariot would end up being dragged along on top of Messala's likeness.

Joe brought the two teams around the end of the spina with the two chariots locked together. The wheel broke, the chariot collapsed, the wreck was perfect—the chariot ended up on top of Messala's replica. Following Messala's wreck, we did drags behind the running team with another chariot following and gaining, right up to the point of trampling him (in these scenes we used Boyd's double). We then substituted a dummy for the team to trample and run over. We also did close shots of Messala's double being dragged under and between the horses, rolling and struggling, and hanging onto the reins which were fastened to a guide on the chasing chariot's tongue. These protruded out in front of the team, out of the camera's view. These scenes were very effective.

I had a special armorlike shell welded onto the underside of the upside down chariot. This shell was hinged so that a man could clamp it around his body, and, when Boyd saw this gimmick, he said, "That looks okay. Why don't I do this one and you get close enough to tell it's me?" I told him that it was safe enough, but that the horses were going to kick back a lot of sand.

"I can take it." Boyd grinned.

So we clamped him in the clam shell and took off. We dragged him the full length of the straightaway and got some great closeups. When we finished, he looked like a man ready to receive his trained seeing-eye dog. We took him to first-aid, they washed the sand out of his eyes, and he came back grinning and ready for work. When you have people like Heston and Boyd, it makes the job a pleasure.

As I was leaving the studio that evening, I ran into Mr. Wyler. He pulled me aside.

"I understand you did the Messala wreck today."

"We sure did," I replied with a grin.

"How was it?"

"Mr. Wyler," I said, "when you do Boyd's closeup lying on the track, just make a quick cut from him to a hamburger stand—only make the sign read 'Messala-burgers'."

"It must have been good," he laughed. "I'll see you after the screening."

We finished the race shortly afterwards. I knew that Mr. Wyler was due to view the rough cut on Sunday. I met him on his set the following morning.

"Well," he said soberly, "I ran the race yesterday."

His serious expression alarmed me. My stomach sank.

"What's the verdict?"

"Yak," he said with his face breaking into a slow smile, "All I can say is—my stuff has got to be great to match it."

TWO

Early Broncs and Brannigans

Some of the things that people tell me I've done, I don't really remember doing—I've mainly been interested in doing, not in recollecting. So when people start saying, "Remember the time, Yak, when you pulled that harebrained stunt?" Well, most of the time the stunt that they describe is true and I'll only argue about how harebrained it was. If you don't use your head in stunts, you don't live this long to tell about them. It's exactly because they weren't harebrained that I'm still alive and I'm writing this book.

With so many close races in my life, it is only fitting that I entered the world in the midst of one. On November 29, 1895, a terrific rainstorm was pounding a little ranch house in the Snake River Hills of Washington. Set at the foot of a high hill with a canyon on both sides, this little house took quite a beating whenever the weather turned sour—the storms that hit eastern Washington state at the turn of the century are some of the nastiest on record. That cold, driving rain could break up the unpaved country roads into rivers of mud that could bog down a wagon for days. Knowing this, my father—six feet four-and-a-half inches tall and weighing two hundred and thirty pounds—was nearly wearing out the floorboards with his pacing. He had a vested interest in this race and he was worried. One of the contestants was a country doctor trying to make it through sixteen miles of rain-whipped mud in a two-horse buggy. I was the other contestant, but I was traveling via the long-legged bird called the Stork. From all accounts the bird must have been anxious to finish the race, since it pulled up at the Canutt family home some two hours ahead of the doctor. The folks who know me will claim that when the doctor arrived I had torn a strip off the sheet, made a loop in it, and commenced to rope the bedpost. They also claim that I later cut my teeth on a branding iron.

Now I confess that I've always doubted both stories. Still, I can rope, even though I don't remember learning. I also own a full crop of teeth that I don't exactly remember getting. And as I said, when it comes to recollecting, I don't argue. When someone shakes out one of those stories, I just slip them a grin and let it ride.

The facts are that I pulled the scale down to twelve-and-a-half pounds. They branded me Enos Edward Canutt, named after two uncles: Enos, after one of my father's brothers, and Edward, after one of my mother's brothers.

When I joined the Canutt family, it included my father, John Lemuel Canutt, my mother, Nettie Ellen, a brother, Alexander Hamilton, and a sister, Sally Treen. Following me came another brother, John Maceo, and our younger sister, Anna Adaline. Three boys and two girls, all in good health and of sound minds. Of course, there has been some doubt regarding me, considering the line of work I followed for the first fifty years.

The first couple of years of my life are a bit hazy. I remember I had the feeling that the world was made just for me. I suppose I got into the same sort of mischief all small boys do. I know I got tanned a few times—my father didn't completely believe in the adage "Spare the rod, and spoil the child."

As I grew older I learned how to swim, shoot, trap mink and muskrats, and I caught a great number of coyotes—there was a bounty on them and all pelts could be easily sold. And, of course, I rode horses—lots of them. In fact, I don't even remember my first horseback ride. It just seems that I had always been on a horse.

Our old ranch was on the Penawawa Creek, about seven miles from where it emptied into the Snake River. The Penawawa is actually formed by two streams, one from each of the canyons on either side of the house. One gave us water for irrigation, the other was great for trout fishing. The willows and red birch, the long, green grasses and wildflowers that framed the streams in all directions, had the kind of simple beauty that looks like it always had been and always will be.

My grandfather had put up every building on the farm himself. He built the house, the barn, cellar, smokehouse and fruit packing shed right by the creek. He picked a good spot. We had a little wheat land, some very good bunch grass pastures, some bottom hayfields, and a few cows and horses. But our main source of livelihood was our thirty acres of orchard—some of the finest cherries, peaches, pears, prunes and watermelons Washington state could offer.

In those early days, no railroads went up to the Snake River Hills, as they do today. In the cool of the evening, we used to haul our fruit to the loading platform on the banks of the river and the old stern-wheeler boat would pick it up the next day and carry it some thirty miles up stream to Lewiston, Idaho. After they had received it, the fruit brokers would mail us back a check.

I did my share of picking, cleaning, and hauling, but it was my older brother, Alex, who rode to the river landing at Penawawa and brought back the receipt for each shipment.

One day, before starting out, he asked me to go with him. Elated, I scrambled up onto the horse behind him and we were off. I felt great. My big brother was taking me along. Down the road we galloped, but before we arrived, he explained with some carefully chosen words why he was taking me with him. On his previous trip he had had an argument with a lad by the name of Elmer Swift, a son of the ferryboat operator. Alex was, of course, a little bigger and a couple of years older than Elmer and the idea of a fight bothered him. Well, my pulse sped up and my eyes sparkled—I thought my brother wanted me to see him in action. I had never had more than a few harsh words with any kid, and had never seen a fight, though I had heard about a fight or two that my Granddad had had.

My Granddad was the kind of colorful man of the frontier that you can't help but remember. He was a fraction under six feet tall, and weighed a trim two hundred pounds. From all reports, he was a man who, in his younger days, loved adventure and a good rough-and-tumble fight. He crossed the plains in a covered wagon and settled in Roseburg, Oregon. After my father was born he migrated to the Palouse country in Washington.

I remember hearing Dad and an uncle tell of the fights that

my Granddad had back in Indiana. Before crossing the plains he fought his way into the number one spot in his section of the country.

Remembering that story on the way to the boat landing and looking forward to what I thought was going to be my first look at a fist fight, I was bursting with excitement and felt proud that my brother wanted me along to see it.

Then Alex dropped the bombshell: "He's too young for me, so I told him that the next time I came I'd bring my kid brother to fight him."

This was a shock. "Alex," I said uneasily, "I don't know how to fight."

"Don't worry," he replied, "just double up your fists and go after him. Punch him in the nose a couple of times, and when his guard comes up, hit for his stomach. If you remember that, he won't last long."

That sounded pretty simple . . . what did I have to worry about? What Alex didn't explain to me was that the poke in the nose or stomach could be delivered by the other fellow, too.

We arrived at the boat landing, a small portable platform that could be moved back during high water. It sat right at the water's edge where the river was deep enough for the boat to dock alongside. We were only there a short time when a young lad rode up on a barebacked pony. He came over to the landing and looked me up and down.

"Is this your kid brother?" he asked Alex.

I stared at him and had the feeling this wasn't going to be so simple. He was a little bigger than me and more mature.

Alex looked at me and said, "Remember what I told you."

I knew if I backed out I'd never live it down, so I made a couple of fists and started swinging. Then something exploded on my nose, setting me back on my heels, and the blood began to flow. I couldn't see for a second or two, but I kept fighting, and finally I landed one on his nose which started to bleed. I tried one for his stomach and that had a good effect. It slowed him down some and while he was trying to get his breath, I zeroed in on his nose again.

He started crying but fought harder than ever. Then I started squalling and we got into a clinch and fell off the platform into the river. Alex fished us out, and Elmer went to his horse, mounted and headed home.

That experience saved me a lot of bloody noses in later years. I found out that fighting wasn't the most pleasant way of expressing your manhood. On the way home, I got to wondering what Dad and Mother would say. I had heard Dad tell Alex never to start a fight, and never to run from one—just be sure that he was right. I didn't even know how this trouble with Elmer got started. Dad lectured both of us but especially Alex because he let someone else do his fighting for him.

Keeping a family of five rambunctious kids in line was no easy task and, all in all, I'd say my father was firm but fair. He loved to talk—Alex and I winced as much before his stern lectures as under the strap—and he loved to farm. A man of the earth and a man of the people—he could have made a success out of either, but the combination just didn't work out.

A year after I was born, he was elected a member of the Washington State Legislature. Following his term in office, he returned to the old ranch but I guess politics is like any other vocation—once it gets into your blood it's hard to shake. A few years later he was the principal campaigner in the election of Alfred E. Mead for Governor of the State of Washington. The governor appointed him state oil inspector. This led to the whole family moving to Green Lake, a suburb of Seattle, where my sister, brothers and I attended the Green Lake School.

Always a maverick, Dad didn't get along very well with the state bureaucracy. During Governor Mead's administration, my father and the Governor had a misunderstanding which finally developed into outright animosity. Dad resigned and we returned to the ranch shortly after.

The ranch was pretty well run down but we soon had it in working order. The buildings had never been painted and they had bleached to a dark driftwood color which people now try to copy with antique paint. To me, the old ranch in its antiquity and the Penawawa canyon in blooming season were rare strokes of beauty. Orchard blossoms along the streams ranged from white to deep crimson, and the locust trees were loaded with clusters of white and pinkish flowers. To travel along the winding road through the canyon at this time of the year was like riding through a fairyland. If you had ever sat on one of those hills, gazed on the overall beauty and inhaled the fragrance that rose from those orchards, it's likely that you would never forget it.

After a taste of city life I suppose that I was hungry to get my fill of all that the country had to offer. The year we returned to the ranch was a turning point in my life. It was the year that I rode my first bronc.

Alex had bought a horse and was breaking him to ride. He called him Buck and that horse did a good job of earning the name—you could never tell when he was going to turn on and had to watch him every second.

Then one day, he threw Alex and dragged him some distance. Alex was laid up with a fractured skull for several weeks, while Old Buck ran loose in the pasture, getting fat and wild. I had been wanting to try my luck on a bronco. In that part of the northwest, a man who was a good bronc rider was a bit of an idol—much like the astronauts today. (I have since come close to being put into orbit myself by a bronc a time or two.)

Every day I went out to the pasture and studied Buck. Knowing what he had done, I just couldn't stand by and let him enjoy that green grass.

We had a hired hand, a Japanese man by the name of Koontario Ingey, whom we called Kay for short. He agreed to help me get Buck into the corral. We got a rope on the horse, haltered him and led him through the gate onto a flat piece of ground near the house. The ground was well cultivated—part of it was a well-grown potato patch—and I figured that if I was overmatched, I would at least have a soft place to land. We put a blindfold over Buck's eyes, to keep him quiet, then saddled him. The saddle was my father's and he had riveted the stirrup leathers so that no one could raise or lower them. I put on a pair of spurs, and tied them down. I had seen this done a few times when some cowboy was getting ready to ride a bronc. At the time I didn't know why, but with them tied down, you can get a pretty good hold.

With Buck saddled, I climbed aboard. With the reins in my left hand and the saddle horn in my right, I told Kay to jerk the blindfold off. He did and old Buck exploded. With his head down, he swapped ends, turned his sides to the sun (what rodeo riders call a "sunfish") and bawled like a bear in a trap. After a few jumps I knew that I could ride him, and I really went to work on him with the spurs. This made him buck harder, but as long as that saddle horn didn't come off, I was safe.

As Buck started to slow down, I heard someone hollering. There was no mistaking the voice. It was my father. He had heard the commotion and came running.

"Get off that horse!" he hollered, more alarmed than mad.

I turned the horse around and could see my mother coming from the house. I rode the now subdued Buck over to where Dad was standing and got off. Mother was frightened and certainly I knew that Dad was more than a little ruffled. He took the reins and handed them to Kay, telling him to take the horse to the barn and unsaddle him.

"Dad," I said rather lamely, "I just wanted to give him a lesson."

Dad turned and I knew he didn't like what he saw—the potato patch looked like a tractor had been doing circles and figure eights in it.

He looked at me and answered gravely, "You just wanted to give him a lesson. Well, son, I am going to give you a lesson." And he did!

I had my first taste of a bucking horse and I liked it. It was like a successful vaccination. My mind was made up, I was going to be a cowboy, a horse breaker. My greatest dream now was to eventually ride in the bronc-riding contest that was one of the main attractions each fall at the Colfax Fair.

To be a serious contender in any bucking contest you must be in good physical condition and have a lot of riding practice. It didn't take long for me to learn that all horses didn't buck the same. Some will come out of a chute or away from a snubbing horse, run a few feet, then down goes their head and up they go, landing stiff-legged; some will do long straightaway jumps while others will come out of the chute and sunfish, turning their sides to the sun; still other horses may leave the chute in long, fast jumps, kicking at the sky—and in my opinion, the stout, kicking horse will give you your roughest ride.

Once in a while a spinning horse will show up and leave you completely dizzy. The best you can do is to get a reride. I used to love drawing a fast, crooked, high-jumping horse. They are showy and good horses to win on. In my opinion, old No Name was the greatest. He was a big sorrel and when he came out of the chute kicking at the sky and rooting at the rein, he was hell to ride. I was on him seven times, five were qualified rides. I lost a stirrup once and he bucked me off the other time. After you see a horse buck, you can judge pretty well how to go about making a good ride on him.

Like any good parents, my folks didn't want their children doing anything dangerous. Bronc riding was something that I had to pursue on my own—and I guess this decision is what most people would say was the start of my career.

By 1906 most county fairs, Fourth of July celebrations, established yearly picnics, rodeos, and Frontier Days and Roundups, featured bronc-riding contests. As almost everybody knows, bronc-riding and steer-roping contests sprang up almost simultaneously throughout the West during the 1870s, a side event to the Saturday afternoon quarter-horse races.

After the success of Buffalo Bill Cody's first Wild West Show in 1883, every community with a bit of western spirit started its own Wild West show. By 1905 the Miller Brothers had their Wild West show in full swing and even brought in Geronimo to kill his last buffalo; unfortunately, he missed.

By 1906 the first Roundup at Pendleton, Oregon, one hundred miles to the Southwest, and soon to be one of the most celebrated rodeos in the country, was still three years away. But there were a number of shows around Colfax that gave me the chance to break in my boots.

Most of the shows owned a string of good bucking horses but they also used stock from one or more of the several horse contractors. These men were always searching for good bucking horses, and kept a large number on call.

Many of the best bucking horses came from farms. In fact, No Name, the greatest of them all, was from a plow team. A great many of the ranchers in Whitman County knew that a good bucking horse was worth more than just another horse, so I was able to get a lot of practice trying them out. Frank Hanna, a nearby rancher who furnished stock for the Colfax Fair each fall, was happy to share my secret. I rode many broncs for him. Hanna, as a young man, had been a good rider and he gave me a lot of help. I worked for him off and on for the next three or four years, and I got to where only a top horse would bother me. I had great confidence in my ability to ride. I don't mean to brag, but by the time I was fourteen I could mount a wild bronc with the same assurance that I had when mounting a well-broken horse.

During the fall of 1911, when I was not quite sixteen, the *Colfax Gazette*, the only newspaper in the county, had a page advertising the fair which was to take place the following week. They had contracted a small group of cowboys that had just finished the Pendleton Roundup. The group included John Spain, who had won the bronc-riding championship, Ben Corbett and Ben Joury, both pros, and Buffalo Vernon, who specialized in what was then a new event, bulldogging. These were the top names in the group. In addition, Spain owned several bucking horses that he had brought along. The ad in the paper looked good, and everyone wanted to see the champs in action. Dad decided to take the family to Colfax for the week. I was working for Frank Hanna at the time and went in with him.

Spain had a little bucking horse called Hot Foot. He was a black horse with a white face—a good-looking horse that certainly knew all the tricks. He would rear up to the point of going over backward, and that, naturally, would cause a rider to loosen up in case he toppled. But Hot Foot would spin and catch himself, and with the rider a bit loose, he would really turn on. If a man didn't know his tricks, he generally got dumped.

Hot Foot was not used in the contest, he was used only as a come-on. Spain would offer fifty dollars to anyone who could ride him by contest rules. This meant that you had to spur the horse over the point of the shoulders during the first jump and one hand had to be kept free of the horse at all times. Of course, none of the riders who knew Hot Foot's tricks were allowed to try. I saw him buck a local man off the first day of the show and I was itching to ride him. I couldn't enter the contest without my father's consent, so I was a spectator.

On the second day I went to the fair early and wore my spurs. I could hardly wait for them to lead Hot Foot onto the track in front of the grandstand. When the announcer made the offer of fifty dollars to anyone who could make a qualified ride on him, I quickly clambered over the fence and accepted the challenge. They saddled the horse and just as I started to get on him, two big hands grabbed me from behind. I knew the feel of those powerful hands—it was Dad. He had one hand on my collar, the other on my britches at the belt line. He took me kicking to the fence and boosted me over. I was really humiliated. I wanted to show the Champ I could ride his horse. Anyway, the crowd in the grandstand gave me a good hand.

During the following spring, a couple of tough, local bucking horses appeared. One was a big black that belonged to John Carroll, a rancher who lived near Wilcox. This horse had bucked off everybody who had been on him. The other horse was a blue roan with an equally good reputation, which was owned by a local farmer named Roody. He was a medium-sized animal that stood about fifteen hands high. I pleaded, bargained and tried to cajol each horse's owner, but neither would let me try without my Dad's consent.

I asked a man named Joe Pierce, who had seen me ride a lot of horses, and who knew Dad real well, to talk to my father to see if he would okay a shot for me at the big black. He did, and the way Dad took it, I am not too sure my secret rides had been unknown to him.

Dad said, "Joe, what makes you think the boy can ride that horse?"

"Mr. Canutt," Joe replied emphatically, "I've seen him ride a lot of bucking horses, and I've seen the black turn on. I'll bet a hundred dollars he can ride him."

Dad thought a moment, then turned to me.

"All right," he said, "I'll let you try him under one condition. If he throws you, that will be the end of your bronco riding. It's up to you."

I bit my lip. If I made a blunder, if the horse had a little luck, it was the end of my dream career. It was now or never. "Okay," I said finally. The time and the place were set: a big alfalfa field had just been mowed and cleared. The ground was firm, not hard, which was perfect for the horse. The owner naturally wanted to see the horse keep his reputation.

The day arrived for the ride—wagons, buggies, hacks and people on saddle horses began to arrive. It was a frighteningly big crowd for a one-man show. I felt myself getting a little nervous, but I played it down. That is, I thought I had, until my Dad came up and said, encouragingly, "Now, son, wipe the sweat off your brow, and get on that horse just as if you didn't know I was here."

His encouragement gave me a lift and confirmed my suspicion. Realizing he knew more about my past bronc riding than I had thought gave me all the confidence I needed.

When you are going to ride a bucking horse, you've got to saddle him first, and then get on him—not an easy thing to do. One way is to put the horse in a bronc chute, which is an oversized crate enclosed on both ends and one side with heavy rails. The fourth side is a gate that swings open into the arena. The horse is saddled, the rider climbs down on him from the rail. "Take his rein," he says. "Turn him out." The gate is swung open and out they come.

However, in this case I would be riding from a snubbing horse, one that is trained to work with men saddling a bronc. This is a two-man job. One holds the bronc and the other works from the snubbing horse's saddle.

The black was led in and tied to the snubbing horse. The man who led him in held the snubbing rope, and the man on the snubbing horse slipped a blindfold over the bronc's eyes. I then put my saddle on him and climbed aboard. The minute I got on him I knew I was home free. I said, "Let me have him."

They pulled the blinds and turned him loose. As he whirled from the snubbing horse, I slammed both spurs into his shoulders. He was the most powerful horse that I had ever been on. He popped my head a couple of times until I could see stars, but I kept working him with my spurs, from his shoulders up to the back saddle skirts. He loosened me up a couple of times, but never enough to worry me. He bucked for about twelve or fifteen seconds, then broke and started running. Before the pickup rider could get to him, he bucked some more and quit. The pickup man got him and I stepped off smiling. When I crossed the field to where Mother and Dad were standing, I could see tears in Mother's eyes. Dad seemed a bit shaken too.

"Well, son," he said after a moment, "when do you want to ride Roody's roan?"

I wasn't about to wait long for this little piece of forbidden fruit. Close to Roody's farm there was a place where we used to play baseball. It was known as Dusty and it wasn't quite a town—it had a store, a post office, a few sun-bleached buildings, and a wonderful baseball diamond. That following Sunday, Roody brought his roan to center field and secured him to the snubbing horse. I looked the animal over closely, then saddled him and climbed on. He was a very different horse—he was a showy, bucking bronc. He went high, fast, and crooked. A good rider could ride him with ease. He was the kind of bronc you could win on. Even before I stepped off him, I knew I'd be riding his type again—and enjoying it.

My dad seemed well pleased—these were the two toughest horses in the region—and I could tell that he, as well as my mother, were not only plenty proud of me—they had accepted the rodeo life I wanted. I was walking on air. I knew it was time to launch my bronc-riding career.

THREE

On
The Circuit

The Whitman County Fair was held each fall in Colfax, Washington, about sixteen miles from our ranch on the Penawawa Creek. In 1912 I was sixteen, six feet tall, a strapping one hundred-and-eighty pounds and primed to test my stuff in the big leagues. Hard work during the summer had put me in good physical condition and, after riding through Frank Hanna's string of broncs, I felt ready for the bronc-riding contest that was to come.

A week before the fair I helped move Hanna's horses into the fairgrounds. Other ranchers had brought their stock in and several riders who were to compete in the show had also arrived early, so we took turns at trying out the new horses. There was one outstanding horse brought in from up near Spokane. In fact, they called him Little Spokane. He was a beautiful blood bay who looked like a thoroughbred.

It happened to be the turn of another rider when we saddled Little Spokane. The horse was very quiet and I had some doubts about him being a bronc. However, when he was turned loose, he really put on a show, and threw his rider with ease. I tried to get a ride on him before the rodeo but his owner refused. He was the best bucking horse that I had seen up to this point, and I knew he was going to make anyone who got on him take a deep seat.

The day before the show started, the fairground was alive with activity—concession stands and stalls, merry-go-rounds, popcorn, hot-dog vendors, and show tents with acts that ranged from sword swallowers to fire eaters—enough attractions to make any kid's eyes pop.

I went to bed early that night and tried to get a good night's rest, but I couldn't get my mind off the bronc-riding contest. When I did fall asleep, that new bronc, Little Spokane, kept showing up. He bucked me off at least a dozen times. When I awoke the next morning, I felt as if I had put in a tough day on the threshing machine. During my rodeo career I never could figure out how I could win so many contests in the arena and lose them in my dreams.

The fair opened with a lot of hullabaloo and the bronc-riding contest was soon on. I had drawn Pomp, a big, dapple gray horse that belonged to Hanna. I had ridden him a couple of times at Hanna's ranch without any trouble. The first ride was on Little Spokane, who threw his rider. Then a local hand by the name of Ben Oaks made a showy ride on a good horse, and a couple of cowboys rode very well.

When my name was called, I felt a little nervous. I didn't quite know why. I knew I could ride old Pomp in good shape, but there is always the chance of losing a stirrup, or touching the horse's rigging with your free hand. It boiled down to one thing—it was my first ride by the rules. I would have to remember both spurs in the shoulders the first jump, then rake ahead and back until he quit. There was no ten-second gun then—you had to ride until the bronc quit and started running.

They led Pomp out to the snubbing horse, set the blinds and I saddled him up and climbed aboard. As he was turned loose, I grabbed him in the shoulders with both spurs and raked him every jump he made. He did a good job of bucking, then jumped over a fence that separated the racetrack from the center field, and ran down the track with the pickup man in pursuit.

At the gate leading to the stables, a cowboy was leading out a horse and old Pomp ran square into them. Both horses were knocked down, throwing me over the top of the animals. I hit the ground hard and it really jarred me. I limped away from the pileup, but it had me worried because we still had three more days to go. I got a good hand though, and a good mark on the ride.

On the second day I drew Roody's bronc and Ben Oaks drew Little Spokane. I was up first. My hip was still pretty sore but would just have to take a little punishment. When they pulled the blind and turned the bronc loose, I hooked him in the shoulders and he went into the air, hit the ground and reversed ends. The pain shot down my leg like an electric shock, but I gritted my teeth and kept working him. He kicked high behind with every jump and swapped ends. He sunfished and then bucked straight away, going high and kicking at the sky. Roody's roan did the best job of bucking he had ever done.

When he quit and the pickup man was gathering him in, I knew by the applause and yells from the audience that the ride must have looked good. I watched the rest of the contestants, knowing the only man I had to worry about, Ben Oaks, was now getting on his mount, Little Spokane. They cut him loose and the battle was on. Oaks managed to qualify and I figured it would be close, for this horse was the best bronc in the string. Fortunately for me, the riders too are judged, and not just the horses.

I got the high mark of the day, but just barely, and Oaks was still a contender. I spent that evening sitting in a hot tub of water and rubbing Doctor Nepaw's Snake Oil into my lame hip.

The third day went along okay. Little Spokane threw one of the other riders who had been doing fairly well, so it looked like Ben Oaks and I were the top finalists. The last day the judges gave us our mounts—I had Little Spokane and was to ride last. By this time Doctor Nepaw's Snake Oil had my hip in pretty good shape.

The saddle bronc-riding started, and there were a couple of good rides made but their average caused me no worries. However, Oaks had made a spectacular ride, and to beat him, I knew that I would have to go all out. When Little Spokane was turned loose I locked both spurs in his shoulders. He went straight up and nearly came over backward but spun and caught himself. This maneuver loosened me a little but I recovered and went to work. The best broncs often bring out the best in you and the more he bucked the more I raked. I felt the contest was in my hands and I aimed to win it or be bucked off trying. Little Spokane was the fastest bronc that I had ever been on. Even though he loosened me up a couple of times, I hung on.

The judge's decision was announced: I had won my first bronc-riding contest!

I could already feel my career taking shape. Deep down inside I felt that I would become a champion. But during the next year or so things seemed to fall apart at the seams. Mother and Dad separated and divorced, a shock to all of us. To this day, I have never been able to figure out what happened. They were fine parents, intelligent, and with a good moral sense of responsibility. I guess it was just one of those unfortunate things that happens in this mysterious life.

Anyway, I decided to get away from the home base for a while and see how people in other walks of life lived. I went to Bovill, Idaho, and hired out as a teamster in one of Blackwell's logging camps. Many of the workmen there were foreigners. The buildings were made of huge logs. I'll never forget the odor in those bunkhouses at night. When the men pulled off their shoes and socks, the stench was indescribable.

When the dinner bell rang and the cook hollered "Come and get it," get it they did. The clashing of knives and forks sounded like a group of knights dueling. I can't say I made many friends there. At the end of dinner one evening, we were each given a piece of pumpkin pie. The man sitting across from me finished his pie off in a couple of bites, then reached over the table, grabbed my pie and devoured it.

I half rose in my chair to do something, then, as I caught his blank look, I sat down. I had to feel sorry for him. I let the incident pass but soon left that tender community.

I went back to the ranch country were people spoke my lingo, where you could saddle a horse and ride over a hill. In fact, I got into the habit of wanting to see what was on the other side of each hill, and then the next hill, and so on.

When I look back to the years of 1913–1914, I find that I was just a bit off the main line—had there been hippies in those days I might have joined them. After drifting about for a while I finally got it all together, and went back to the rodeo circuit.

"Rodeo" is the Spanish word for the roundup of cattle for branding. Today we use the word to mean an exhibition of cowboy skills. This meaning goes back into the 1800s, and I have read of a roping contest that was held at Santa Fe, New Mexico, in 1847.

What might have been the first appearance of this great Western sport was staged by Buffalo Bill Cody in North Platte, Nebraska. He had advertised for riders, ropers and Mexican *vaqueros*—cowboys—for a Wild West show that he had planned to open in Omaha in May, 1883. Riders, ropers and vaqueros showed up in such numbers that Buffalo Bill had to put them through tryouts to compete for the jobs.

The Mexican vaqueros were considered expert riders and ropers—a vaquero has been known to tie the end of a lariat around his neck and rope a running horse by the front feet while standing on the ground. "Tailing the bull" is another of their favorite sports. While on horseback, they pass the bull on the run, reach down and catch his tail and spin his rear end around, making him fall. They originated rope spinning and trick and fancy roping.

The vaqueros of Buffalo Bill's show have been given credit for bringing the first rope spinning and trick roping to the United States—their trick and fancy roping astonished the American cowboys, who were quick to adopt their techniques for themselves.

The Miller Brothers' 101 Ranch Wild West Show was never considered a rodeo. Wild West Shows paid their performers a salary; in rodeos you paid for the privilege of competing for purses and trophies. My research shows that Prescott, Arizona, had the first commercial rodeo in 1888, where purses and trophies were awarded for bronc riding and steer roping.

If I were asked where the rodeo got started, my answer would be that it was born in Mexico, raised in the U.S.A., and came of age in Cheyenne, Wyoming, in 1897 with that city's Frontier Days. For that event, the Union Pacific Railroad ran special trains to bring in thousands of spectators from the East. Seats sold for fifteen to thirty-five cents, and the show was a great success.

In 1912 a group of ranchers in Calgary, Canada, backed the Calgary Stampede with the largest money prizes ever offered up to that time. The show in Calgary was the start of a series of successful rodeos that continues to the present day.

In September, 1914, I went to Walla Walla, Washington, for their Pioneer Frontier Days. This was my first major rodeo. After signing up at headquarters for the saddle-bronc riding and wild-horse racing events, I took a cab to where the rodeo was to be held. I wanted plenty of time to look around.

The grounds were buzzing with activity. I joined a couple of cowboys standing by the inside rail of the race track watching the workouts. At that moment a tall cowboy on a well-groomed horse rode by, spinning a maguey rope in what is known as the "Ocean Wave"—a trick that takes a lot of practice to do on the ground, let alone on a horse. He spun the rope in a rolling loop, from the right side of the horse around in front to the left side, and then rolled it up over the horse's rump and on around, all with the utmost grace and ease. I could do a little rope spinning but this guy was in a class by himself.

"Who is that guy?" I asked one of the cowboys. As soon as I said it I regretted it. They both eyed me up and down.

"You follow rodeos?" one of them finally asked.

I had always tried to follow the shows in the papers, but with travelling and everything else I had been out of touch for a while.

"This will be my first major show," I confessed.

The bigger man of the two stuck out his hand. "My name is Daniels, Tex for short. This waddy here is Frank Cable."

I smiled, glad to make the acquaintance, and introduced myself. Then Tex said, "That fellow spinning the rope is Chester Byers, the greatest trick roper that ever coiled a maguey."

I had heard of Byers. My eyes caught another roper lassoing a horse. I remarked that this fellow was also good.

"Yeah," said Tex. "That's Tex McCloud."

His name also rang a bell. It was a great thrill to see all these top hands in the flesh. This was the heyday of rodeo, and often you could catch one big name at a local contest. At the major events they all showed up and a fan like me could walk around bug-eyed.

They were working out roping and bulldogging steers in the center field. They turned them out of a chute at one end of the grounds and ran them across center field to the catch pens, or corrals, at the far end. This not only gets the cattle familiar with the course and catch corrals, but gives the ropers and bulldoggers a good chance to work out their horses. The steer ropers took advantage of the opportunity to take some roping practice at the same time. They used a breakaway honda that separates when the loop tightens on the steer's horns, leaving him free to run into the corrals.

Bulldogging was still a new rodeo event in 1914. It was first introduced by that great Texas cowboy, Bill Pickett, who starred in the Miller Brothers' 101 Ranch Wild West Show in 1903. He would ride into the field after a running steer and dive from his horse, Straddler, onto the steer's head. He'd grab the animal's horns, twist his neck, and throw him to the ground. With the steer flat on his side, Pickett would sink his teeth tight into the animal's lip, holding him down, and throw his hands up in a victory salute. Pickett named the event "bulldogging." Buffalo Vernon was the first man to repeat the act at the Pendleton Roundup in 1911. It was George Fletcher, another early contestant, who cut out the lip bite. He taught the art of bulldogging to other cowboys, and it soon became a regular event in rodeos.

I was later to meet Bill Pickett himself. Scout Mash, an old-time cowboy who knew Pickett from way back, introduced me to him, saying, "Yak, I want you to meet the man who bulldogged the first steer."

I shook hands with Pickett. He was a medium-sized black man with gray hair; I judged him to be well beyond his fiftieth year. He was pleasant and courteous—a fine man. I had many talks with him, and during one of them I asked him how he came to throw his first steer. He laughed and said: "It's an odd story, and I have it first hand, right from the horse's mouth." Along with another cowboy, Pickett had been trying to drive a steer into a slaughterhouse corral. The steer had different plans. He would turn and run back, and when Pickett crowded him, he would charge the horse, hooking at him. This happened several times.

"Finally," Pickett said, "I got mad and when he charged my horse again, I dove right onto that steer's head, and holding his horns, I tried to break his neck. I twisted his neck until his nose was pointing up. I grabbed his lip with my teeth, and kept twisting, and down he went."

The other cowboy was amazed. "If you can do that to other steers," he said to Pickett, "you should join the 101 Ranch Show. The Miller Brothers would certainly feature that kind of an act." Pickett practiced and perfected the act and became the star of the 101 Ranch Show.

The Miller Brothers decided to take the show to Mexico City, Mexico. Unfortunately, bullfights are the big deal there, and the rodeo show failed to attract an audience, and just about went bankrupt. It was Zak Miller who figured out a stunt that might get them out of the hole they were in. He made a deal to use the bullring, put on their regular show, and finish with a special attraction: Bill Pickett, on his horse,

Straddler, would ride into the ring alone. One of the Mexican fighting bulls would be turned out into the ring. Pickett would dive off his horse onto the bull and hang onto the animal's head for ten minutes.

The Miller Brothers had posters put up all over the city, advertised the event in the paper and succeeded in filling the bullring to capacity. The regular show finished, and it was Pickett's time to do the impossible.

Bill rode into the bullring alone. There were to be no capes or safety men, just Bill Pickett on his horse—just as advertised. The one thing that Zak hadn't figured on was that in Mexico, when you advertised something that you were going to do and collected money for it, you had to do it or go to jail.

The bull was turned in, a big, black Mexican fighting bull, with a set of horns that curved ahead and up. The strength and speed of a fighting bull is nothing less than fantastic; I have seen one of these black demons pick up a horse and rider on his horns, and toss them both upside down with ease.

The bull looked around, and seeing Bill on his horse, charged. Bill's horse had been well trained for steer bulldogging, and he would go up alongside a steer for a jump, but this was quite different. Bill tried to maneuver into a position to make the catch, but Straddler, not knowing the difference between a fighting bull and a steer, was unaware of the danger. The bull made a fast turn and caught the horse in the lower hip with a horn, tearing a deep, one-foot long gash which brought a squeal from the horse.

Pickett, thinking only of his horse, whirled him around and rode out of the arena.

The audience figured this was not what had been advertised, nor was it what they had paid their good money for. Not about to take it peacefully, they began to shout and scream insults. The police began to pour in.

Zak Miller got to Bill in a hurry and handed him a quart of whiskey. "Take a good slug and get back in there, and on the bull's head," he said.

"I drank about half of that quart," Bill said, "and got back on Straddler." He paused a moment, then looked at me. "I was really scared. I figured that if I didn't go in, Zak would probably kill me, so I decided to take my chances with the bull. I rode back into the ring, and the bull charged as he saw us. I spun Straddler and dove right on the bull's head between his horns. I locked my hands together under his neck and scissored my legs around his nose. This put my stomach right on top of his head.

"I really hung on! The bull tried to flip me loose, but I clung there . . . It seemed a long time . . . then they started throwing bottles at me, why I don't know, but one hit me in the side of the face here, and cut clean through." As he said this, he turned his face and touched the scar, which was about two to two-and-a-half inches long.

"Then the gate opened," he continued, "and cowboys and cape men came in and helped me turn the bull loose." He had actually stayed on the bull's head close to fifteen minutes.

There is probably a tougher way to spend fifteen minutes, but with all my experience in thrill events, I couldn't tell you how. It's an incredible story, but I heard it told by too many men to disbelieve it. They had all witnessed it and their accounts were all the same. I really had to admire that great man.

Bill Pickett was killed in 1932, while roping a bronc. The Cherokee Strip Cowboys' Association erected a marker at his grave honoring him, and Zak Miller wrote a poem to his memory. Bill Pickett was a man with many friends; everybody who knew him had words of praise for him.

In 1914, I was a week away from trying my hand at bulldogging. I was there to check out the broncs. One caught my eye right away. It was a bronc that a cowboy was just starting to ride into the center field. When they turned him loose from the snubbing horse, that bronc whirled away. The rider went to work with his spurs high in the horse's shoulders. I have never seen a horse go any higher. Head down, bucking and bawling like a mad bear, he used all the tricks in the book. As a cowboy might say—he went high, wide and handsome. The cowboy was trying to keep a deep seat, but this horse kept him loose. The horse made a couple of fast straightaway jumps, and then made a half turn and kicked at the moon with both hindfeet. That did it! The cowboy went into the air, end over end, and hit the ground with a thud that probably jarred his kinfolks back home. I have never seen a bronc waste a cowboy any cleaner.

I just had to learn something about that horse, so I walked over to the group. The Indian that owned the bronc was talking to a distinguished-looking man, who was sitting on a horse. They had apparently been discussing the price of the bronc. The man said that he would take him, and asked if they had any more as good as that one. The Indian said one of the other men had a horse that he thought was as good. "However," he added, "I have never seen the horse buck." "Bring him out and we'll see what he can do," said the gentleman on the horse.

The Indian turned and, in the Nez Percé language, told the owner of the horse to bring him out. The man left to get the horse.

This Indian looked familiar. He looked at me and grinned. Then I remembered meeting him during my travels at a carnival in Moscow, Idaho, where I rode a horse called Flaxey that had thrown him a day or two before.

He was the greatest Indian rider that ever lived: Jackson Sundown, a full-blooded Nez Percé and a nephew of the famous Chief Joseph of the Nez Percé War of 1877. In fact, Jackson wears three scars—they are bullet wounds from the white man's guns, received while fighting alongside his famous uncle in that last of the Indian Wars.

In 1916 he won the bronc-riding championship of the world at the Pendleton Roundup. At the age of 50 Jackson Sundown was not only a competing champion, but a great man—well respected, friendly, proud, and intelligent. He never smoked or drank.

Jackson sold the first bronc, a horse he had named Cul de Sac. This horse turned out to be one of the great broncs of his day. The other Indian came back with his horse. He was a roan, fifteen hands, two inches high, halter broke, and he handled nice. The man on the horse looked at the cowboy who had been thrown. He was very pale from that hard fall, so the gentleman said, "You'd better go over and have Doc look you over." Then he said to me, "Are you a bronc rider?"

"Let's saddle him up," I said, "and you'll be the judge."

I borrowed the cowboy's saddle and spurs. They snubbed him up, and I saddled him and climbed aboard. I hadn't heard the name of the man on the horse, but I had a hunch that he had a reputation.

Then they turned him loose. I grabbed him in the shoulders with my spurs and he came undone. He bucked very good and high, swapped ends quite a bit, and kicked high behind. He went well for ten or twelve seconds, and then started to slow down. I took the horn with my right hand and stepped off and held my feet, also hanging onto the rein.

When you get off a horse this way, before he has completely stopped, it keeps them in the habit of bucking—they actually think they have thrown you. The man rode over to me and said, "That was a nice ride. What do you think of him?"

I looked at the horse and said, "Well, he's pretty young. He will either develop into a good bronc or quit altogether, in which case, he'll make a good saddle horse."

The man asked me my name, and introduced himself as George Drumhiller. I shook hands with him, and said that I was very pleased to meet him. I told him that I had heard a great deal about his ranch on Rock Creek, his race horses, and his son, Allen, who from all reports was one of the top Relay and Pony Express riders.

"That seems to be the opinion of a lot of people," Drumhiller said. Then he asked me if I would like to work with them, saying, "We have a few more broncs to try out, and you can work with the snubbing crew and corrals. It won't interfere with your contesting, and it will take care of your entrance fees and expenses."

I thanked him and went to work. During my rodeo career, I saw a great deal of both George and his son, Allen, and had the greatest respect for both of them. In the racing field, the name of Drumhiller was, and still is, widely known.

Before the show got underway, I had ridden a few tryouts and drew a very good bronc for my first ride. In the first go-around in the bucking contest I had the advantage of seeing some of the top men make their rides before my turn. There were two or three good rides made—Red Parker had drawn Cul de Sac, the horse Sundown had sold to Drumhiller. Cul de Sac did a beautiful job of bucking and Parker rode like a champion, raking the bronc from his shoulders to the back skirts of the saddle every jump. I knew it would take something out of the ordinary to top his ride.

I had set the under stirrup leathers well ahead and, using a couple of wood screws, made them secure to the underside of the front tree bars. This would allow me to spur ahead with ease and shorten the upswing when spurring back. By taking a little shorter hold on the rein I could lean forward more. This allowed me to hit the back of my saddle cantle board with my spur rowels, a feat that not many cowboys could accomplish.

I saddled my bronc and climbed aboard. When they turned him loose, I hit him hard in the shoulders the first couple of jumps. He really came undone, getting plenty of altitude and kicking high and crooked. When my spurs came out of his shoulders on the second or third jump, they went all the way, slamming the rowels hard against the cantle board. I continued hitting the cantle all through the ride. I could hear a terrific roar from the grandstand and I knew that I was making it look good. The old horse was really jarring my teeth. At this time in rodeos, your ride was judged to the point where your horse broke and ran or stopped. There was no time limit. I was going strong but, close to the finish, I blew a stirrup, which disqualified me.

Spurring that high back, you must bend your knees completely, which gives you a little slack in your stirrup leathers, which, in turn, can very easily cause you to lose one. To have this happen on my first ride was a great disappointment. Mr. Drumhiller tried to cheer me up by saying, "You know you were making a money ride until you lost that stirrup."

I thanked him and said, "My first ride in my first major show, and I blew it."

He grinned and said, "It may be your first, but it won't be your last. You'll make it okay."

Those words made me feel better. It was a good first lesson. It's the overall points and finish that count and only the grand finals pay off.

The show finished with Red Parker winning the bronc riding, and George and Burt Weir winning the steer roping. I had watched the bulldogging very carefully and decided to give it a go at Pendleton, which was to take place the following week.

In fact, it was at that Pendleton Roundup that I earned the nickname that I would carry through life. I was palling around with a couple of cowboys who were from the Yakima country. We were trying out some rodeo broncs three or four days ahead of the Roundup. These two friends were great believers in a bit of firewater to settle their nerves, so I joined them in a skirmish with a quart of Old Crow. When we finished the bottle we practically flew out to the roundup grounds. Those pals of mine couldn't get to the broncs quick enough. The Old Crow really had them wound up. We hadn't even passed through the gate when a wrangler rode in leading a bronc. He hollered, "Who wants this one?"

One of my friends yelled back in a loud voice, "Give him to me, and I'll show you gents how they ride these fuzztails over in Yakima."

They snubbed and saddled the bronc and he climbed aboard. When they turned him loose the cowboy let out with a Commanche war cry and slammed both spurs high in the horse's shoulders.

He was big and stout and those spurs really hit the firing pin. The bronc exploded like a charge of T.N.T. He went into the air, threw his head up, giving the rider a slack rein, and at the same time kicking high behind. The cantle board hit my friend with such force that he turned a complete somersault in the air, hit the ground with a grunt and gave the bystanders cause for a real howl.

The next bronc was brought out and my other pal shouted, "I'll take that one." He did, but in reality the bronc took him.

When the bronc left the snubbing horse, he made a couple of jumps and then started spinning like a lopsided top. The longer he spun, the faster he turned. The cowboy left him like the blade of a windmill that had been torn off in a storm. Above the hilarious laughter, I heard a voice say, "All them Yakima boys ride alike." Well, all the razzing was a little embarrassing, so I decided to give them a little help.

"Bring another one of your good broncs out," I yelped, "and I'll show you what a Yakima bronc rider can really do."

The laughing and kidding was really on. The wrangler brought out a little bronc that, in my condition, looked like a lost cause. I saddled him and climbing aboard, calling loudly, "Turn this field mouse loose!"

They let him go, and that scrawny fuzztail made me look like a rank amateur. I never realized how much of a wallop that Old Crow really had. From my point of view, looking down over the front of my saddle, that bronc had two very fuzzy heads. They quickly transposed to four or five spurred boots with my feet in them and nothing but the blue sky on beyond. The little bronc was gone. I hit the ground with a painful thud, to the joy of the spectators who were in hysterics. The Yakima buckaroo stock had hit an all-time low.

A photographer got a picture of me upside down above that bronc and to carry on the rib, captioned it "Yakima Canutt leaving the deck of a Pendleton bronc." The cowboys picked it up and started calling me "Yakima," which was soon cut to "Yak." However, the name has been a good show name—people seem to remember it.

Yakima is an Indian name and it has caused a great many

people to think that I am an Indian. I used to get a kick out of questions as to my Indian blood, especially during some of the parties at the end of the rodeos. Of course, I always obliged them. One time I would be a Sioux and the next time a Umatilla, or a Nez Percé.

I enjoyed the little game until the Indians themselves started trying to find out what tribe I belonged to. When I would try to explain to them that I wasn't an Indian, they would give me a questioning look. I remember White Cloud, who was a well-educated Indian, saying one day, "Yakima, what tribe are you from?"

"I'm not Indian," I replied.

"You ashamed of it?" he asked, with a scowl.

"White Cloud," I said, trying to sound convincing, "if I was Indian I would be very proud of it, but I have traced my ancestry as far back as possible, only to learn that I am Scotch and Irish on my mother's side and Dutch and German on my father's side."

White Cloud turned and looked down, mumbling to himself, "Scotch . . . Irish . . . Dutch . . . German." He gave me a sympathetic look, shook his head and walked away.

My disastrous ride and the publicity surrounding it taught me a good lesson: alcohol and bronc riding don't mix. In the future I would save what little drinking I did for after the contests.

Following this rule (and breaking a few others along the way) I did pretty well over the next few years. I had found my career, had caught the rodeo madness and was enjoying every moment of it. Hoot Gibson had one of the best remarks about the peculiar attraction of this "wired" circuit. Hoot was only a year older than I, and he too was young when he caught the fever. By 1912 he was hanging around Pendleton, exercising the horses and taking more than a few successful shots at the big money. He once said, "It takes a lot of courage for a man to pay out his dollar to enter a rodeo and then, after not winning a red cent, walk away saying, 'Sure lucky I didn't get hurt.'"

Luckily, I won more than I lost. I was building a good reputation as a bronc rider, bulldogger, and all-around cowboy. In my own mind I knew that I was headed for the championship—but then I suppose that was every boy's dream. In 1915 I won a second at Pendleton and firsts in a great many small shows. My name was becoming better known and I started receiving letters from rodeo promoters inviting me to compete in their shows.

Compete I did! By 1916 I was a cocky twenty-one year old who felt that he was already an old hand at even as tough an event as bulldogging. In 1916 I had signed up with C. B. Irwin from Cheyenne, Wyoming, to do several shows. The big one was a twelve-day event at Sheepshead Bay in New York, and on one day of the show, ex-President Theodore Roosevelt was an honored spectator.

It had to be that day, of course, that I had a really wild experience. I had complained to C. B. that the horses I was using for bulldogging were a little slow. "All right, Yak," he answered. "I'm going to bring out Toby Grey for you to ride in the bulldogging."

Toby Grey was a quarter horse who had won a good number of races. When the steer left the chute Toby, not being trained for bulldogging, reared up and gave me a bad start. But when he straightened out he was overtaking the steer so fast I had to start leaving the horse ten or fifteen feet before getting to the animal. I managed to get hold of his horns with a perfect catch, but I was traveling so much faster than the steer that I practically jerked him off his feet, and we went into the wildest hoolihan I was ever mixed up in. The steer turned end over end, breaking off both horns, and breaking a rib for me. It also knocked the breath out of me. I got to my hands and knees, trying to regain my breathing, and the steer, with both horns dangling, stood alongside me, shaking his head and bellowing.

A humane officer rushed over and shot the steer, which all but fell on me. Then he squatted down in front of me with his gun still in his hand. I thought for a moment that he was going to shoot me as well, and at that moment I wouldn't have cared much. I finally got my breath and I could hear the excited officer saying, "You are under arrest."

"What for?" I gasped, feeling my bruised ribs.

"For cruelty to animals," he answered.

C. B. Irwin paid the fine, but he wasn't about to let me forget it. The next day he collared me, "Hey, Yak, you want Toby Grey again?"

"Only if you give him a couple of sleeping pills to slow him down," I replied. The tape on my chest made it hurt to laugh.

That was just a broken rib, which we didn't pay a lot of attention to. The only time that I was so badly hurt that I couldn't finish the show was when I was coming out of the chute on a bronc when he fell and I wrenched my knee. After having a nurse put hot and cold packs on it all night, I wrapped and taped it up good and tried to ride. When I used my spurs, it hurt so much that I gave up and told the pickup man to come and get the horse.

Another time, I was bulldogging at Weiser, Idaho, when I started to jump for the steer and my horse crowded so close that he put me right on top of the steer's head. One of his horns went into the corner of my mouth and tore my upper lip pretty bad. A doctor took me in his car to his office and when I looked into the mirror, I didn't think he would ever put my mouth back together. However, after working on it for an hour or so it looked pretty good. He gave me ten or twelve stitches, then with some cotton on the wound, he taped it down and took me back out to the rodeo grounds. I made my final ride and won the contest. The doctor came over and said that was a fine ride and inquired how I felt. I said fine and lit a cigarette. The flame touched the cotton and it practically blew up. I slapped it with my hand to put the fire out and tore a couple of stitches out.

"What in hell was that?" I asked. "Gun cotton?"

"That's what it was," he replied, mildly.

"Why in hell didn't you tell me," I demanded. He grinned and took me back to his office and replaced a couple of stitches. During the next year, it looked as if I had a hare lip. Finally I went to a good plastic surgeon, and he did a very fine job of fixing my face.

I was lucky with that one. I had a friend, Jerry Wright, who was killed in the same kind of accident. He was bulldogging a steer at a rodeo in Parsons, Kansas. As he was making the catch, he landed on top of the steer's head, hoolihanning him, turning him upside down. The steer's horn ran through his upper leg and severed the big artery. He bled to death on the way to the hospital.

From New York, we went to Pittsburg, Kansas, for a three-day show, and from there we went to Kansas City, where we played to big crowds, and also put on a big parade. During the parade, whenever we passed a saloon, a group of us would leave the parade and ride right in and line our horses up at the bar. To our amazement, the owners and bartenders got quite a kick out of it, and we each got a drink on the house. At the next saloon, another group would ride in, have a drink and return to the parade.

One of the big hotels had a barroom, we tried to ride through the revolving door and got a horse stuck in it. We finally got him out, but we were then ordered to stay in the parade. It seems that the publicity of these pranks really drew the crowds to the show, and this show was very successful.

The following season I traveled with a group of contestants who played the Northwest and Canada. There were several circuits for a cowboy in each season, and I tried to mix it up from season to season. During that season I was pursuing more than the big money. I had become interested in Kitty Wilks, one of the competing cowgirls. With her riding habit on, she couldn't have weighed more than a hundred pounds, but she was a great lady bronc rider and a good relay race rider, and had won the Lady's Bronc-Riding Championship a couple of times.

We were competing in a show at Kalispell, Montana, when we decided to get married. I was just twenty-one, and she was twenty-eight. We had everything set to say the "I dos" the day after the show finished. The last day of the show I finished winning the bronc riding and the bulldogging and five or six of my good friends decided to take me out for a bachelor dinner that soon turned into a drinking contest. Early in the evening a big lumberjack crashed our party and became a bit of a nuisance. When I told him to scram, he threw a haymaker at me which I sidestepped and laid one on his chin, which luckily put him out.

There were three or four saloons in the town and, of course, we made the rounds. By eleven or twelve o'clock we were well plastered. While drinking and verbally riding broncs, Ben Corbett, a great all-around cowboy and later a fine Hollywood actor, came over and said, "Look who's at the other end of the bar."

I glanced that way and saw it was my friend, the lumberjack, having a beer and bothering no one.

"So what?" I said to Ben. "It's a public place, isn't it?"

By this time I was practically hanging onto the bar rail with one hand in order to stay on my feet.

"Yeah," Ben answered, "but I just heard him say you were a double-crossing so-and-so."

"That's right," chimed in White, one of the other cowboys. "I heard him."

In my alcoholic haze, this was enough for me and I weaved my way to the lumberjack. "What's the idea you saying I'm a double-crossing so-and-so?" I asked accusingly.

The man was fairly sober now. "I never said anything about anyone," he replied shortly.

"Ben, come here," I called. He and White joined me, and I said, "Did this fellow say I was a double-crossing so-and-so?"

"He sure did," Ben said.

I let go and hit the lumberjack right between the eyes, but it never fazed him. He landed a haymaker on me that sent me sprawling clear across the barroom. I got up, shook the fog out of my eyes, and went back and laid another haymaker on him. But old John Barleycorn had taken the power out of my punches. The lumberjack hung one on me and I took another sprawling trip across the room. Even in my condition, I realized that I had to keep away from those haymakers. I crossed the room and swung with everything I had, and ducked his counterpunch. He grabbed me and slammed me to the floor. As we rolled, I got a good hold on him, and he started choking me. I pulled his head around and rammed a thumb in his eye. That did it. He let out a squeal, tore loose and got to his feet and beat it.

I learned afterwards that this poor fellow had not said a thing about me or any of the gang. Corbett and White, witnessing my run-in with him earlier that evening and knowing that I had had too many drinks to be a real challenge in any kind of donnybrook, figured it would be very funny to get me into a fight and marked up a bit for my wedding the next day.

When traveling with a group of rodeo ranahans in those days, you had to watch your step. If anything could happen, it did! As fate would have it, their sinister prank worked. I took a look at myself in the mirror the next morning, and what I saw wasn't good. I looked like I had finished second in a skirmish with a wildcat!

Everyone at the wedding was happy except the bride and groom. The Justice that married us eyed me peculiarly and glanced around suspiciously. I think he expected to see a man with a shotgun. However, he smiled and proceeded with the "do yous" and we responded with the "I dos."

After the congratulations and good wishes were all over, the little bride couldn't get me behind closed doors fast enough. I thought nothing of that. It seemed natural. But once the door was closed, I found out that Webster had left a lot of words out of his dictionary, words to express just what kind of a no good character a man really is. It didn't take long for me to figure out we should have been saying "I won't" instead of "I do."

Now don't get me wrong. We all know, it takes two to make a bargain or kick up an argument. This marriage turned out to be one of those undeclared vest-pocket wars. It was an unhappy one that terminated three years later when I acquired a divorce. It was never contested—seeming to be one-hundred percent mutual.

Ex-president "Teddy" Roosevelt poses with his Western friends after enjoying the rodeo show at Sheepshead Bay, New York, in 1916. Yakima Canutt is second from left, seated.

Yak ready to ride from a snubbing horse.

Yak winning the Bronc Riding at Walla Walla, Washington, in 1917 on Cul de Sac.

On furlough from the Navy in 1918, Yak demonstrates his skill "bulldogging" a steer.

Monte Vista, Colorado, 1920. The horse is Corkscrew, the rider Yakima Canutt.

William Gibbs McAdoo presenting Yak with the Roosevelt Trophy (first leg) awarded to the winner of the highest point score in the two biggest rodeo shows of the time: Pendleton, Oregon, and Cheyenne, Wyoming. Others in the picture are, from left, Dorothy Morrell, Donna Card and Tom Grimes.

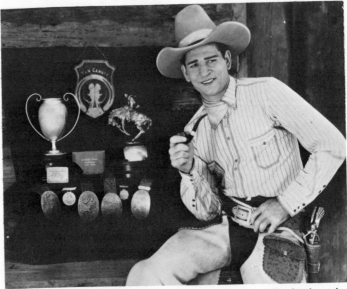

Yakima Canutt, at the end of his rodeo career, proudly displays the Colorado Springs Bronc Riding Cup (1922), his Roosevelt Trophy and four Police Gazette Championship belts won in 1917, 1919, 1920 and 1923.

FOUR

Mixing Rodeo and Reels

All was set and ready for the 1917 Pageant of the West, the Pendleton Roundup. As usual, this "biggest little town in the Northwest" was in ornate holiday dress—Western style. However, the ornamentation was dominated by Old Glory and the colors red, white and blue, and many of the colorful lavaliers bore patriotic slogans which replaced some of the usual cowboy phrases that were so familiar during the Roundup; slogans such as "Let'er Buck," "Hook 'em, Cowboy," "Bite 'er Lip," and "Take a Deep Seat, Cowboy." The reason—the country was at war!

President Woodrow Wilson had gone before Congress on April 2nd, and asked for a Declaration of War against Germany. On April 6th, 1917, Congress passed a joint resolution declaring war on Germany.

In spite of that fact, one of the largest crowds ever came to the Pendleton Roundup that year. Each year, a beautiful silver-mounted saddle and cash prizes were awarded in the steer-roping and the saddle-bronc riding events. In addition, the riders were competing for the top prize of them all—the Police Gazette belt for the All Around Cowboy Championship of the World.

The show got underway with its usual clocklike precision—at one P.M. a pistol shot was fired, the gates of the arena were thrown open and the grand entry was on. Led by a color guard and the President of the Roundup, hundreds of cowboys and Indians dressed in colorful attire entered to the accompaniment of Bob Fletcher's famous Roundup Mounted Band. The entire procession rode the full circle of the track in review.

After the introductions, came a series of spectatular events: exhibition bull and bareback bronc riding, cowboys' flat race, trick and fancy roping and riding, and the very popular Indian squaw race. Then hundreds of Indians, men, women and children, dressed in their colorful costumes, entered the arena, weaving and interweaving, performing their ceremonial dances. After this eye-catching event, the main competition began: steer bulldogging, steer roping and tying, and saddle-bronc riding. These were the "go for broke" events that would crown the World Champion!

I was in the second division for the bulldogging and wouldn't compete in this event until the second day. The saddle-bronc riding followed the bulldogging. There were sixty-nine bronc riders in this event, and most of these were professional cowboys. In a contest with that many competitors you've certainly got to have what it takes to emerge a winner. A little luck helps, but luck alone just isn't enough.

Half the contestants in the saddle-bronc event would ride on the first day of the Roundup and the other half on the second. Then the fifteen or sixteen men who had earned the most points would advance to the semi-finals on the third and last day. Following those rides, the three top men would compete in the grand finals for the World's Championship!

On the first go-round, I drew a horse called McCay, a sturdy looking pinto. He was a good bucking horse, and had gotten out from under some good riders. Waiting my turn, I watched my competitors make some very good rides.

Finally McCay was brought to the snubbing crew. He wasn't a big horse, so I had taken my stirrups up one hole. I intended to make my ride as flashy as possible.

I saddled McCay and turned to see if the judges were set. They gave me the nod and I stepped aboard. When my mount turned away from the snubbing horse, I grabbed him high in the neck with both spurs. He squealed and went for altitude, high and crooked. I necked him for three or four jumps, and then, leaning ahead a bit, I started spurring from the points of his shoulders clear to the back saddle skirts.

The crowd let out with applause. Then I slammed my spur rowels against the cantle. I turned my head and looked toward the judges, but I kept those spur rowels clanking against the cantle. The roar from the crowd was music to my ears. McCay was bucking very crooked, that is, he was sunfishing.

When he gave up and started to run, I sailed my Stetson high in the air.

The pickup man took McCay in tow. I went over the pickup horse, behind the rider, and hit the ground running, circling back to retrieve my hat. I had reason to believe that I had paved the way to the semi-finals. Tossing my hat in the air when a horse quit bucking became a habit, and somehow it always added to the applause from the audience. To this day, when I meet one of the old timers and bucking horses are mentioned, they will remind me of the way I used to sail my hat into the air.

The steer roping was next on the program. George and Charley Weir were top men for time the first day. These two brothers were a hard pair to beat. Their names will always remain among the great ropers of their day. George Weir won the steer roping in 1915 and 1916, with his brother Charley close behind in second place in 1916. At this 1917 show, Charley beat George for first place.

The second day, I watched the rest of the saddle bronc riding. As always, there were some good rides made, but I had the feeling that I was still in the contest. I bulldogged a steer, but I was a bit slow in getting to him, and had no chance at the day money for that event. Jess Stahl set a record that day for one steer—that record was to stand at Pendleton for many years.

On the third and last day of the Roundup, the crowd coming to see the finals of "The Olympics of the West" not only filled the grandstand and bleachers, but all the standing room as well! It was the largest crowd ever assembled to watch this show.

This was a big day for me. I was close to realizing the dream that I first dreamed when I was eleven years old and I rode old Buck in the potato patch. My mother and stepfather were at the Roundup, but Dad couldn't come—he was at the old ranch. I would have given my right eye if he could have been there to see me. I had the feeling that this was my day.

In spite of being confident of my ability, I somehow felt as though I had eaten butterflies for breakfast. I think that the contestants in all competitive sports must have that feeling until the starting gun fires. The few times that I have been a bit nervous getting on a bronc, it was not from fear of the horse, but because I was competing. The minute I got into the saddle, though, I felt at home and sure of myself.

My marks in the first round of bronc riding were high enough to get me into the semi-finals, where I rode a horse called Corbett against fourteen other cowboys. Only one man was thrown! As the judges sat on their horses, each checking his book to pick the three riders to compete in the grand finals, I sat on the inner track rail and watched the others. Three or four were holding a serious conversation, others were stall walking. I knew that I was not the only cowboy with a slight case of the jitters. The audience seemed unusually quiet as they watched the judges. Then, all of a sudden, they seemed to come alive. One of the judges was riding over to the announcer. Their choices had been made.

I found myself holding my breath. Then, loud and clear, amplified by his megaphone, came the announcer's voice.

"Ladies and gentlemen, the cowboys picked to ride off the grand finals for the Championship of the World are: Yakima Canutt . . . (applause) . . . Bob Hall . . . (applause) . . . and Dave White . . ." (applause). I had made the finals!

We drew for mounts and then the judges asked me to go first. The name on the bit of paper I pulled out was a surprise. I had drawn Cul de Sac! I now knew that it was up to me. I had the horse you could win on.

Dave White drew P.J. Nutt, a big bay that was one of the best. Bob Hall drew Angle, another good horse. Lew Minor had won the Pendleton championship on him in 1912. We were all well mounted and with luck any one of us could win or lose.

I was first to ride, which certainly gave the other two a chance to see what they had to beat. I had my mind made up to go all out. I saddled Cul de Sac and was very careful not to cinch the saddle too tight, as this could affect his bucking, yet I made it tight enough so that it'd stay in place without affecting my riding. The judges gave me the go-ahead nod, and it was so quiet you could feel the tension of the crowd.

With my left foot in the stirrup I eased into the saddle. Holding the rein with my left hand and my hat in my right hand I said to the snubbing crew, "Let me have him!"

They did, and as he turned away from the snubbing horse I grabbed him high in the shoulders with my spurs. With his first jump I knew that he was right. Cul de Sac always bawled and squealed as he bucked. He was fast and crooked and would do something a little different every three or four jumps. I spurred from the shoulders back to the saddle skirts every jump. I was really going all out.

The horse hit the ground and went into the air in reverse. He followed with a straightaway and a high kick behind. That loosened me and raised me several inches above the seat of my saddle.

Ordinarily when a cowboy gets loosened, he will settle down for a jump or so, but my mind was made up to go all out, and I kept my spurs really working. Cul de Sac hit the ground hard and made another reverse, and as I slammed my spurs into his shoulders I turned my head to look at the judges for the space of a few jumps.

I finished the ride kicking back. My spurs hit the cantle a few times and as the old horse quit and started to run, I sailed my hat into the air.

The crowd responded with a thundering ovation. The pickup man got to me and took Cul de Sac in tow. I stepped off and retrieved my hat, then waved and smiled at the audience. I went to perch on the track rail and to watch Dave White and Bob Hall make their rides.

White saddled and mounted P.J. Nutt—not a showy horse, but one that had bucked off a lot of good riders. When P.J. turned away from the snubbing horse, he made a high jump with a terrific kick behind. Dave had his spurs in the horse's shoulders and this high kick loosened him to the point where it took him a couple of jumps to settle down. The judges are very critical of the first jumps that a horse makes, and I would say you can lose very easily at the beginning of your ride. Dave got straightened out finally, and finished with a qualified ride, but I felt that Bob Hall was all that stood between me and the Championship.

The snubbing crew turned Angle loose and he raised his feet ahead and up. Hall was driving his spurs into the horse's shoulders. As Angle leaped ahead, hitting the rear end of the snubbing horse, he was thrown out of stride and Hall was jarred a bit. However, both man and horse made a quick recovery and made a good showing—much better than White's ride.

As I sat there wondering if there was anything that could keep me from winning, John Spain, who had played a lot of shows with me the year before, and who had become a good friend, came over, sat down and said with a big smile, "Congratulations, Yak, you've got'm sacked."

"It's never over, John," I said, "until that fellow up in the crow's nest gives it to the audience."

"Well," John answered, "he's picking up the horn now!"

And out of the megaphone came the announcement, "In the cowboys' saddle-bronc riding for the World's Championship," a slight pause, "Yakima Canutt first, Bob Hall second, and Dave White third."

The years 1918 through 1923 saw me in the winner's circle a great many times. However, we were at war and, despite my western background, I always had a yen to join the Navy and see the world through a porthole, so to speak. In 1918 I went to Spokane and was sent to Bremerton, the 13th Naval District, and put in the Ordnance Class of Gunnery. In the fall of 1918 I was given a thirty-day furlough to go to Walla Walla and Pendleton to defend my rodeo title. I played Walla Walla first and won the saddle-bronc riding. The following week at Pendleton I drew a horse called Monkey Wrench. I had ridden him several times. He was a good bucking horse and had never given me any trouble. I started my usual spurring routine, but on the fourth or fifth jump he turned me into a complete somersault and away went my title.

Soon after I got back to camp, the Armistice was signed. I had enlisted for the duration of the war, so in the spring of 1919 I was discharged and went home. A short rest left me itchy to get back to the rodeo circuit.

In picking rodeos, I always tried to make the major shows. There were three big ones in Texas starting with El Paso in February and going on to San Antonio and Fort Worth in March and Wichita Falls in April. Then I'd head north. Tex Austin generally had big shows at Soldiers' Field in Chicago, and Madison Square Garden and Yankee Stadium in New York City.

I'd catch some smaller shows and go on to Cheyenne and Bozeman, Montana. Then up into Canada for the Calgary Roundup and back to the U.S. to Walla Walla, Washington, and the Pendleton Roundup. I'd finish up with Weiser, Idaho, and the War Bonnet Roundup at Idaho Falls.

Of course, there were always new shows coming up, but Tex Austin always had the big ones. So when I read in *Billboard* that Tex Austin was putting on a couple of good shows, one at Indianapolis, Indiana, and one in Danville, Illinois, this was good enough for me. I packed and headed for Indianapolis.

I finished in the money there in both the saddle-bronc riding and bulldogging. With this money and another five hundred dollars that I won by picking Jack Dempsey over Jess Willard, I was off to a good fresh start. I went to Cheyenne, always my jinx show, where I won seconds and thirds, but never a first. And from there I went to The Calgary Stampede. It was one of the top events of the circuit, and had the finest bucking horses of the time.

The first day of the show I drew a horse called Fox, who was one of the greatest. When I saw the horse, I remembered him from a rodeo at Sheepshead Bay in New York in 1916. But the horse's name at that show was I Don't Know. They kept changing his name because too many riders would turn him down. At the Sheepshead Bay show he bucked a rider off for ten consecutive days. Jim Massey, one of the best, was among the riders he had thrown. I heard Jim say that no one could ride the horse under the current rules. A rider had to use a three-quarter-inch manila rope for a rein. Anyway, I made a three-hundred dollar bet with Jim, and rode the horse to a standstill the day after the show finished.

When Fox came out of the chute at Calgary, he really turned on. He bucked the full length of the very large arena. It was one of the toughest rides that I ever had. In fact, I wasn't sure that I was going to make it. When I got off I could hardly stand—my legs were that gone. But I won the day money on that ride.

The last day I drew a horse called I.B. Dam for my final ride. In those days, when a rider got hurt he was allowed a substitute. An injured cowboy, by the name of Walt Whitten, had drawn Fox. I was picked to make the ride for him. Of course, we would split whatever I won. Since Fox was harder to ride than I.B. Dam, I chose to ride him first. He charged out of the chute and, about the fifth jump, he loosened me up and hit me with the cantle. My right leg went over the top of his neck, which twisted my left foot in the stirrup and hung me up. He bucked in a small circle, kicking at me every jump. He was a powerful horse and my weight finally tore the spur and sole off my boot. I came loose from the stirrup and rolled end over end. I was lucky to walk away from that one. My left leg was a little lame, but I rode I.B. Dam anyway and won the bronc riding. I still have the beautiful diamond-studded gold medal.

The Pendleton Roundup Association had sent a man to Calgary to buy three top horses. He bought Fox on the strength of his performance in bucking me off. A month or so later I drew him in the finals at the Pendleton Roundup of 1919 and won the championship on him. He had been renamed No Name by this time.

A big rodeo was to be held in Los Angeles and I had heard of a horse named Pancho Villa. His owner, Lucky McFall, claimed no one had ever made a qualified ride on him. I had never been to Los Angeles, so I decided to play that show mainly to take a seat on this celebrated bronc. On my arrival in L.A. I met with Lucky McFall and made a deal to ride his horse the first day of the rodeo. I was to get two hundred-and-fifty dollars if I qualified.

Douglas Fairbanks was among the celebrities who took in the show. Doug always liked to get close to the action so he came over to the chutes and kidded with us until the entertainment started. He also upped the Pancho Villa purse with a two hundred-and-fifty-dollar check. When I came out of the chute I hit the horse with the spurs and he really went high and fast. He was a good, showy bronc with power. I made a qualified ride, received the five hundred, and thanked Doug for the extra money.

I decided to stay in Hollywood for the winter. I had met quite a few screen personalities during the rodeo. Westerns were very big in Hollywood at that time, and many of the stars were former rodeo contestants and cowboys. Tom Grimes and Ben Corbett, close friends with whom I had rodeoed, now worked in pictures, and promised to show me around.

I went to the Fox Studio with Tom Grimes and by luck ran into Tom Mix. He was getting ready to make a picture and during our conversation he said, "Yak, as long as you're to put in the winter in Hollywood, how would you like to work in one or two of my pictures?"

"When do we start?" I asked.

"Next week," he said.

He took me to the Casting Office and had me put on the payroll as an extra. I thanked him for the job, and got instructions from the Casting Director on where and when to report.

The first day of the picture I came on the set clean-shaven and dressed in one of my most colorful rodeo costumes. When Tom saw me he came over and greeted me with a broad grin.

"Hey, Yak," he said, "I'm the star of the picture. You're going to work with the outlaw gang, but that won't start for a couple of days. Wear faded Levi overalls, an old hat and shirt, and let your whiskers grow."

The next morning I came to work with the proper wardrobe on, but no whiskers. I was twenty-four years old and naturally, I enjoyed a little night life. Whiskers just didn't seem proper.

During the day a group of spectators came to the set to watch the filming. They circled around Tom and started asking him all sorts of questions. Tom Mix was first "discovered" by the Miller Brothers when he was a bartender in Oklahoma City. His outstanding talent was that he was one of the last of the great Western storytellers. He spent a number of years traveling with various Wild West Shows and he did, in fact, work at mastering riding, roping, bulldogging, bronc riding, and shooting but his main attraction was always his tall tales. Most of the exploits in these tales exceeded Tom's (or anybody's) capacity to perform. Tom was a showman extraordinaire. That morning on the set, he entertained the crowd with several of the wild adventures he had had before entering motion pictures. He had captured horse thieves and fought bands of outlaws single-handedly. To make some of his yarns a little more believable, he would turn to one of his cowboys and say, "You remember, Tex, when that outlaw shot my horse out from under me."

Tex, knowing who was buttering his bread, would answer with an awed, "Do I remember! Boy, that was a day I'll never forget."

When the group left, I turned to Mix. "Tom," I said, "you're a bit reckless with the truth, aren't you?"

"What do you mean 'reckless'?" he retorted half-angrily. "They wanted to be entertained, so I took a few sequences from my pictures and turned them into reality." Then he calmed down a bit and added, "Look, Yak, when you're in show business, you've got to meet people and entertain them. As long as a lie don't hurt anyone, there's no harm done." Then he gave me his big winning smile. "They ate it up, didn't they?"

"That they did," I said, not wanting to use the word "yes." I had heard that a little too often in my two days on the set.

After three or four days of shooting, the director called for the outlaws. He took one look at me and frowned with annoyance. "You're supposed to have whiskers," he said coldly.

I was left out of the scene, and when it was finished Tom came over to me. "Yak, you're the most stubborn cowhand I've ever known," he said. "Now dammit, let your whiskers grow." I didn't want to run around with whiskers, so I never went back. In fact, I never even returned to the studio for my salary.

During the winter I did work in two or three pictures. Ben Corbett took me to a studio that was starting a twelve-part serial titled *Lightning Brice*, which starred Jack Hoxie and Ann Little. Paul Hurst was directing. Paul was also doing the villain in the picture. I did a couple of horse falls using a Running W (more on this later) and a fight with the villain.

As my first scene in a picture, this fight scene was pure comedy. Shortly before the picture started my friend, Ben Corbett, came to me and said he thought that I was going to be cast in the part of a sheriff who has a fight with Paul.

"What gave you that idea?" I asked.

"Well, Paul wanted to know if you could fight."

"What did you tell him?"

"I said you're damn right he can fight."

A little later Paul called me over and confirmed Ben's prediction. "Mr. Hurst," I said, "this is my first picture work and I don't know anything about motion picture fighting."

"You know how to fight, don't you?" he asked.

"I should know how," I said. "I've had quite a number of them."

Paul nodded his head with a satisfied grin, "That's fine. Now this is the scene. I'm in the jail cell here, and I'll put on a sick act—screaming and hollering. You come in and I beg for a drink of water. I have already picked the lock. When you turn to go after the water, I shove the door open and leap on your back."

"Then what do I do?"

"You start fighting."

Everyone had a good laugh. I thought they were ribbing me. With the camera ready, Paul entered the cell and I got in my starting place. Paul then told the crew to hold everything and ordered the grip to bring a bucket of water and a couple of towels. Everyone on the set had another laugh.

Then Paul added, "Also, get the first aid kit and have it handy."

Another laugh by all. I was getting more nervous by the minute.

"You'd better tell me what to do when you jump on me," I said to Paul.

"You'll soon find out," he grinned.

Not only was I nervous but I was getting a bit irritated.

"O.K. I'm ready," I said, wondering just what was going to happen and why everyone was still chuckling.

When the camera started rolling, Paul began hollering and pounding the wall. I entered the scene and crossed to the cell door.

"What's wrong with you?" I demanded, trying to sound rough.

"Water, please, water," he pleaded.

I said okay and, as I turned to go for his drink, he shoved the door open and leaped on my back. I spun around, then snapped back, getting him in front of me. We threw a few punches and he went into a clinch. I hip-locked him and, as we went to the floor, I put my left hand out to break the fall, but he grabbed my left wrist, pulling my arm to him. My head hit the hard floor and I saw more stars than an over-anxious astronomer. We separated, got to our feet, and exchanged a few more punches. I had made up my mind to let him set the pace and play just as rough as he wanted it. He again rushed towards me and tried to get in a clinch with me. I used a wrestler's gag—I grabbed his right wrist with my left hand, raised his arm and ducked under it, and at the same time I grabbed his leg and was able to flip him over my head. He landed against one of the big arc light stands, and knocked down the light with a shattering crash.

I stood there looking at him. My head was really ringing from the jam that I had taken on the floor. I expected him to be mad but he rolled over and sat up laughing uproariously, then got slowly to his feet.

"Let's see, where were we," he said, stretching to flex his bruised back muscles.

"We were on the set," I replied, enjoying the friendly grins on the faces of the crewmen, "not out here among the lights."

I did a deputy sheriff in the picture, *The Girl Who Dared*, starring Edith Sterling. I was happy when we finished that show. It was close to spring and almost time for the beginning of the rodeo season.

Before leaving Los Angeles to play the 1920 rodeo circuit, I received a letter from the Secretary of the Tri-State Roundup at Belle Fourche, South Dakota, which said that they had a very famous bucking horse named Tipperary, who had thrown or disqualified over eighty cowboys. The rodeo sponsors wanted me to come to Belle Fourche for their Fourth of July rodeo and as they worded it, "*try* to ride Tipperary."

I had always wanted to ride that horse but, for some reason, we were never at the same rodeo. Tipperary was a medium-sized bay who looked like a thoroughbred and was owned by a Mr. Charley Wilson.

The letter also contained a contract which stated that I was to ride contest rules, with one addition. I had to ride Tipperary to a finish. No pickup man was to get near until he stopped bucking. I was to pick a judge, the committee would pick a judge, and the two judges would pick a third judge. I would be supervised in the saddling of the horse by Wilson. This supervision was to make sure that the horse wasn't cinched too tight. If I qualified I was to receive five hundred dollars for the ride, but nothing if I lost. The letter further stated that there was good prize money in the bronc-riding and bulldogging contests, and that I could compete in these, and make all the bets I wanted. All in all, it sounded like an interesting challenge, so I signed the contract and mailed it back.

Tipperary had built a fantastic record. He had thrown more cowboys than any horse I ever knew. I was told by Mr. Wilson that I would be the eighty-third man to try him. Of course, the majority of them were come-alongs, but I knew several top hands who had tried him and bit the dust. Three or four were winners of big shows—Sam Brownell, a winner at Cheyenne was disqualified; Leonard Stroud, who won a lot of first prize money, was thrown. I never forgot Stroud's advice to me when he heard that I was going to take a seat on the famous bronc.

"Yak," he said, "watch out for that third jump."

In talking with other cowboys who had tried the old horse, or seen him in action, I found that they all had the same comment. The rider was always thrown quickly. With this information and my experience with bucking horses, I figured that Stroud's warning was worth remembering. It takes a jump or two for a horse to really get under way.

On my arrival in Belle Fourche, I met the committee and entered the saddle-bronc riding and bulldogging. When asked who my judge was, I told them that I would have him there on the day of the ride. I met Wilson, the rancher who owned the horse, and after talking with him, I figured he was a trustworthy man.

I had a couple of days before the show opened, and after meeting with members of the Roundup Board, I knew that I wouldn't have any trouble getting a bet up on my ride. However, the morning of the day I was to make the ride, I went to headquarters to see the committee. Mr. Wilson was also present. I told them that we had kidded about a bet for a couple of days, and I thought it was time to get serious. I wanted to make a bet. One of them asked me how much I wanted to bet.

"You fellows name it," I said. "I will cover a couple of thousand."

That was a mistake. I should have started off with smaller bets. I guess they figured that if I had that much confidence in my riding ability, and, of course, holding the World's Championship as a back up, they were bound to lose. They decided to save their money, so I got no bets!

The rodeo drew a capacity crowd, and I was to open the show with my ride on Tipperary. Wilson brought his horse out for the introduction. They had always bucked him away from a snubbing horse and didn't want to put him out of a chute. It made no difference to me. Everything was set, and Mr. Wilson turned to me.

"Yak," he said, "we've asked you to name your judge and never got an answer. The committee picked me as their judge. Now who have you selected?"

"Charley," I said, "I'm going to also pick you, and aside from that, I'm going to place the saddle on the horse and let you cinch it."

He did, and just before I got on Tipperary I said, "Charley, watch very close. I'm going to hit him in the shoulders to start him and once again before he gets into his second jump."

"You can't do it, cowboy!" he grinned.

I stepped aboard, and the bronc was cut loose. I hit him in both shoulders with my spurs, and he whirled away from the snubbing horse in a high jump. His second jump was a fast straightaway jump. I raked my spurs from high in his shoulders and set them in his sides by the cinch. I figured that with this long, fast, straight jump he was getting up momentum for that next "third" jump, which had made him famous. And, just as I figured, he practically exploded. He went into the air with a combination jump that felt like he was breaking in two. He kicked high to the right, swinging his front legs and head to the left. Actually, it was a sunfish with a kick added. It popped my head and loosened me, but that tricky maneuver threw him out of stride and I really went to work with my spurs. He bucked to the end of the arena, and stopped at the race-track fence. I stepped off and led him back to Wilson, as the crowd gave me a great ovation.

"Well, Yak," he said, and his eyes were actually showing tears, "you rode the old horse, but I don't believe you could do it again."

"Let him rest up," I answered, "until tomorrow or the next day. I'll take him on the same deal, or a good bet."

"No, Yak," Charley replied, "I'm taking him back to the ranch. We may make a deal though, for you to come back next year, and take another seat on him."

I received the five hundred dollars for my ride, and won a good part of the purse money in the saddle-bronc riding and bulldogging. I will say one thing for Mr. Charley Wilson—he was an honest gentleman.

Between that show and the show the following year, old Tip bucked off three or four more cowboys. For their 1921 show the Belle Fourche Rodeo Committee brought in a horse called Black Diamond which had acquired a good reputation. They made a deal with me and another top rider, Oklahoma Curly Roberts, a contestant from the South, to come to the show.

On the first day, Curly was to ride Tipperary, and I was to ride Black Diamond. On the last day of the show, I was to ride Tipperary, and Curly was to ride Black Diamond. Curly asked me about old Tip's style of bucking.

"As you know," I said, "we all ride a little different. But I'll give you one good tip. Watch that third jump!"

At this show the horses were to be bucked out of a chute, and the regular committee's three judges were to judge the rides. When the show was ready to start, Curly set the saddle on Tip, and Charley Wilson and his men cinched it. Curly set his boots into the stirrups, and adjusted his rein.

"Turn him out!" he yelled.

The gate was swung open and out he came!

Curly hit the old horse in the shoulders with his spurs and old Tip went to work. He loosened Curly on the second jump, and turned him end over end on the third. Curly got to his feet, shook his head, and walked away.

I was next. When Black Diamond came out of the chute, I went to work on him, and he proved to be a good bucker, fast and crooked. I kept my spurs busy and that black really kept *me* busy. I qualified, but it was no armchair seat. Barring Tipperary's explosive third jump, I think that the black was the better bucking horse.

The rodeo went along fine, and the last day started with my ride on Tipperary. I set the saddle on his back and Wilson and his men cinched it. I got on the horse, adjusted my rein, and told the chute men to turn us out.

As the gate opened, I grabbed him in the shoulders with my spurs and once again on the second jump as he hit the ground. I then set my spurs low in his sides by the cinch, and tightened my hold on the rein. His third jump was high and fast, kicking to the right and rooting his head to the left. This was his "secret weapon" jump, and he was so used to losing his man with it that when my hundred-and-ninety-five pounds still held solid in the saddle above him, he lost his balance and nearly fell. However, he righted himself and went on bucking, but he was all mine. I spurred him right to the finish, and again won the five hundred dollars for a qualified ride.

Before Oklahoma Curly mounted for his ride on Black Diamond, he asked me if I could give him a tip on the black.

"Curly," I said, "after riding the horse, and knowing how you ride, I'm afraid I can't help you. However, the main thing is to keep him between your legs." But Curly wasn't able to do it. Black Diamond threw him very quickly.

The committee presented me with the Tipperary Medal, which is a very beautiful token made of gold and inscribed: "Tipperary Medal, Belle Fourche, S.D., Presented to Yakima Canutt, Making the only qualified rides ever made on Tipperary—Presented by the Tri-State Roundup, Belle Fourche, S.D. 1920 and 1921."

Tipperary, that great horse, was inducted into the

National Cowboy Hall of Fame in Oklahoma City, the same day I was, in 1976.

Looking back over my rodeo years I am very proud of my record. In the south, Fort Worth was the top show. I had the honor of winning the saddle-bronc riding three years in succession—1921, 1922 and 1923. In fact, some of the cowboys called it Yak's show. At Wichita Falls in 1921, following the Fort Worth show I won both the bulldogging and the saddle-bronc riding. In the Tex Austin show staged at Soldier's Field in Chicago I placed first in the bronc riding and second in the bulldogging average.

At Pendleton, I won first in the saddle-bronc riding during the years 1917, 1919 and 1923, and second 1915 and 1920. I was first in the steer bulldogging in 1920 and 1921, and took home the all-around Police Gazette belt four times, in 1917, 1919, 1920 and 1923. I also won the first leg on the Roosevelt Trophy, which was given for the most points accumulated at Cheyenne and Pendleton, the two top shows of the time. This was a beautiful trophy given by the Roosevelt Hotel of New York in honor of that great American, Theodore "Teddy" Roosevelt. You had to win three times before you could claim it. However, they gave a small one for each one- or two-time winner. The first winner of the Big Trophy was a great cowboy, Bob Crosby, who won in 1925, 1927 and 1928.

After my win of 1923, the rodeo committee arranged for William Gibbs McAdoo to make the Roosevelt Trophy presentation in Los Angeles. McAdoo was the son-in-law of President Woodrow Wilson and served as Secretary of the Treasury from 1913 through 1918. He was also a senator from California from 1923 through 1939. After having been in Los Angeles during the winter of 1919 and having met a great number of screen personalities, I was very happy to visit the city again.

Tom Mix, who attended the presentation, also had stables and horses in Edendale where he kept his famous horse, Tony. He had a couple of bucking horses, and a particular one that he was really high on. After he saw my ride on that runaway scrubtail, he sent one of his men after his top bronc.

My old rodeo friend, Tom Grimes, came over to me and said that he had heard Tom tell his man to bring out his top bucking horse and get me bucked off. When the horse arrived and I got ready to saddle him, Tom stood by to watch the saddling.

"Well, Tom," I said, "as long as you're going to get me

bucked off, you might just as well win a little money. I'll make you a wager of anywhere from a hundred to a thousand dollars that I really comb him down and qualify."

He grinned but said nothing. I mounted, and when Tom's wranglers turned him loose, I really went to work on him with my spurs. I raked so much hair out of his shoulders and sides that it looked like the shedding season was on. When I got off, Tom walked over, smiling amiably.

"That was a nice ride, Yak. What do you think of him?"

"Tom," I replied, "he's a nice, showy bronc, but I don't think he'll make the big league."

After the presentation was over I decided to stay in Hollywood for a while. One morning I was pleasantly surprised by a phone call from one of Hollywood's top motion picture agents, Mr. Edward Small. He said that he would like to have a talk. I went to his office where he told me that an independent producer by the name of Ben Wilson had called him and wanted to talk with me about doing a series of Western action pictures. I signed a contract with the Small Agency to handle the deal.

Mr. Small took me to the Burwillow Studio located on Santa Monica Boulevard in Hollywood where we met Ben Wilson. He had seen the Roosevelt Trophy presentation on a newsreel at a moving picture theatre and liked my looks as well as my riding. A deal was made for me to star in eight action Westerns for him. They were called "blood-and-thunder quickies," in the silent era. I was happy. I had never tried to be an actor, yet here I was about to star in a series of eight pictures, with an option for a second series.

During my first year in the picture business I ran into Tom Mix many times and we became friends. I had formed a rather critical opinion of him during my earlier stay in Hollywood, but after really getting to know the man, I found him to be a fine human being. He was generous and had a good moral sense. He took great pride in his showmanship, and in my opinion, he was a showman without a peer. I once heard him talking to a friend who was complaining about someone who had been gossiping about him. "It don't make a damn bit of difference what they say about you," Tom said, "as long as they keep bringing up your name."

Tom once received an invitation to a dinner party during the filming of a motion picture in San Francisco. The guests were the elite of the city, including the governor of the state and high officials. It was a black tie and gown dinner affair. Tom arrived wearing a purple tuxedo, high-heeled white boots, and a ten-gallon, white Stetson hat. He was photographed from all angles and made the front pages of all the papers. To him this was showmanship.

I recall a parade that I was riding in during a rodeo at Yankee Stadium in New York. I always dressed a bit fancy at rodeos and especially in the parades. (In fact, Tom Mix once borrowed one of my two-toned shirts and had his tailor make several patterns from it.) As the parade neared the stadium we passed a group of youngsters gathered on the curb and one of them hollered at me:

"You can't ride like Tom Mix."

At the time I was holding the World Championship. But to those kids Tom Mix was their champion. That same sentiment was expressed by kids everywhere. He was also a champ at the box office, and in my opinion, he was a very important factor in the popularity of action Westerns.

Tom loved good cars and speed. On his way back to Hollywood from a weekend visit to Arizona, he failed to see a a detour sign where an underground culvert was being repaired, his car crashed through the construction and rolled over, killing him in the wreck.

Tom's death was a great shock to his many friends and fans, besides being a great loss to the motion picture industry. His name will live on, and rightfully so. He will long be remembered as one of the motion picture industry's greatest showmen.

The first script I was given for Ben Wilson's series of action Westerns was one called *Ridin' Mad.* As I studied the script, the memory of how flustered I got in some of the movie scenes that I did during the winter of 1919 came back to haunt me. The more I read and studied, the more convinced I became that I was not an actor. For a week or so before the starting date, I couldn't sleep. I was scared to death.

I would gladly have exchanged some of the intimate scenes for a single-handed fight with a grizzly bear. I was a wreck when I arrived on the set the morning we were to start shooting. I had spent one of the worst nights of my life, a sleepless one of rolling and tumbling and, worst of all, a dream about being in front of the camera and freezing with stage fright.

The director, Jack Jacard, realized that I was new to the acting profession and spent the forenoon photographing my rides in and away from the set, which was a beautiful San Fernando Mission. This, of course, was a big help, but the last scene before lunch was a bit of dialogue with the leading lady, a very fine actress, Helen Rosson, who was playing my sister in the picture. They gave me all the help they could. Of course, that was in the silent picture days and your blunders in dialogue did not mean too much. Had it been a talkie, I'm sure it would have been the first and the last day of my acting career. When we stopped to eat, I was so tied with nerves that I went behind the Mission and lost my lunch.

We finished the first day's work and when we arrived back at the studio, I went straight into Mr. Wilson's office. He looked up from the script he was reading.

"Well, how did it go?"

"Mr. Wilson," I replied emphatically, "today's work has convinced me that I'm not an actor. You'd better get another lead. I'm going back to the rodeos."

Wilson studied me a moment, then called the director, Jacard, in from another office.

"Yak says he's not an actor," he told him. "He wants to quit and go back to rodeoing. What seems to be the trouble?"

Jacard shrugged, "There's nothing wrong. It's his first day and he was a little nervous. He'll be okay. His work wasn't too bad and I'm not worried."

Wilson looked relieved at Jacard's reply. "I have the very thing you need," he said to me. He then broke out a bottle of bourbon and after two or three good jolts, they convinced me that I would make it as an actor.

The second day I stuttered and stammered through my scenes and at the end of the day, I was happy to hear the director say, "Wrap it up!"

When we got back to the studio, the film editor had the rushes of the first day's work ready to run for Jacard, Mr. Wilson, and me. That was the first time I'd seen rushes in a small studio projection room. The others knew the blunders would be lost in the cutting process, but I felt like hiding.

After seeing that stuff I said to Mr. Wilson, "I imagine you'll be glad to let me go back to the rodeo now."

"You're crazy," he laughed. "When those scenes are cut and put together, they'll be fine."

I couldn't believe he was serious, but he was.

"I guess you don't have to be crazy to be in the picture business, but it sure helps," I said.

After a few more days, I settled down and felt a little more at ease, especially in the action scenes. I did flying mounts, hazardous fights, chases, and a leap on the villain from the balcony. It didn't take too long for me to realize that there was a lot of room for improving the action routines. One of the hardest things for me to learn was that, when doing action, I had to forget what was practical and do the scene in a more spectacular way.

I recall doing a couple of tricky mounts in one of my early pictures. One called the "crooper mount" was a leap frog over the horse's rump and into the saddle. The other mount was running at the horse from a three-quarter angle and leaping six or eight feet into the air toward the animal's back with my legs spread open like a pair of scissors. I landed with my left foot in the stirrup and my right hand catching the saddle horn as my right leg went over the horse. This was a very showy mount and usually got a hand from the audience.

Someone told Douglas Fairbanks about the trick mounts that I had been perfecting. He called me and said he would like to see them. I had the studio send him the reel of film that the mounts were in. After seeing them, he called and thanked me, saying he was getting ready to film *The Gaucho* and wanted to do a couple of showy mounts and dismounts.

Doug was a great showman and loved doing things in a spectacular way. I saw *The Gaucho* and he had really topped my trick saddle mounts. He did one of the mounts by using a back crank on the camera. He started the scene sitting in the saddle, then turned a back flip off the rear end of the horse, landed on his feet, and ran out of the scene backwards. When the film was run at the forward motion, he ran up to the horse, turned a flip into the saddle and galloped away.

Doug was a fine athlete and worked out regularly. I made it a point to go over quite often. He loved to compete in all fields of athletic sports and when there were six or seven of us in his gym, he would flip a coin to see who was his first contestant.

Doug could beat me in a running jump, but in a standing jump, I almost always beat him. In his game of badminton—or Dougminton, as he called it—he had no trouble beating any of us. In fact, if there were a lot of spectators present he would play two of us at a time and give us a rough go. He was a great sportsman and a real man's man. It was always a pleasure to visit with him. I never forgot one bit of advice he gave me after he had watched me make a running broad jump.

"Yak," he said, "when you're doing jumps in a picture, cut your distance down a foot or two so you can land a little more gracefully. If you extend yourself you look awkward. Always put the bounce in it." He was right and I made use of that advice many times.

When we finished *Ridin' Mad* and it was cut and put together, I could hardly believe my eyes. For a quickie, it was a very good Western. I didn't care too much for my acting, but Wilson and Jack Jacard said I looked okay and would improve with experience.

Mr. Wilson was also doing a series of Western comedies with a star by the name of Richard Hatton, and while the writers were preparing my next story, I agreed to play a part in one of his films. I did not have to work on any pictures except my own, but I wanted all the experience I could get. This picture was to be made at a ranch, owned by the Giltabrand family, near Simi, California. They had a number of double-room cabins placed among big oak trees and the main house had a fair-sized dining room. Mrs. Giltabrand ran the place and did the cooking. A couple of cowboys worked for her, supplied the stock, and played extras as well.

Another small Western company was already at the ranch shooting a picture. The star was a cowboy, Bill Patton, whom I'd met during my first visit to Hollywood in 1919. He was a very close friend of Richard Hatton, the star of our film. Hatton was strictly a city man and our nickname for him was "Fearless Richard" since he was actually afraid to go out at night unless someone was with him. However, he could ride a horse and that's all that seemed necessary to some quickie producers.

I arranged with our director to set up a gag with Patton and the director of the other company. They put out the word that Patton and I were deadly enemies of long standing. When the Hatton company came in the first evening from work, Patton came over and greeted Fearless Richard warmly. Hatton then turned to introduce me:

"Bill," he said, "have you met Yak?"

"Yeah," Bill replied, glaring ominously at me, "I've met him."

I glared back and walked away. Fearless Richard was dumbfounded. Later, he came over to me and seemed concerned.

"I'm sorry, Yak," he said, "I didn't know you two were on the outs."

"I know that you and that so and so are good friends," I answered, "so tell him that if he'll just tend to his own business there'll be no trouble."

Then the two directors stepped in and one of them said that one thing they didn't need on location was a fight, so hold it down. We could tear each other apart after we finished, but there would be no fighting while we were working.

The next day Bill and I had some rough words, and the cowboys working with Bill took him away. Then Fearless Richard came over to me.

"Yak," he pleaded, "please don't get into a fight with Bill."

"What do you mean, fight?" I said. "I whipped him a couple of times three or four years ago. He knows that he can't beat me with his fists and that means only one thing. He wants trouble, and that means gun trouble."

"Oh no," gasped Dick. "One of you might get killed!" I nodded grimly and walked away. By this time, the crews on both pictures were getting jittery and the two directors were really helping to build up the tension.

The following day, when we finished work, our director told me to load my gun with blanks. Bill was going to start an argument in the dining room during dinner. I saw Bill as he left his cabin and he was wearing his gun. I slipped a blood capsule into my pocket, put my gun on, walked into the dining room and took my seat at our table. Bill was seated on the opposite side, watching my every move. I sat down and started putting some food on my plate. All was quiet with the exception of a couple of dudes from Bakersfield, who had been taking a horseback ride and were staying overnight. They were talking about a big rattlesnake that they had killed on the back part of the ranch.

"That's not the only rattlesnake around," Bill remarked loudly, looking right at me.

Our director, who was sitting next to me, tried to calm

Bill, and Bill's director also started soothing him and finally everyone started eating.

Then Fearless Richard, who was trying to break the tension, asked Bill, "How did things go today?"

"Not so well," Bill said, again directing his words at me. "You know we haven't got the great star your company has."

"You can say that again," I said nastily. "What your outfit needs is a star with a little of that stuff they call talent!"

Bill lunged to his feet and went for his gun. I deliberately fumbled my draw and let him get the first shot. I doubled up and fell, slapping the blood capsule to my forehead, then came to my feet shooting. The gun fight and the blood must have looked pretty realistic, because I've never seen people clear a room so quickly. Some went out through an open window, taking the screen with them, and, believe it or not, there was a one-legged man dining who jumped clear over the table and was among the first out.

At this moment, Mrs. Giltabrand's daughter, Juanita, came through the kitchen door with a tray of food. The shot and the blood on my face caused her to drop the tray and faint deadaway. While this was happening, the two dudes from Bakersfield grabbed Bill and me and were trying to keep us from continuing the battle. Then Mrs. Giltabrand rushed in. She helped revive her daughter, then grabbed a double-barreled shotgun and ordered both movie companies off her ranch.

Sobered by what could have been a tragedy, since Juanita had a heart condition, we all did some fast talking and apologizing, and finally Mrs. Giltabrand agreed to let us stay and finish our respective pictures.

Kernville, California, about one hundred-and-fifty miles northeast of Los Angeles, with beautiful mountains and valleys, was a fine location for Westerns in the twenties. The north and south forks of the Kern River joined a few miles down-river from the village. From this point they flowed through Kern Canyon to emerge from the mountains onto the lower San Joaquin Valley near Bakersfield.

The main part of town, built in the old western style, was owned at that time by the Brown Company. They had a hotel, a court with many cabins and a big store. They could accommodate a large picture company or two or three small ones. In the early days it was called "Whiskey Flat" and was a rough spot that boasted a number of shootouts. In fact, two or three of the old-timers were still living there in the twenties.

On my second or third picture, Ben Wilson decided to send the company to Kernville. I was happy to go there, since I had heard so many stories about the town and its bad men. The Walker brothers were, if the tales were true, a bit on the bad side, and the man who furnished horses and equipment to the picture companies had a rather rough reputation, too. His name was Wofford and the yarns coming out of Kernville pictured him as a knife man.

We left Hollywood in the afternoon, but because of bad roads, it was night when we neared the outskirts of the village. Then we heard a siren and shortly afterwards an ambulance passed speeding for Bakersfield.

"There goes one of Wofford's victims," I joked, but sure enough, when we arrived, we found that was the case. It seems Wofford and one of Newt Walker's hired men had an argument during a card game. Wofford got up to leave and the man stopped him at the door and slugged him. During the fight the man went for a gun and Wofford pulled his knife and trimmed the guy down to size. From all reports the cowboy had asked for it. He recovered and was back in Kernville before we finished the picture.

While filming that picture I was doing a scene where I rode my horse down a bank to the edge of the river. The camera was reset and I was to overlap the end of the last scene and ride into the river and swim the horse through the gorge. I was having trouble getting the horse into the water when Newt Walker decided to help me. He'd been drinking and was known to have an itchy trigger finger, so naturally I didn't want to get into an argument with him. I asked him in a nice way to please stay back of the camera, but he insisted on helping and picking up a large willow stick he remarked:

"This will put him there."

I had one of our boys hold my horse and I walked over to the prop truck, took the blanks out of my forty-five and loaded it with live ammo. I went back and mounted and said to the director:

"Let's try it again."

Newt came in to help once more and I told him patiently, "Newt, please go back of the cameras—you're just making things worse."

"I'm helping you," he replied belligerently.

"You're drunk and in the way," I said angrily. "Now get the hell out of here and leave us alone."

Newt eyed me silently for a long moment, then laughed and walked away.

We got the scene on the next take. Wofford was coming down the trail when Newt stopped him and told him what had happened. He wanted to come back down to the river and see which one of us would leave. Wofford talked him into going home. He then came over and asked me what the trouble was. I told him and he looked a little worried.

"Don't figure it's over, Yak," he said. "I know him. He'll call your hand, so be on guard."

"Thanks for the tip," I answered. "I'll try to play it right."

The next day we were shooting some scenes in front of a country store in Isabella, a small town a few miles from Kernville. I finished a few scenes and, of course, was wearing my gun but had no live ammo in it because that's a mite dangerous when you're pulling a lot of fancy draws, spinning the gun in and out of the holster.

I had just spun it into the holster, when I felt something poke me in the back. It was Newt. He spun his gun and poked me again, a sarcastic grin on his face. I could see the lead bullets in the side of the cylinder.

"You'd better be careful," I said coolly, "that gun is loaded."

"Sure it is," he chuckled, "an empty gun is no good!"

And believe me, at that point no one knew that better than I. Newt put his gun back in the holster, still grinning.

"Let's you and me go behind the store and have a drink," he said.

"Sure, why not," I replied. I put my hand on his shoulder and as we came to the back end of the store, I noticed an old-fashioned Chick Sales—a privy.

"Hey, Newt, I've got to go," I said. "I'll be right back." Without giving him time to object, I stepped inside and shut the door. I quickly put six live cartridges in the cylinder of my gun. I holstered it, then went back to Newt and had a drink with him.

"Thanks for the drink," I said casually, as he put the bottle away. "They're about ready to shoot so we'd better get back."

Newt hung around the set for awhile and every time I looked his way he gave me a mean look. I answered with a grin and a wise crack. He just couldn't put it all together. Finally, he told me to be careful and went home. I think that he had some idea of what had taken place in the Chick Sales. It just may be that that little building saved my life.

However, Newt Walker was destined for a tragic end. Shortly after I left Kernville, his brother shot him and his partner, then went to his cabin and took his own life.

In the picture, *Branded a Bandit*, directed by Paul Hurst, we again went to Kernville. Paul, like me, loved action and this film was loaded with it. In one sequence I was doing a fight with the heavy on top of a bluff that overhung the river. We fought to the edge of the bluff and went into a clinch. The camera was reset across the river at water level. At that point, Cliff Lyons, a stunt man, came into the shot, doubling for the heavy. We overlapped the previous scene, fought to the edge of the bluff, went into a clinch and spun off, falling to the river below.

We continued fighting and Cliff, who was a good stunt man but the world's worst swimmer, had a big problem. We would fight a bit, then I would have to help him out of the river to keep him from drowning. Hurst finally got disgusted and stopped the cameras.

"Give me those clothes," he ordered. "I'll show you how to fight in the water."

He changed into the double's wet clothes, and ordered the cameraman to pan with us.

"We'll fight in mid-stream for a few feet," he told me, "then I'll shove you under water and swim to that rocky point with you after me. You catch up as I get to that shelf. I'll turn and swing at you, you duck, and the force of the swing will carry me into the water.

"Then," I said, "I jump or dive back in and we fight some more, right?"

"Right."

We got into the river and the cameraman shouted, "rolling!"

Paul was a good swimmer and we put on quite a fight. Paul pounded me under the water and headed for the rocky point. I kept very close to him as I had a plan to change the fall a bit. Just as Paul got on the ledge, I quickly climbed up on the rocks and grabbed him. Hanging on tight, I went backwards off the bluff. We hit the water and went under.

When we surfaced Paul started to laugh, but I still carried

on the fight. He got a bit of water in his lungs and began coughing, so I dragged him to shore.

"Why did you grab me and do that Gilligan fall?" he choked when he finally got his breath.

"Well, Paul," I said, "I figured it would be better to do it that way than to have you ride me into a big splash!" Paul enjoyed that prank as much as I did.

On another occasion while filming in Kernville, I really got into trouble and had to be hauled back to Hollywood to a hospital.

We were getting ready to film a spectacular stunt where I was to jump my horse off the edge of a cliff some forty feet above the river. The grips and carpenters had built a smooth runway that was sixty or seventy feet from the trail to the edge of the cliff. At that point, the water below was very deep.

The director had shot all the tie-in scenes leading up the the stunt: scenes where I was, as usual, chasing the villain, who rode his horse into the river aiming to swim him through the gorge. I had cut crosscountry to arrive at the top of the cliff and had seen him below. Then the cameras were moved to cover the stunt itself.

I had fastened a pair of blinkers over my horse's eyes and had eyes painted on them so that they looked normal to the camera. The blinkers were held in place by an elastic band that went under the horse's neck and fastened between the eyes with a metal pin and a cord. I could pull this cord and release the blinkers just as we went off the runway. A horse with blinkers can be ridden at a slow lope if the track is perfectly smooth.

I led my horse to the end of the runway, mounted and signaled the director I was ready. The director had the cameraman roll the cameras, then gave Cliff Lyons (who was doubling the villain) the cue to start his horse swimming at a given point. He gave me my signal. I started my horse in a mild lope down the runway but, just before he got to the takeoff, something happened. Whether one of the blinkers had loosened or moved so that he couldn't see ahead, I will never know, but within a few feet of the bluff edge, he stopped and whirled. I tripped the blinkers so that he could see, but it was too late. He stumbled and threw me off and over the edge of the runway. I landed, head first, about ten or twelve feet below and slammed my nose into a big, egg-shaped rock. The horse remained unhurt on the runway, but I was a mess. My nose was badly broken and I had skinned my hands trying to stop the fall.

The accident delayed the picture for about six weeks. When we resumed filming, they had to shoot all my close shots from a side angle. My nose was crooked and I looked like a prize fighter who's had more than his share of long counts. Later, when the injuries were completely healed, I went to a plastic surgeon for repairs. He rebroke my nose and straightened it. It was such a fine job that I really think it looks better now than it did before.

Once I got the hang of it, those Ben Wilson Westerns were a real pleasure. I starred in eight of them a year from 1923 to 1926. And while I was not in the big time with stars like Tom Mix, Buck Jones or Fred Thompson, I was living comfortably and building up a following. I got my share of fan letters and requests for photos, and was in demand for personal appearances at theatres, fairs, and rodeos.

I thought that my time had come, when, in 1926, I was loaned to Hal Roach to play the leading role in *The Devil Horse* (not to be confused with the Nat Levine serial of 1932). Hal Roach was the producer, Fred Jackman the director, his brother, Floyd Jackman, was head cameraman, and George Stevens, who was later to become a famous director, was the second cameraman. This picture was the biggest and best of the films in which I played the leading role.

We set up a complete camp on the shores of the Little Big Horn River, not far from the Custer Battlefield. We built a log fort for the Indian battle scene and at times used as many as four or five hundred Indians.

The plot called for a lot of action, and I did it all. I played a pioneer whose wagon train had been wiped out when he crossed the wilderness as a child. There was a moving scene where the child is captured by the Indians as he is playing with his pet colt.

I played the child grown to manhood. In the picture, I'm having a running fight with four or five Indians. They overpower me and sentence me to be tied to a tree at the mercy of the Devil Horse.

As you might have guessed, the killer stallion turns out to be my former pet colt. He recognizes me, unties my ropes with his teeth, and we ride off, to the Indians' amazement.

I had pretty good luck working with horses, but when you

find out that a horse is actually a killer stallion, you know that you have to be on your guard. Rex, the "Devil Horse" of the picture was a big, beautiful well-trained black, but every so often he would get mad and try to kill anyone near him. After he killed his keeper he was sold to Hal Roach. In his first film, *Black Cyclone*, Rex knocked down the leading man, Big Boy Williams, and really ripped him up. If the trainer hadn't run in and settled Rex down, Big Boy would certainly have been killed.

Although the tree scene went fine, things didn't run so smooth later on when I was doing a scene where Rex was to run to me during an Indian battle. He had made the run three or four times, but the director didn't like any of them. After a couple of more runs, I warned the director that the horse was getting mad and we better let him cool off. He said, "Let's try one more take." After that "one more" it was time to call an ambulance.

The old horse charged and, when he got within about ten or twelve feet from me, he laid his ears back, opened his mouth and came at me with everything he had. I tried to duck, but his upper teeth hit my left jaw and his lower teeth got my neck. I was knocked to the ground and he reared above me, striking down with his powerful front hooves. I rolled away frantically and, when he rushed at me to bite, I kicked him on the nose and rolled away again. The trainer ran in with a buggy whip, but the horse kept right after me. I finally rolled over a bank and escaped.

Some of my other stunts in this picture were just as hazardous, but the finished effect was quite striking. I worked closely with George Stevens and he knew his trade. He'd use wide angles to make falls look higher and slow camera speeds to make movements appear faster. After finishing that picture I worked with Stevens on several of the Ben Wilson Westerns and learned a good deal from him.

One day George said to me, "Yak, I'd like to direct a couple of pictures for you."

"You're a good cameraman, George," I replied. "Why don't you stay with what you know. I don't think you'd make it as a director."

Fortunately for the thousands who've enjoyed *Gunga Din*, *Shane*, *Giant* and many others, he didn't take my advice. In a few years he was among the top directors in Hollywood.

When 1927 rolled around my contract with Ben Wilson expired and I didn't have any series contract. But I wasn't worried. My personal appearances would carry me over nicely until another starring series came along. I made a number of personal appearances during the spring and summer, then booked a show in Seattle, Washington, where the Chamber of Commerce was staging a rodeo for a worthwhile cause. At this show I was to make an exhibition saddle-bronc ride, and bulldog a steer each day. In addition to my exhibition rides, I had the privilege of entering the competitive events.

The announcer really spread it on with my introduction each time I rode into the arena. He made it sound as if I was a top man in the picture industry and, of course, mentioned that I was an ex-champion cowboy. I didn't believe everything he said, but it sounded good, so I took my bows in stride.

One thing that I had learned from my motion picture experience was to make use of the spectacular. During exhibitions, I did not have to follow rodeo rules, so when they turned my steer out for the bulldogging, I'd ride to him and dive onto his head, hoolihanning him end over end. The crowd would really give me a big hand, but I'd get some dirty glances from some of the contestants.

The evening after my first appearance, I went to a party, which, like most parties in those prohibition days, was an occasion where the popping of corks could be heard quite regularly. The party lasted into the wee small hours. When I finally got back to my hotel, I left a call for eleven o'clock and hit the hay. The clerk forgot my call and when I woke up I had to hurry to get to the grounds in time for the show.

As I got out of my car, I heard the announcer starting my introduction and my horse wasn't even saddled. One of the cowboys, a short-legged fellow, offered me his mount. I mounted and when I got my feet in the stirrups, I felt like a jockey. Then I heard the last few words: ". . . ex-champion cowboy of the world, Yakima Canutt!" The gate was opened and at a full run, I started across the centerfield. The crowd was giving me a good hand, and I turned sideways in the saddle and doffed my hat in acknowledgment.

I was just about in the center of the arena when the horse that the short-legged cowboy had so generously given me dropped his head and bucked me off. Turning a somersault in the air, I hit the ground with a thud and sat there for a moment, humiliated beyond description. The crowd as well as the cowboys were in hysterics. Finally, I got to my feet, made

Novice film actor Yakima Canutt with
Dorothy Woods in *The Ridin' Comet*.

A realistic fight scene in *Desert Hawk*, 1924:
Yak and Ben Wilson.

Ruth Stonehouse, Joe Rickson and Ben Wilson in *Two Fisted Sheriff*.
Yak stunted in this 1925 Western.

Yakima Canutt and Bob Steele in Republic's *Arizona Skies*.

"Bulldogging" can apply to other riders as well as to steers.
Here Yakima Canutt bulldogs Cliff Lyons, another well-known stunt man,
in an early Republic Western.

A young John Wayne and his pals (Gabby Hayes is at far right)
challenge Yak at gunpoint in a Monogram Western.

Yak gets the upper hand of Wayne in this "blood-and-thunder quickie" from Western Adventure Pictures.

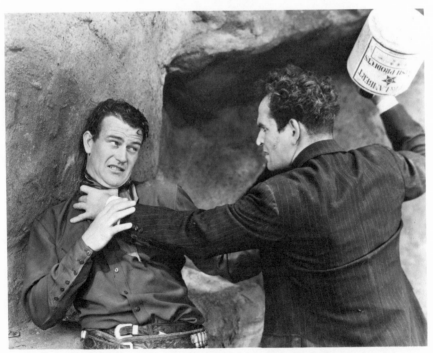

John Wayne at the receiving end as Yak attacks with the first weapon at hand in an early thirties Monogram "talkie" Western.

an exaggerated courteous bow and limped over to the bronc chutes. My next act was an exhibition of bulldogging. I did a fast catch, hoolihanned the steer end over end, and took a big hand from the crowd, a gratifying change.

After the show finished, I drove to Colfax and visited my mother and many old friends for a few days. When I returned to Hollywood I still didn't have a job. At that time the great change from silents to talkies was underway. The first talking picture, *The Jazz Singer*, had just been released and the film industry was in a turmoil. By 1928 all the pictures were talkies. I realized that I was in trouble. I had had the flu in 1918, while in the Navy, and my vocal chords were permanently damaged. My voice lacked resonance, a quality needed for good recording. When I heard it for the first time on a sound track, I thought they were kidding me. It sounded like a hillbilly in a well. But I was not alone. A number of fine silent film actors vanished from the screen. This, along with a slump in the business due to the great depression of 1929, made it a bit tough to make ends meet. I started doing bit parts and a few stunts when I could get them.

After a year of this, I found myself in tight straits. To be blunt, I was in hock up to my ears. I had never been a failure and I certainly wasn't about to give up. I tried to analyze what was it that I had that the picture industry needed. Then it dawned on me that the majority of the films being made lacked excitement and thrills! I realized that so much more could be done than what everybody was doing. I could just see that in the pictures I had been involved in. A whole new field in the action end of the motion picture industry seemed to open up before me.

FIVE

Thirties Times Three

In the late twenties there were very few all-around stunt men. Most of them specialized in certain kinds of work. Those who did high falls into nets or pads were called "high men." Swimmers and divers were "water men," although most of them also added fights and car chases to their credits. Then there were a few cowboys who did falls from horses, stagecoaches and wrecked wagons.

Of them all, I'd venture to say that cowboys probably had the best potential to be all-around stunt men because of the wide range of rodeo events that demanded a certain versatility on the part of the participant. Much like the professional stunt man sizing up all the angles of a stunt he's going to do, any cowboy worth his salt spends a good deal of time casing the bronc or steer before he goes out of the chute. In the gab session with the cowboys around the steer pen he's checking out the steer's color, the length of the horns, the size of the neck and the development of the muscles—you want to know your quarry. With a horse you want to know how he'll react to the rear flank cinch, whether it'll be best to draw it tight or loose. You'll want to watch what kind of buck he uses. If his head is held low, you'll need a long rein, if high, a short one. How does the horse react to packed dirt, to turf, to dust? What's his background and temperament? These are all important points for the cowboy to know. I remember that Lee

Cowles even kept a little book with him, listing all the horses and their tricks.

So all in all, I figured that I had years of experience, especially when I took into consideration all that was involved in creating thrills—I had the physical ability and the know-how needed to construct the right equipment.

I got work fast because I was usually able to do the stunts on the first take. I soon discovered that a producer was always happy when he could save time, and that always meant that there might be another call for me on his next picture. I started building a name as a stunt man who could do a job well, and in a minimum of time.

However, I was still in debt and owed several thousand dollars, which I found tough to pay off. At the end of each job, which ran from one to four weeks, I would hold out just enough to carry me through to another picture. Then early in 1930 I received a letter from an agency in Chicago, wanting to book me with a rodeo outfit for a series of state fairs. Candy Hammer, a man I had met during my rodeo days, wanted to stage the shows, which were to open in Trenton, New Jersey, and finish in Dallas, Texas. It was just the working vacation I needed. I made a deal with Candy and left for Trenton within a week.

Before leaving, though, I was invited to a party at the home of Claude C. Rice, a police officer in Hollywood. I had been on a few fishing trips with him, but had never been to his home. He was a big, jovial man and had often spoken of his wife and adopted daughter, Minnie Audrea, who worked for the Telephone Company. Audrea caught my eye immediately and, I have to confess, she made a lasting impression on me. She was pretty, twenty-three and twelve years my junior. This seemed safe. After one unsuccessful marriage, I was trying to dodge any romance that might become serious. I had a nice time at the party and a day or two later left for Trenton.

It was like old home week to be, yes, back in the saddle again. I not only surprised the rodeo hands, but myself as well. On that trip I drew and rode thirty-five or forty good bucking horses without making a disqualified ride. I also found that my work in motion pictures added to my popularity in the arena.

The shows came off nicely and, much as I enjoyed working with Candy's outfit, my thoughts always seemed to be with a certain policeman's daughter in Hollywood.

We finished the last fair at Dallas and I headed back to Hollywood where I lost no time in getting on the phone. Audrea and I started dating and during the following year kept steady company. That is a year that I can look back on with many pleasant thoughts.

The picture industry was still in a slump, owing to the change over from silents to talkies. The depression was certainly having its effects, too. Financing was a problem and jobs were scarce. Fortunately, I had good connections with a couple of independent producers, one of whom was Nat Levine, head of Mascot Productions.

Nat was one of the smartest operators that I have ever known. Originally he was a film salesman, but quit that end of the business to come to Hollywood where he organized the Mascot Company. Within two or three years he was the serial king of the industry. In those days, it took from four to six weeks to make a fifteen episode serial. Nat had his company so well-organized that he turned them out in twenty-one days. I worked on most of his pictures, writing action into them, for which I received fifty dollars an episode. I also ramrodded the action, hired stunt men and did the major stunts. It was hard work, but the pay was good and it was a great testing ground for ideas.

Much of my work at Mascot was under "Breezy" Reeves Eason. Between Breezy and Levine you couldn't ask for better teachers. Breezy had come to movies much the way I did. He was an expert horseman and he had stunted for ten years before he started to direct. He was often a bit wild on the set and he took risks with his actors, but he had a great eye for action and he moved fast. I recall one day when he shot 104 scenes between sunrise and sunset, including a wild stallion fight and several good stunts. When you tell that to some of the new breed of picture people, they just can't believe it.

Nat Levine was not only a sharp operator, he knew how to handle people. He could get more work out of a crew than anyone I have ever known. Sometimes he would come out with the kind of impossible order that would ordinarily send people into tantrums. However, with Nat's crews and actors, it would have the opposite effect. They would laugh it off and Nat would laugh with them. He was a shrewd businessman who had a keen appreciation for what people were going through.

I remember when Otto Brower was directing *The Devil*

Horse in 1932. Harry Carey was doing the lead and I was doubling him in all his stunts. I had written a real hazardous ending for the first episode, but with the understanding that we would shoot it on the last day of the picture. This would give me the benefit of fulfilling my contract, whereas if we were to shoot it first and I got hurt, I'd lose my contract money.

This stunt was rough. In a sequence with a wild stallion that Harry Carey was trying to capture, his horse falls and the wild stallion attacks him. He grabs the stallion by the ears with one hand and swings his body under the animal's neck, straddling the neck in an upside-down position, and locking his spurs on top of the horse's withers. We used a trained horse for the first part of the scene where he charges Carey. After Carey got hold of the trained horse's ears, I took over. Then we substituted the trained horse with a real rodeo bronc that was full of fight. I rigged a strong strap around the horse's neck so that I could hang on at either ear. Then, with three cameras set and ready to shoot, we put a blindfold over the bronc's eyes and got him quieted down with the help of a couple of cowboys.

I got a good hold of the strap and ears and, as the cameras started turning, the two helpers eased off the blindfold and dashed out of the scene. The horse stood for a second or two, then, as he started to rear, I swung my body under his neck and hooked my spurs over the top of his withers. He reared high and spun around trying to strike me with his front hooves but, because of the position I was in, he could only hit me with the forward part of his front legs. Those spurs tickling his withers sure set him in motion—he practically exploded, rearing, spinning and doing everything he could to shake me loose. I was able to hang on, but with my two hundred pounds hanging on his head, he was thrown off balance and he finally fell hard to the ground.

The next thing I knew, bells were ringing, birds were singing, and I could barely make out a couple of cowboys who seemed to be trying to help me. I dazedly asked them what had happened and one of them said that the bronc turned a somersault and lit on top of me. I felt as if an Indian war party had just finished a dance on my chest. One of the men drove me to the hospital in Hollywood, and then went to the studio to report. Nat was surprised to see him.

"What are you doing here?" he asked gruffly.

"I brought Yak into the hospital," the driver answered. "He got hurt in the horse fight."

"Did they get the scene?" was Nat's first question.

It sounds a little cold-blooded, but actually, he was a very kind and considerate man. I once made a one-thousand-dollar deal for two weeks' work in one of his pictures—good money in those days. We went to Kernville for the filming. On the first day, the first scene I was to do was a fall from a running horse. As I put pressure in the stirrup in order to make the fall, the stirrup strap broke and I missed the prepared bit of ground and drove my shoulder into a granite rock.

I was in the hospital in Bakersfield for three weeks. Mr. Levine kept a close watch on me, and when I was ready to leave, he sent a car for me. He also sent a one-thousand-dollar check for the contract I was never able to fulfill, and which, legally, he did not have to pay. But Nat was that way.

Another time during the making of the serial, *The Lightning Warrior*, for Mascot I was to do a jump from a rock ledge about eighteen feet high, onto a horse which was saddled and standing below. I had put blinkers on the horse so that he could see out ahead, but not up. Lee Duncan, the owner of the movie dog, Rin Tin Tin, was to have the dog follow me out of the scene. I got everything set so that I could make the takeoff noiselessly. I then asked everyone to keep quiet until I hit the saddle. I especially made it clear to Duncan, who had not been very cooperative.

When all was ready, the director gave me a signal and, just as I took off, Duncan screamed at the top of his voice at his wonder dog. My horse jumped and took off and I landed in the rocks. I wasn't hurt, but I was mad. I got up and limped over to Duncan.

"Mr. Duncan," I said, angrily, "I'm going to try this stunt again and if you holler before I hit the saddle, I'll whip you but good!"

Duncan glared at me and walked away while we got the horse back in place. I made the jump, Duncan sent Rin Tin Tin in, and he followed me out of the scene the way the script called for.

That night after dinner Nat Levine called me to his hotel room. "Yak," he said gravely, "Lee Duncan said I would have to fire you or he would take his dog and go home. Let's hear your side of the story. What happened?"

I told him exactly what had occurred.

"Well," Nat said thoughtfully, "if he meant what he said, I guess he'll just have to take his dog and go."

Duncan didn't leave, and from then on he was a little more cooperative. Nat Levine would back you if you were right.

At Mascot we were under a lot of pressure to come up with spectacular action sequences in a hurry. This made us try all sorts of things, and it was there that I created some of my most famous stunts, including the one which I did in *Stagecoach*.

I first did it when I was doubling Jack Randall in *Riders of the Dawn* in 1937. The gag was this: I was riding shotgun on a freight wagon that was being pursued by a small group of Indians. Two of them pulled up alongside the wagon. I shot one and the second Indian leaped from his horse onto the lead team, trying to turn them off the road. My gun jammed so I dropped it in the wagon and leaped to the wheel team. With the aid of a couple of crossbars attached to the harness hames of the wheel and swing teams—bars that were concealed from the camera—I went into a stand on the first bar and leaped ahead to the swing team. From the second bar, I leaped onto the Indian who was trying to turn the lead team off the road. We engaged in a hand-to-hand fight with the team going at a full run. Then we slipped and fell to the wagon tongue between the two lead horses, where we continued fighting until the director called, "cut."

For a longer shot, I tied an Indian dummy to my ankle and, when we got lined up with the camera car which was running at a side angle, I overlapped the fall and ended up on the ground, hanging onto the wagon tongue. I dragged between the horses for a short distance with the dummy's hands tied to my ankles, then I turned loose and as the wagon passed over me, I caught a prepared hand hold on the wagon reach and dragged under the wagon for a few feet, kicking and flipping the dummy around. In another scene I had a stunt man by the name of Cliff Lyons get under the wagon with me and in close travel shots we fought until I finally kicked him loose. While I was still dragging on the ground, I worked my way under the wagon, using the under-carriage for handholds, then climbed up in it from the back and on over to my original position on the wagon seat.

This gag turned out to be one of my best stunt creations and to this day it has never been duplicated in its entirety by anyone else. I was paid a thousand dollars each time I did it and in those days, that was really big money. I performed it once at a benefit show in the Los Angeles Colosseum before an audience of eighty thousand people, and stole the show.

A third important person entered my life in the early thirties—or rather a fourth, since I must certainly account for the wonderful event that took place on November 12, 1931—my marriage to Minnie Audrea in Yuma, Arizona. We took our time returning to Los Angeles, driving along the Mexican border to San Diego, and then up the coast. There were no freeways in those days and the towns we passed seemed small and precious, perfect settings for my new-found joy. The November weather was like spring.

Shortly after we got back to Hollywood, I received a call from Nat. He had just closed a deal with John Wayne who was to star in a serial titled *Shadow of the Eagle*. At that point Wayne had just made a few "B" Westerns and had not yet come into his own. Nat wanted me to double Wayne and to beef up the action. I was also going to play one of the villain's henchmen along with my friend, Bud Osborne.

I had never met John Wayne but Bud had worked with him a number of times. One day, when we were having lunch together, I asked Bud what kind of fellow Wayne was to work with.

"Yak," he said, "you'll love him. He's really great. And when it comes to ribbing, he'll hold his own—even with you."

"If he likes to rib," I said, "let's start him off right. You tell him to be very careful about what he says or does around me, that I'm Nat Levine's stool pigeon, and that I report to Nat each night and tell him everything that happens during the day. But don't tell him this until he and I get acquainted."

The first day of the shooting John arrived on the set and Bud introduced me to him. He was very friendly and said he was happy I was going to double him. He had heard a great deal about me and my rodeo achievements and was also familiar with my standing as a stunt man.

The afternoon of the second day I told Bud to break the news to him about my being a stool pigeon. I stood off to one side making some notes in my little red book, and peeking out from under the brim of my John B. Stetson hat, when Bud walked over to Wayne and began giving him the low-down on my spy activities. John looked at me in amazement, then turned back to Bud and shook his head in disbelief. A little later I walked up to him and asked: "Well, how's everything going?"

John just looked at me but said nothing. I took out a pack of cigarettes, lit one and offered the pack to him.

"Have a smoke," I said.

He gave me a dirty look.

"No thanks," he replied curtly, and walked away.

I knew we had him hooked. John was, and still is, a man who believes in loyalty, whether it's to friend or country. One time I heard him say that there was only one thing worse than a stool pigeon and that was two stool pigeons.

The rib had been going along for about a week when I had Bud and one of the other actors take Wayne behind the set for a drink. I went around the opposite corner. John took a swig, and as he handed the bottle back to Bud, he saw me. I looked at my watch and then made a note in my little book. That did it. He blew his top and I made a hasty retreat. A little later I got to Bud and a couple of the fellows who were in on the gag, and told them that they had better straighten John out about me. I knew I couldn't out-run him, and I wasn't about to fight him.

When they told John it was all a joke, he laughed heartily, even though it was at his expense.

"I'm sure glad it was a gag," he grinned, "but you've left yourself wide open, Yak." And that I had! There was never a dull moment on the set when we were together.

I worked with John more than with any other star on the screen. In the early thirties he also made a great many Westerns for Trem Carr's Monogram Productions in which I was his double and also played parts. On one picture we were shooting on a western street. As his double I was to ride up to the front of a two-story hotel, catch hold of a rope dangling from a projecting flagpole, swing up onto the balcony and go through a window. The first time I tried it, the horse slowed down and, of course, I had to have enough speed so that the momentum would carry me up onto the balcony. To liven the horse up a bit, I took a willow switch and made a couple of dry runs, using the switch on the horse's rear quarters. There happened to be quite a number of spectators present and on my second warm-up run, Wayne called to the crowd: "Folks, when you see this picture, remember that it's not John Wayne whipping that horse!"

"Yes, folks," I answered, turning my horse to face them, "and when you see the picture, remember it's not John Wayne doing the stunt either."

Everyone laughed and, as always, Wayne laughed with them.

In one of his Westerns, *Paradise Canyon*, we had to do a rugged fight and, believe me, Wayne can put on a better fight than the majority of stunt men. In fact, we worked together so often that the director usually left us to choreograph our own fight scenes. John and I were both so competitive, both so eager to top whatever previous bit we had worked out, that this might have been dangerous if we hadn't become such close friends.

At one point in this particular fight, I was supposed to throw Wayne in a flip over my head, so they had me double him, and another stunt man double me. The action started and I crashed through a table, ending up sitting on the floor with my back to the camera. I was just starting to lose some hair at the time, and had a small bald spot on the top of my head that showed prominently in the scene when my hair fell away. No one noticed it at the time, but when they previewed the picture at a local theatre, everyone saw it.

After the show, Wayne, the director, and the producer really chewed me out. Of course, on those medium-budgeted pictures, they wouldn't go back and shoot the scene over.

From then on, whenever I doubled for Wayne, he would say, "Get the shoe blacking on that bald spot!"

So much had been said regarding my lack of hair on top that when we were doing another picture a few weeks later, I decided to really give them something to talk about. I asked a lady that I knew in New York to write me a fan letter. When it arrived, I took it out on the set. I got the producer and Wayne together and told them I was sorry about the bald spot showing up but, after receiving this letter, I could understand why they got so upset. Wayne took the letter and read: "Dear Mr. Canutt, I saw you last evening in the picture *Paradise Canyon* with John Wayne. It was a good picture and you did some fine work in it. Why don't the producers get smart and give you a break. Wayne must be getting old. I noticed that he is getting bald-headed."

John looked at the postmarks on the envelope, which were authentic, and passed the letter on to the producer. He didn't think it was funny.

"Yak," he said, "you're going to have to watch that damn bald spot when you're in a scene."

John gave me that eagle eye and I knew that he had a

hunch how I came by that letter. He was due to get back at me.

Later in that picture we were doing a sequence where John was fighting a couple of us in a saloon. He knocked one heavy down and I swung at him. He stepped to one side and knocked me through the glass in the big front window. The camera outside caught me as I tumbled out end over end, stopping under a hitch pole at the edge of the sidewalk.

When I got up and started to run for my horse across the street, John leaped out of the window over the hitch rail and made a flying football tackle on me. I have never been turned over so many times so fast. To this day, I "ouch" every time I see a fast tackle in a football game. I had been paid for the letter.

In another Wayne picture the director had the camera set at the bottom of a steep hill where the ground levelled off abruptly. I was again doubling John and was to ride fast down the hill and exit close to the camera. The cameraman was worried about a double riding that close to the lens, so John said that he would do the ride. I had been coaching him for quite awhile and he was becoming a real horseman, so no one was worried. As he mounted, I told him to bring the horse over the top of the hill in a run, but to be sure and check him just before he hit the bottom where the ground levelled off. I stepped over behind the camera to watch.

John came over the top of that hill really carrying the mail and raced down the steep ground, never checking the horse. I held my breath as he hit the level ground, sensing the horse couldn't collect himself. He fell, turning a real hoolihan and John did a spectacular fall. I hollered at the top of my voice for him to get on the horse and ride out.

John rolled to his feet and, as the horse got up, he jumped on and rode him out by the camera. They used it in the picture and it really looked wild. As he got off his horse, he said to me with a grin, "I heard you holler 'get on him and ride out', and that I did."

Those are the things that can happen to anyone, and they really give the producer a scare. Many of the stars are capable and willing to do their own stunts, but with a tight schedule and thousands of dollars tied up in a picture, it's too much of a gamble. Should a star break a leg, an arm, or even get his face skinned a little, the overhead goes up while the actor recuperates. Should a stunt man get injured, he can be replaced without any loss of time. A stunt man is always a good insurance policy for any action picture.

John is a very capable action man, and he once doubled me in a gag. In 1934, we were doing a picture called *'Neath Arizona Skies* and, as usual, I was a villain. I was supposed to be making a getaway on one of the little, motored handcars that railroads use when they make minor repairs on the tracks. John was to make a flying mount on his horse and race over the hill to intercept me in a canyon. He was to gallop alongside the handcar and leap from his running horse onto the car. Pauley Malvern, who was handling production, knew that I always doubled Wayne and did my own part as well. However, he overlooked bringing out another stunt man. We were getting set up to do the stunt when it dawned on the director, Robert North Bradbury, that if I doubled Wayne, someone would have to double me.

He mentioned this to the producer and they both were really upset. Not one of the cowboys working with us that day was large enough to double either Wayne or myself.

While they were trying to figure things out, John looked questioningly at me and I nodded in agreement.

"Which one?" I asked with a grin.

"Give me your wardrobe," he answered.

We changed clothes, and I doubled John and John doubled me. I made the transfer from the running horse to the handcar in a full shot and we started fighting. We switched back to our own clothes for the closer shots. In the fight, John knocked me off the speeding car and down a steep bank. Then he leaped off the car after me and we finished the battle in a dry wash.

Working with John Wayne got to be a steady and welcomed habit. In another picture that we were filming in Kernville the villain was to jump his horse into the Kern River and swim him through a narrow gorge. Wayne was to ride his horse to the top of a bluff overlooking the river, where the villain would have to pass. As his double, I was to take his place, tie my lariat to the saddle horn and, with the horse holding my weight, slide down the rope to a slanting ledge about thirty-five feet above the river. When the villain swam by on his horse, I was to run down the ledge, dive into the water and fight him.

While the camera was getting set up, I checked everything on the stunt. There was a large, flat rock at the bottom of the ledge. The rock was in about three feet of water, and extended twelve feet or so out into the river. I tossed a few large stones off the ledge, and knew that I would have to leap out at least twenty feet in order to miss the dangerous rock below. However, I didn't take into consideration the fact that, when you are running down a steep slant, your weight becomes more for the muscles to lift in a jump.

The tie-in scenes leading up to the stunt were filmed, then I changed places with Wayne on top of the bluff. At the call of "action" I slid down the rope to the ledge, hurried to the slanting edge and took off toward the villain in the water below. The second I left the ledge I knew that I would never make it. I also knew that I would break my leg if I hit the flat rock in the shallow water.

I snapped my head back and fanned my arms, trying to flatten my body so as to use as much of the surface of the water as possible. I hit the water in a lean-back sitting position, but managed to raise my feet up and out. The three feet of water did a great deal for me. I hit the rock and my right hip took most of the shock. The water was so shallow that my head never submerged, but a terrific pain ran from my right hip down my leg, then it felt numb.

By that time, John Wayne was in the water and had hold of me. I told him to let me sit for a bit, which he did. He then helped me up to my feet and out to the bank. Fortunately, the numbness soon left my leg, and I was able to finish the picture. My hip was black and blue and sore for two or three weeks. But, by picking up the scene with a close shot of John in the water where I had landed, they were able to save the stunt.

John always had a great sense of humor about his increasing popularity and he was quick to share the exposure he received with his colleagues. As early as 1932, when we had only worked together on a few films, I suspect that it was John's say-so that landed me a stunting spot in Warner Brothers' *The Telegraph Trail*, starring John. The timing on that job was particularly important since Audrea was expecting. The money from that picture more than paid the hospital bill for our first son, Edward Clay.

When my brother Alex's baby arrived and he and his wife, Elva, were picking a name, I kidded them, suggesting the name of *Tapadaro*, the Mexican word for a saddle stirrup covering. They turned it down, so I said I'd keep it for my first son. A few days after Edward Clay was born, I received a letter from Alex asking me how Tapadaro was. Edward Clay has been called "Tap" ever since.

In other ways, 1932 was not the best of years. A few months after Tap's birth, I worked on a picture directed by Otto Brower which featured Tom Keene. In one scene I doubled Keene in a transfer from a horse onto the wheel team of a heavy, runaway covered wagon. We were doing this in a travel shot and the team was very fast. As I rode alongside the wheel team, my horse shied away and I did a long dive over the near horse and went down onto the wagon tongue head-first. I grabbed the tongue, but in trying to right myself I got a leg tangled with one of the horse's legs and that tore me loose from the tongue. I hit the ground rolling beneath the team.

I was wearing a wide belt with a Colt six-shooter in the holster and one of the horses stepped on it and tore it off. I pulled myself into a ball, but the front axle of the wagon hit my right shoulder blade. I spun under the wagon and one of the big wheels cut my cowboy hat right off of my head. I got to my feet and started to brush the dirt off my trousers. For a moment I thought I had escaped without an injury. But when I tried to raise my right arm, I knew my shoulder was hurt. Later the x-rays showed the shoulder blade was broken in four pieces.

I was lucky to get off that easy. If my head had been two or three inches closer to the wheel, I would have rounded out my existence for sure. It's nice to know that luck is on your side in a mix-up of that kind. The doctor had me keep my arm in a sling for three weeks, and told me that I wouldn't be able to work that arm in any drastic movements for six to eight weeks. I was just to take it easy.

A couple of days earlier I had made a deal to double an actor in a scene that called for him to be knocked off a cliff, about thirty feet high, into a fire net. The company was shooting at night and didn't know exactly at what time the director would get to the fall scene. It was only a few minutes' drive from my apartment to the location, so the assistant told me to stick around the house at night. When they got within an hour of the scene he would call me. After leaving the doctor, I got home and with Audrea's help, took a hot bath, had a bite to eat, and went to bed.

The phone rang around one A.M. The assistant director told me that they would be ready for the fall in an hour or so. I said okay, still half asleep but, as I hung up, I suddenly realized that because of my accident I had completely forgotten this stunt. I tried to call two or three other stunt men, but no one was home. So Audrea helped me get my shirt on and I drove the car to the location with one hand. When I arrived, the wardrobe man helped me into my double's clothes, a tussle in itself. I just told him that I had a very sore shoulder—not unusual for a stunt man.

The camera and lights were ready when I went up to my spot on top of the cliff. I carefully explained to the man who was supposed to knock me off to be sure and make a clean miss since I had to do a half turn in order to land on my left side. Everything worked perfectly. He threw a punch and I took off making a turn and landed on my left side. The jar caused very little pain. I went back to the wardrobe and was being helped into my own clothing when the producer came in to thank me. He saw the trouble I was having getting into my shirt and was quite concerned.

"What's the trouble?" he asked. "Did you hurt yourself?"

When I told him what was really wrong with me, he blew his top.

"I thought you were the one stunt man with brains," he said disgustedly, "but I guess you are all alike!"

I always remembered his words and I never again risked my reputation as a top stunt man to do a gag that I knew I wasn't physically prepared for.

I recovered completely from my shoulder injury, but for the next year or two it was really tough. Jobs were scarce and the money was small. In the winter of 1934, I signed a contract with a Mr. McCall, an Australian who had engaged a group of thirty cowboys and girls to play a couple of rodeos down-under. He wanted me along as the star of the show, which was to open in Melbourne. I was to receive five thousand dollars and first class transportation for me and my family. If the show failed I was guaranteed my full pay.

Audrea and I had a marvelous trip and found the Australians to be fine people. The show opened in Melbourne and played to good crowds for three days and then it rained steadily for a week. Everything was flooded and we were forced to close when the backers withdrew their support. Many of the American cowboys didn't receive any money but all had round trip tickets and were able to get back home. I had a solid contract and so I was paid in full—more money than I had seen in a long time—which made the trip back to the U.S. on the steamship "Mariposa" all the more enjoyable.

When we arrived home I was able to pay off the last of my bills and instead of moving back into an apartment, I leased a house which we furnished. I felt like a king. For the first time in the last few years I was free from debt and the picture business was picking up. Mr. Herbert Yates of Consolidated Film Laboratories, Inc., along with Nat Levine of the Mascot Picture Corporation and Trem Carr of Monogram, merged and formed Republic Pictures. They took over the New Mack Sennett Studios located in Studio City. I had worked in many Monogram pictures with John Wayne and had also handled the action in most of Mascot's serials, so this newly formed company was a windfall for me.

I soon became top stunt man at Republic. I handled the action and did parts in many Gene Autry films, *The Three Mesquiteers* series, and several serials including *The Lone Ranger* and *Zorro*. Many times I would receive a script which would have blank pages and scene numbers in the main action spots with a caption saying, "See Yakima Canutt for action sequences."

Republic was looked upon by the major studios as a blood-and-thunder factory where they turned out Western pictures on an assembly line, but it was the best equipped studio in the business and the crews were second to none.

In those early days, the studios weren't completely unionized, as they are today. In fact, a prop man and grip could handle any job that came up. I recall a picture that we were shooting in Red Rock Canyon near Mojave, California. I was to drive a covered wagon that was being chased by Indians, and two other stunt men were in the wagon with me. An Indian was to throw a burning torch into the wagon, setting it on fire. Roy Wade was the prop man and he had a helper who was supposed to be a good fire and powder man. We got the wagon in position and Wade and his Man Friday started soaking the wagon cover and interior with gasoline. When I told them that they were using too much gas, their answer was, "You do your job and we'll do ours!"

In the scene that we were to film, I was to get the team really running while the wagon burned, then jump to the wheel team, then to the lead team; the other two men were to jump to the wheel team and in those positions race on through the scene. All was ready and I put the team into a fast run as the Indians were closing in.

As we entered the scene, the Indian rode in with the lighted torch and tossed it in the rear of the wagon. Suddenly a flaming inferno exploded behind us. Fire flew clear out of the front end and the other two stunt men leaped off either side of the vehicle, landing unhurt. I jumped to the wagon tongue between the wheel team, intending to try and drive them to safety, but the fire was so hot I couldn't take it. I jumped over one of the horses and hit the ground, rolling to safety. As the wagon passed me it actually set the dry grass alongside the roadway on fire. The team made a sharp turn, upset the burning wagon and tore loose. The pickup men caught the horses, but the wagon had to be replaced. The following day we did the gag but with much less gasoline.

Handling explosives is such a tricky business that I was never about to risk my life on someone else's bad arithmetic. Roy Wade was a fine prop man, but I'm sure that everyone who worked with him and prop men like him were glad when the production companies began hiring specialists in special effects. On another of Republic's blood-and-thunder Westerns we had just stopped for lunch when the director told Wade to set up an explosion for the next scene.

The scene was a western street on Republic's back lot. Wade and his assistant were sinking a five or six inch pipe mortar in the center of the street for the explosion. Before leaving for lunch, I spoke with Wade and told him to get everything set but to leave the mortar empty so that I could supervise the loading. I was to ride a horse over the explosion and I wanted to make sure the charge was right. When I got back from lunch Wade said the mortar was all loaded and ready, so the director started lining up the shot.

"Wait a minute," I hollered. "I told Wade not to load the mortar until I got back. I happen to know from experience that he isn't very good with explosives."

I asked Wade to dig out the mortar. He went to work grudgingly and took out enough powder to have blown up the entire street, and there was still some left.

"How much more powder is in there?" I demanded.

"Not enough to make a good explosion," Wade replied sullenly.

"Yak, if the explosion is too small," the director said, "you'll have to do the stunt over."

"I'll settle for that," I nodded.

I measured from the top of the mortar to the powder and

said it would be big enough, if not too big. I told Wade to fill the mortar with loose Fuller's Earth and lamp black. The ground had been dug up in front of the explosion and topped with sand, so I stood the horse at the edge of the soft ground, a yard or so ahead of the mortar. I had them put the explosion switch on the hitch rail with a strong fishline tied to the trip, then stretched it across the street and tied it to a porch post just high enough to hit the horse's breast and trip the switch for the explosion.

When everything was set I got on the horse with my hand-bag of loot—the hardware man was set to throw the tied sticks of dynamite at me as I rode in on a getaway. When the director hollered "action! come on!" I put the horse into a run and the man threw the sticks of phoney dynamite. They hit the ground just behind the horse at the same moment that the horse hit the fishline and the explosion went off. The horse turned end over end. I hit the ground rolling, and the town marshal had me covered before I could get to my feet. I might add that the explosion broke a lot of windows in the store fronts on the street and my ears rang for a day. Had I not made Wade take most of the powder out of that mortar, I think the horse and I would have had it.

The Republic years were some of the greatest. As their offerings proved successful, the studio began taking chances on non-western serials, giving me a chance to devise different kinds of stunts.

At the end of that year Audrea and I were expecting our second child. Only this time I wasn't worried. I had money in the bank and assignments at other studios between Republic productions. One day that winter I got a call from Warners. They were redoing *Telegraph Trail*, the John Wayne film that was such a timely job for me in 1932. Warners wanted to use all the action sequences and some of the same cast, and hired me to play the Indian chief that I had played before. The writers added some new scenes to fit Dick Foran, the lead in the new version. We finished shooting on the fifteenth of January, 1937, and on the nineteenth our son, Harry Joe, was born.

The next few years were the best of my career thus far, not only from a financial standpoint, but because I was being given better opportunities to show my stuff.

Even though I wanted to get into directing, I had been willing to wait until I had the chance to do it right. Back in

1935 Willis Kent, producer of six-day blood-and-thunder pictures, called me into his office one day.

"Yak," he said, "you want to become a director, don't you?"

"Yes," I said, "that's my goal."

He handed me a script. "Here's your first job," he said. "Take it home, read it, then drop in tomorrow and we'll make a deal."

I thanked him and took the script home.

It was titled *The Circle of Death*. Mr. Kent had written the story himself and it was really dreadful. I read and reread it, trying to figure out a way to change it and give it a little color, but I just couldn't see how I could make a picture out of such a weak story. In addition, Monty Montana, the lead, had never been in front of a camera before, so there wasn't a great deal going for a director. I knew that if I directed the picture and it flopped, I'd get the blame. I took the story back to Mr. Kent, but before I could say anything, he asked: "How do you like the story?"

"Now, Willis," I said, "don't get mad. You wrote the story and must like it, but I don't believe I can make a worthwhile picture of it. However, there is an Indian part in the story that I'd like to do. If you'll get an experienced director, I'll do the part and help in any way I can to build up the action."

"You're crazy," he snorted. "I give you a chance to become a director and you turn me down. Okay, you can do the part and keep on batting your brains out doing stunts."

He hired an actor to direct the film and I did the part and stunts. After we finished the picture and a cutter had put it together, Willis invited all the people who worked on it to a studio screening. The director never showed up. Once the screening got underway, I was sorry that I came. It was really a lost cause. Every time something bad showed up, Willis would turn to me and say, "Yak, why did you let him do that?" After the screening was over, he cornered me, "I have never seen a picture directed so badly," he said angrily. "Why didn't you straighten him out?"

"Willis," I answered, "you don't tell a director how to do his job. He tells you what to do."

The more we talked, the madder he got.

"You could have made a good picture out of it," he said accusingly.

"I don't think anyone could have made a good picture out of it," I replied curtly.

He looked coldly at me. "I offered you a chance to direct," he said, "and you turned me down. You'll never work for me again as long as you live." We always seemed to be good friends over the years, but he was as good as his word. I never worked for him again.

In 1939 Republic pulled out all the stops to produce their first million dollar picture, *Man of Conquest*, a classy, historical epic based on the life of Sam Houston. Ten thousand dollars and a good three months were spent scouting locations for the climactic "Battle of San Jacinto." The producer was Sol Siegel. The director, George Nicholls, Jr., even worked with McArdle's famous painting of the battle in planning the scenes. They finally shot it on the Salt Springs Reservoir, about thirty-six miles outside of Stockton, California.

Richard Dix, who hadn't really had a role equal to his talent since he did the popular Yancey Cravat in the 1931 *Cimarron*, was cast as the tall Texan. Dix really threw himself into the role. He brawled so realistically that he broke a few fingers during the shooting and had to wear flesh colored adhesive bandages for most of the film.

Many of the stunts in the movie were to be difficult and dangerous and so, of course, I found myself once again teamed with Breezy Eason, the second unit director.

In one scene, I was to drive an ammunition wagon through a lot of action, and then it was to be blown up. I had special effects rig it for the blowup. I had a barricade built out of two-by-twelves behind the seat to protect me. A shade top on the wagon hid it from the cameras. I had them cut all the way into the middle of the wagon bed and fasten it together so it would separate when the ammo exploded. A hook was fastened onto the back half of the wagon which would drop and stick into the ground, and a cable was secured to the front half of the wagon so the rear half would turn end over end. The ring that was on the rod would automatically slip off as the rear end turned over. I fastened a cable to the outside of the front half of the wagon, made two complete wraps around it, and tied it to the wagon tongue.

One of the stunt men asked me, "What will the wagon do?"

I said, "When the explosion goes off, the back half will turn a front flip. The front half will spin like a top."

"You want to bet?" he grinned dubiously.

"If you want to throw away some money, O.K. How much?"

He said, "How about fifty dollars?"

"It's a bet," I said.

I drove the team through a lot of background action, then when I tripped the switch the effect really was terrific. The back end of the wagon turned a high somersault. I jumped from the seat onto the tongue and rode on the front half of the wagon, which spun like a top.

When the scene was over, the stunt man came over and said, "Beautiful," holding out a fifty-dollar bill. I looked at the bill and said, "Keep it. I'll have a drink on you tonight."

We then completed a few more beautiful stunts—a wreck between two wagons and the explosion of the ammunition in one of them—and a number of one-, two-, and three-horse falls. We cleaned up the location. With the shooting finished there, we went to L.A. by train. On the train I was talking with Sol Siegel and during the conversation he said, "Yak, how would you like to be an action director?"

I said, "Sol, you have the best action director in the industry in Breezy Eason."

He gave me a stern look and said, "Don't give me that. I wasn't asleep on the show—you were lining everything up for Breezy and doing the stunts, too."

I said, "O.K., then. I certainly want to thank you and I know that I am getting to the age where I should quit stunting. Let me know when you're ready."

Sol replied, "As soon as *Man of Conquest* is finished."

It was true that Breezy had some problems. I had heard that Nat Levine had fired Breezy a few times. Breezy was one of the best, but he had days when he drank more than he should.

I remember one evening during the filming of *Man of Conquest* when Sol Siegel came to me and said, "Yak, Breezy is in the bar getting pickled. See if you can get him out and to bed."

I said that I would try. So I went into the bar and up to Breezy. "Breezy," I said, "we have a lot of stuff to do tomorrow. Don't you think that you have had enough to drink tonight."

He replied, in a rather belligerent voice, "So they've sent you to get me out of here."

"Breezy," I said quietly, "I'm trying to be a friend so don't make it rough for me."

"To hell with them, and you too."

"Look, Breezy, I don't want to see you lose your job and I don't want to take you out of here the hard way."

He looked at me for a moment, then turned and walked out and headed for bed.

The next morning he had a beautiful hangover. He started to set up on the wrong scene. The cameraman gave him a puzzled look. I took Breezy aside and straightened him out on the scene and rode herd on him all morning. Sol came out on our set. I tried to help Breezy without letting Sol know and thought that I had succeeded. We got a good day's work done and Breezy was sober through the rest of the picture.

I sincerely admired him for his ability as an action director, but I always felt that he took too many risks. I stunted in *They Died With Their Boots On*, with Breezy as second unit director, and they had a lot of accidents in the picture. Several men were hurt, including the great Indian athlete and Olympic champion, Jim Thorpe. He fell from his horse and had to spend some days in the hospital. The assistant, Russ Saunders, was setting up the runthroughs and falls, and he kept an ambulance busy. So many fellows were hurt that the company finally assigned me to work with Breezy on the action. After that, we did most of the fights and didn't have another man hurt.

Breezy directed the great action scenes in *The Charge of the Light Brigade*. He had okayed the location, a very rocky place that I would never have picked had I been doing the show. It was so rocky that some of the pits had to be blasted out with dynamite, and a number of horses were killed in the "pit falls." There was also one man killed and a great many hospitalized. It was said that two ambulances were working all the time. I recall that Errol Flynn was outraged by these events in the filming of the picture.

A long time after I directed the chariot race in the remake of *Ben Hur*, I learned some more about the filming of the first one. They had tried to stage the race in Rome, but there were so many pileups, with one man and over a hundred horses killed, that they had to give up and move it to Culver City, California, near the M.G.M. studio.

When they had been filming in Italy, they shot all the horses that got hurt. This is only a guess, but I imagine that the animals were butchered and sold to meat markets, since it was customary to eat horse meat in Italy at that time. The butchers and wranglers could have had something going.

When they filmed the race in Culver City, there were several pileups there, too, and a few horses and men were injured. But, with the way that the race was handled, and the type of equipment used, it's a wonder there were so few mishaps.

SIX

The Big Leagues

Herbert Yates, who then headed Republic, was so delighted by the finished product of *Man of Conquest* that he announced that Republic would be abandoning its run-of-the-mill productions and concentrating on big budget films.

My big break came in 1938. The producers at Republic liked my work and, as the studio began expanding in all directions, my opportunities improved as well. Sol C. Siegel, the associate producer of Westerns at Republic, knew my work better than anyone else and when he started lining up his staff for the first of the studio's larger-budgeted pictures, he assigned Eason as second unit director but handpicked me to coordinate, or ramrod, the stunts. This meant hiring all the stunt men, doing some stunts myself, but most important to me, I would be laying out the action for the direction and writing additional thrills where I thought they'd work.

The film was *Army Girl*. Preston Foster played the young modern officer whose duty it was to prove that mechanized warfare was here to replace the obsolete horse and soldier. George Nicholls Jr. directed and Madge Evans portrayed the heroine, the cavalry colonel's daughter with whom Foster falls in love.

The climax of the action comes when a small army tank competes against the cavalry in a cross-country race. If the tank wins, it means the end of the cavalry and a new era in warfare. This sequence was left to me and I had a great time with it.

We shot most of the action in Lone Pine, California, a beautiful location about a hundred-and-forty miles north of Los Angeles at the foot of Mount Whitney. There I found an embankment that dropped twelve or fifteen feet straight down and had a steep slide of loose sand and scattered sagebrush that extended another forty feet. For the climactic thrill, I had the crew build in a wooden floor of two-by-twelve planks that reached from the upper lip of the bank to within twenty-five feet of the bottom. This slanted floor was secured to cross beams sunk into the embankment side. I then had two-by-fours nailed three feet apart on the floor from the top to the bottom. The floor was wide enough to handle four horses side by side and also acted as a guide to keep the horses straight. When a horse slides, he stiffens his legs and tries to stay on his feet. Therefore, smooth plait shoes were put on each horse, and with the help of the guides, I knew that they could make the slide with ease. The corners of the two-by-fours were rasped and made smooth and the entire floor was covered with a heavy coat of grease.

I next had the crew sink railroad ties a few feet to the side of the main slide and build a platform strong enough to hold up the tank. This platform projected out from the slide about six feet below the lip, like a stair. The crew carved the top lip of the bank and rounded it so the horses could go onto the slide without making the slightest jump. After this was completed, I had the crew cover both the greased slide and the tank platform with loose dirt and sand, and had sagebrush planted on it to blend in with the surroundings.

In the scene, the cavalrymen, riding in columns of four, were to break over the top of the hill, skid to the bottom, and continue on out of the scene. The tank, which at this point in the race is a bit behind, was supposed to come over the top of the embankment alongside the skid, drop onto the concealed platform, turn over and roll to the bottom.

I was to drive the tank and was more worried about a fire than the roll. I had the interior and the motor washed and cleaned, and the gas drained, leaving just enough to get me through the scene. I had our electrician put a blade switch on the dash with a heavy cord tied across the compartment in such a way that I could automatically throw the switch while reaching for the hand holds.

When all was ready I gave the two Humane Society officers, who had arrived the night before, a brief rundown on the scene and what was to happen. They couldn't understand how running horses could go down that slide without falling and were very concerned. Ever since Erroll Flynn rightfully raised hell over the treatment of the horses in *The Charge of the Light Brigade*, Humane Officers were present on most action sets.

I reassured them that the horses were in no danger. On the call of "action" the long line of cavalry galloped over the top of the embankment, hit the slide still in fours, then slid to the bottom and galloped on out of the scene. It worked beautifully. The horses looked as though they were on skis.

I then belted myself into the tank and, with dust effects on the slide and an overlap of the last few sets of cavalry fours, I brought the tank over the brim of the embankment and headed straight down toward my trap platform. As it started down, I thought for a second or two that it was going to do an end-over-end, but it didn't. I couldn't see too well through the small square opening in the tank and, if I hadn't had the foresight to place a high green bush on the trap proper, I would never have seen it, in which case the tank would have turned a few flips.

When the front of the tank hit the green bush, I pulled my right lever back, locked the right track and turned the tank broadside. The left track dropped off the concealed platform. I let go of the guiding levers and grabbed my handholds, cutting the switch. The tank did a spectacular roll to the bottom. I really believe that if the engine had not stopped, I would have been in serious trouble. Because even with the small amount of gasoline in the tank, there was enough gas on me and the interior to have barbecued me. A spark was all it would have taken.

The crew then tore the slide out, redressed the slope of the bank, and we did a number of controlled horse falls to cut into the master scene. As usual, this sequence was finished without any injuries to man or beast and the action scenes in the rest of the picture went smoothly. I'm happy to report that all the stunts using animals won the approval of the Humane Officers.

Even as I was collecting credits and praise for my action work, bigger things were looming on the horizon. From 1935 on John Wayne had a steady contract with Republic to make series Westerns. Wayne's following was growing but, except for Raoul Walsh's *The Big Trail* way back in 1930, all of his films were low-budget Westerns. Then out of the blue John Ford cast him as the lead in the high-budgeted United Artists picture, *Stagecoach*. As I mentioned before, John wasn't stingy in doling out credit and I was very happy when I received a call for an interview with Mr. Ford. I had never worked with him before but had long admired his work and was eager for the shot.

When I walked into his office he studied me for a moment, then remarked, "Well, Enos, how are you?"

Few people knew my real name since I always went by my rodeo nickname. "I see Wayne has given you all the inside dope on me," I said as we shook hands.

"That's right," he laughed. "In fact, he has said so much about you that you're going to find it a little hard to live up to it."

After a short interview and some good laughs, he handed me the script. "Take it home, read it," he said, "and come in tomorrow morning and we'll talk."

I read the script and considered it one of the best Western scripts that I had ever read. It was a good dramatic story with all the audience-capturing elements. It had one gag which had never been done before—arriving at a river crossing, the stage driver, the guard, and the various passengers find the stage station burned down and the ferryboat destroyed by an Indian attack. They attach logs to either side of the coach to float it, and the six horses swim and pull the coach with its eight passengers across the river. I figured this would be tricky, but was sure it could be done.

With the proper time and money, I always say, you can do the impossible. After reading the story and making notes on action and added thrills, I had a talk with Mr. Ford. He shook his head when I mentioned the floating coach and swimming horses scene.

"Forget that sequence," he warned. "The wranglers tell me it can't be done."

"Mr. Ford," I said, "it can be done and I think that it will look terrific."

"Can you do it?" he asked.

"Yes, but it will take some good rigging," I told him, "and cost a bit of money."

"I didn't ask you anything about money. Can you do it?"

"I can do it."

"Okay, we'll leave it in," was his reply.

I went on location with a crew to the Kern River where I weighed the stagecoach, the eight people, and all the equipment. The people in that coach are all well-known now: the driver, Andy Devine; George Bancroft, riding shotgun; John Wayne; Claire Trevor; Louise Plett; John Carradine; Donald Meek, the whiskey salesman; and Thomas Mitchell, the doctor. I've forgotten the total weight, but it was heavy.

I had the company hire a special effects expert from Paramount. He supervised the building of four hollow logs, two to go on each side of the stagecoach. They were made so that they could be secured to the boom poles located on the understructure of the coach, but would allow the wheels to turn. The logs had enough air in them to float the vehicle. The six horses were to be in regular harness and all of them were hooked in such a way that if any one of them quit pulling, he would be towed right along with the others. I devised an underwater cable that was fastened to the front lead tongue with a pelican hook that could be tripped when we reached the opposite river bank. The cable crossed the river underwater and then ran through a pulley to an off-stage truck, which would pull the entire outfit into the water and across to the other side.

Mr. Ford was still a bit skeptical. The rigging took three days. I phoned him when we finished to tell him that we were ready. "Did you do it?" he asked.

"No," I said, "we haven't actually done the swim, but it is rigged and ready."

"Put eight people in the stage tomorrow and try it," Ford said. "Then call me after you finish."

I took seven people and drove it myself. Before we did the gag, I told the effects man, who knew the amount of air it would take to float the coach, to put a mark where he figured the water line would be. He only missed it by about half an inch. Everything worked the first time, so we wrapped it up and went back to the hotel. I told Mr. Ford and he brought the company to shoot the next morning. I had everything ready to go when Mr. Ford arrived on the set. I put on a padded outfit to double Andy Devine and drive the team. I gave the driver of the truck a signal and it went off without a hitch. When the scene was over, Mr. Ford said to me, "Yak, do you think Andy could drive it across?"

Not Andy Devine, but Yakima Canutt doubling him in a river crossing in
Stagecoach. Action director Canutt had the coach rigged to
float as the horses pulled it through the water.

Yak doubles John Wayne in a jump to a team
of running horses. (*Stagecoach*)

Getting into Indian costume for the famous leap from a running horse
to the lead horse of the coach team—at forty-five miles an hour.
The man in the overcoat is *Stagecoach* director John Ford.

The running leap lands Yak, as the Indian,
on the team horse's back.

Yak is shot by John Wayne in this spectacular
horse fall. (*Stagecoach*)

The famous burning of Atlanta scene in *Gone With the Wind*.
Yakima Canutt doubled Clark Gable as Rhett Butler, driving a one-horse
hack through the flaming streets. (From the MGM release
Gone With the Wind © 1939 Selznick International Pictures, Inc.,
Copyright renewed 1967 by Metro-Goldwyn-Mayer Inc.)

Yak as a character in *Gone With the Wind*. He is playing
a renegade, here attacking Vivien Leigh as Scarlett O'Hara.
(From the MGM release *Gone With the Wind* © 1939 Selznick
International Pictures, Inc., Copyright
renewed 1967 by Metro-Goldwyn-Mayer Inc.)

"No problem," I replied. "The way it is rigged, all he will have to do is hold the reins."

"Good," Ford said. "We'll shoot it again so we can get closer with the cameras."

We got the scene ready and, with the principals who could be seen through the coach windows, we repeated the action and everything worked perfectly.

One thing I'll say for John Ford—he picked the most stunning locations available.

We did the final chase and fight with the Indians on a dry lake near Victorville, California. We had a number of saddle and horse falls to do and I had written in a couple of spectacular stunts. Mr. Ford always shot very fast and I knew that any hold-up in waiting for stunt men would rile him.

The running Indian fight was scheduled for three days. To make sure there would be no delays in putting the thrill action scenes in front of the camera, I had a farmer with a tractor disk up about fifteen or twenty acres of the dry lake bed to give us good soft ground for the falls.

After we got the chase started and shot the scenes of the Indians splitting to either side of the running coach, exchanging gun fire with Wayne and the passengers, Mr. Ford waved me over.

"Yak," he said, "we'll do that Indian routine of yours, now. So get into your war paint."

This was the creation I described earlier. It called for special hookup equipment that I had invented and used a time or two before on a couple of quickies. This would be the first time I had done the stunt on a major picture.

We were to start off with me playing an Indian making a transfer from his running horse to one of the animals on the lead team. As I grab the reins and try to stop or wreck the coach, Wayne fires a shot at me from the top of the coach. I take the shot and fall to the ground between the two speeding lead horses. Hanging onto the lead tongue, I drag on my back. Wayne fires a second shot and I turn loose and let the six horses pass by—three on either side—and then the coach passes over me. The distance between the horses as they pass is three feet, give or take a few inches either way, and the clearance under the coach is critical. If you were to double your arms with your elbows up, the front axle would strike them. All in all, it is a gag that you could easily rub yourself out with if you make the wrong move. In order to get all the clearance possible I picked a section of the dry lake bed that had a hard surface so the wheels would not sink into the ground.

Mr. Ford was going to shoot the transfer first, in a traveling shot, with the camera car running to one side and ahead at a three-quarter angle. The three cameras were set and the car ready to start when Mr. Ford noticed that I had a pair of full-length buckskin leggings on.

"Get those leggings off," he ordered. "You're a breech cloth Indian, remember?"

I figured that he didn't know exactly what the gag was but it was too minor to argue over. The worst that could happen from the lack of leggings would be a little skin burn from the hard ground or a glancing clip from a horse's hoof. I pulled them off.

"Okay," I said, "I'm ready."

"How fast will that team be traveling?" Ford asked, still dubious about the safety of the stunt. "I don't want any mishaps."

"Mr. Ford," I answered, "you can figure—for a short run—around thirty-seven miles an hour, give or take a little. And don't worry about me."

We lined up for the shot. I was riding a pinto and had a flat saddle with an iron step fastened to the stirrup leather high on the right side of the horse. With my foot on this step I had good leverage for the transfer. The saddle was covered with an Indian blanket. On the command of "action," I raced the pinto in alongside the team. The pinto tried to shy away, and I had to make a long jump. I lit sprawled out over the back of the near lead horse, but pulled myself over into a standing position on the lead tongue. I started gathering up the reins, which ended that part of the gag.

When everything came to a stop, Ford hollered in a loud voice, "Yak, come here."

I figured that something had gone wrong. I walked over to the camera car and asked, "What's up?"

"A hell of a lot you know about how fast a team can run," he snorted.

"How fast were we going?"

"Forty-five miles per hour."

"If you're right," I grinned, "we just broke the record."

Everyone had a good laugh, but I noticed that it burnt Ford a little, even though he laughed with the others.

"You'll never top that transfer with the finish of your gag," he said.

I knew then that he didn't have any idea what I was going to do.

I stood on the lead tongue, and when the team got leveled off at a full run, I signaled I was ready. While tugging at a set of false reins, Wayne fired a shot at me. I doubled and fell, hanging to the tongue as my back hit the ground. I dragged along, looking back between the horse's flying legs and the undercarriage of the coach. It was a little spooky, but the horses were running straight. Wayne fired again, and I let go of the tongue, keeping my legs together and my arms flat on my body. As the back of the coach went over me, I rolled over and tried to get up and then fell back and laid still. I heard Ford holler "cut!" so I got up and started walking to the camera car.

Mr. Ford was leaning against the camera car looking at the ground. One of the camera operators said that he didn't think he got it, a second didn't know for sure, and the third cameraman said he was pretty sure he had it but couldn't be positive.

"I'll be happy to do it again, Mr. Ford," I said. "You know I love to make money."

Mr. Ford shook his head. "I'll never shoot that again," he replied flatly. "They better have it."

I believe that he thought I was going to fall to the outside of the horses instead of in between them. My bit of acting at the end of the stunt may also have fooled him. He probably thought I had really hurt myself. Anyway, one of the cameras had good footage of the entire stunt and it seems to be the one stunt in the picture everyone remembers.

At the end of the second day, we had filmed a good number of very spectacular falls. One of my stunt men had just done a very good horse fall and he made the mistake of asking Mr. Ford how it was. Ford gave him a sour look.

"It stunk," he rasped. He then turned and said to all of us, "In fact, it was the worst day's shooting 'supposedly' thrill stuff I've ever done, but maybe I can use it."

He went to his car and left. One of the stunt men, burned by Ford's words, said to me, "What the hell does it take to please him?"

"Don't let him get your goat," I said. "He liked the stuff. If he hadn't, he would have shot it over."

The next morning we still had quite a lot of gags to do and that being the last day of action, Mr. Ford called me over and asked me to get my stunt crew rounded up. He wanted to talk to all of them. I got the men together, and Mr. Ford eyed them soberly. "Boys," he said, "we've had two good days of pretty wild stuff. I don't want to see anyone get hurt. This is the last day, so hold it down a bit."

"What's the matter, Boss?" I asked with a grin. "Is your powder getting damp?"

"Okay," he said. "Just hold it down a little."

Everything went well and we had one gag left, a fall in which the Indian hangs in the stirrup and drags a few yards.

"Yak," Mr. Ford said, "we've been very lucky. Let's forget that drag. I'll pay for it anyway."

"Mr. Ford," I replied, "it's all rigged and ready, and the man who is set to do it has done a lot of them. And the safety traps are rigged."

"There are the cameras," he said. "Tell the cameramen where you want them."

He went to his car and sat down to watch from a distance. We set up and the Indians rode from behind the camera. The one doing the fall took it right in front of the camera and dragged for some distance. I looked over and Mr. Ford gave me the "okay" sign and we wrapped it up. It is the only action picture that I ever worked on where there never was a second take on any of the stunts. Every stunt worked perfectly the first time.

That night at the Greenspot Restaurant in Victorville, Mr. Ford, John Wayne, Ward Bond and I sat in a booth having dinner. Wayne and I were laughing over some of the ribs that we had pulled on different people at different locations.

The restaurant was packed, not only with our company, but with many locals and transients. A group of stunt men were sitting at a table in the central part of the room only a few feet away from our table. Among them was Ken Cooper, a cowboy who was always pulling a prank on someone. John and I were laughing about a joke we had played on him during the shooting of a picture at Lone Pine, California, a few weeks before.

Ken had done a horse fall and at the end of the scene, unnoticed by Ken, I slipped a double-pointed stick, about two feet long, under the rigging of his saddle. The Humane Officer on the job went along on the gag and acted his part one-hundred percent. While looking the horse over for injuries, he pulled the double-pointed stick from under the rigging. He looked accusingly at Ken, who was really shocked when he saw the stick. He looked at me for support, but I gave him a dirty look and walked away. The Humane Officer, despite Ken's heated denial, put him under arrest, saying that he could tell the judge how the stick got there. He handcuffed Ken and took him off the set for an hour or two.

Mr. Ford looked over at Ken.

"He likes to rib," he said musingly, then got up and went to Ken's table and talked with Ken a moment.

When he came back to our booth, he sat down and announced that Ken and I were going to have a fight in the cafe. I nodded with an understanding grin and looked over at Ken who was glaring at me.

"What are you staring at me for, you silly-looking idiot?" I said in a loud, belligerent voice.

Ken threw an insult back at me. Keeping my voice loud, I told Mr. Ford that he should leave before any trouble started.

Ken came over to me and Mr. Ford faked an attempt to stop Ken, then let me out of our booth. I met Ken head on and we fought right through the center of the room, knocking tables over while the customers scattered like scared sheep. I made it a point to upset as many tables as possible.

The owner of the restaurant, a big husky fellow, was outside when it started, but finally came in, threw a headlock on Ken, and gave him a pretty good roughing up before he found out it was a phoney fight.

I went back to my table to finish my dinner. The place was a wreck, tables upside down, steaks and catsup and broken dishes all over the floor.

"Now, why can't I get a fight like that in a picture?" Ford said to John and Ward Bond.

"Mr. Ford," I said, "if you'll pay stunt men as much money as this fight is going to cost you, you'll get a better fight."

Mr. Ford was indeed a great director. He was, you might say, a psychologist. He understood people and how to bring out the best in them.

By the time John Wayne made *Stagecoach*, he already had some ten years' experience in making films. But he was new to the big leagues and Ford treated him like the greenest tenderfoot. He harped so much about John's acting and made him so self-conscious that John and I used to have extra sessions in our hotel room in which we'd go over John's lines for the next day again and again. Both Wayne and Ford had indomitable spirits—for all their friction, the chemistry was right. It's no wonder that they went on to make many great films together.

John Ford could be a little more than gruff at times, and he seemed to take pleasure in chewing someone out in a voice that could be heard by all. I've been told that during the filming of *The Informer* Ford had a crony of Victor McLaughlin's take a quart of liquor to Vic's dressing room and get him soused. They were set up to shoot when Vic came on the set. He was really high, and Ford chewed him out in an unmerciful manner. Poor Vic, who loved Ford as a great pal, was ready to burst into tears when Mr. Ford sent him into his biggest scene in the picture. His performance won an Oscar that year.

When we finished shooting *Stagecoach*, Mr. Ford called me into his office.

"You can go home and put this in your notebook," he said, and these are his exact words: "Any time I'm making an action picture and you're not working, you are with me." He then added, "I'll see you at the party tonight."

The company was throwing a big party that night at the studio. During the evening, I was having a drink with Mr. Ford and the cameraman, Bert Glennon, when the film editor came in. He had been running all the film that had been shot on the picture.

After a good look at the film he told Ford, "I really think you're going to have one of the best Western action pictures ever made."

Glennon was getting a little high and he broke in a little drunkenly, "Yes, thanks to Yakima Canutt."

I glanced at Ford who was glaring at Glennon. I moved away but quick. I told Glennon later that not only did he cut my throat, but his own as well.

A year or so later I had a call from the Fox Studio to do a fall from a bucking horse during a parade on *Young Mr. Lincoln*. When I went on to the set Mr. Ford saw me and asked curtly, "What are you doing here, Yak?"

I told him that I had been called to do a fall from a bronc. "Oh," he said, and turned away.

It was a tricky fall. During a Fourth of July parade someone throws a firecracker under the horse, Henry Fonda, as Abe Lincoln, is riding. The stunt worked very well and, even knowing that Mr. Ford had not asked for me, I thanked him for the call and turned and headed for the casting office to get my pay.

"Your gag stunk," he hollered after me.

"Don't say anything about it until I get my money," I yelled back, and despite himself, Ford had to grin.

For all his bluster Ford had a big heart and would go all out to help a friend. He was a great director and the many fine films he left behind testify to that.

Stagecoach launched John Wayne on the path to stardom and I can tell you from having worked with him that he is one star who earned his status. In six out of the eight years between 1949 and 1957 John Wayne was one of the top ten money-making stars. Yet, even with such clear evidence of his long distance public appeal, you still hear criticisms of his acting ability. Many say that he's a great actor, others say that he's wooden.

Now John Wayne is by no means a Shakespearean actor, for which he can be thankful. But he is blessed with a stature and personality that perfectly capture the fearless, red-blooded man of the wide-open spaces. His easy gait and slow manner of talking make you take to him immediately. He's so natural in his acting that some people think that he isn't acting at all—but for my money that's the sign of a great actor.

Like the majority of people in the industry, I was very happy when he won the Oscar for his brilliant performance in *True Grit*. I worked with John Wayne more than with any other star during my stunt career and I am proud to call him a friend. He's more than a great man—he's a national institution.

Stagecoach was not the only motion picture destined to become a great classic that reached the American public in 1939. That was also the year of *Gone With the Wind*, and I am just as proud to have worked on that picture. M.G.M. hired me to double Gable and to play the part of a renegade. I had doubled Gable several times before and it was always a pleasure.

By now the story behind the making of *Gone With the Wind* is almost as legendary as the film itself. Production on the picture moved at a snail's pace and the project was plagued by troubles with the directors, the script, the actresses, the sets and, of course, the ever-changing grand designs of the producer, David O. Selznick.

My involvement with the project began as the filming itself did, with the famous burning of Atlanta sequence. It was on the night that they first lit the flames, and began production on this multi-million dollar epic, that, as legend has it, David O. Selznick first saw Vivien Leigh, the flames lighting up her face, and thus the twenty-month search for the right Scarlett O'Hara was ended.

Shooting that fiery sequence started some storms of its own. George Cukor, the first of three principal directors, Ray Klune, the production manager, Lee Zavitz, special-effects expert, and other top advisors tried to persuade Selznick to build the city of Atlanta in miniature. It would save money and simplify the burning. But Selznick was adamant. He was going to burn an actual city. This city, finally designed by William Cameron Menzies, the production designer, and art director Lyle Wheeler, was built on the RKO-Pathé back lot. It used practically all the old buildings that had stood there for years, including the great wall built for the original *King Kong*. The Selznick Company constructed over two miles of streets and sixty buildings, many of them false fronts erected on the Kong Wall. The burning was to take place at night and the flames and smoke would mask any inconsistency.

For the burning of Atlanta, Lee Zavitz had fitted the walls of the buildings with pipes through which the mixed burning fluids were fed to the atomizers that threw out the flames. The fuel flow was controlled electrically from a pumping station where all the atomizers could be turned on or off instantly. Another control fed a flow of oil or water into the pipes on cue. Well over a thousand gallons of fuel per minute were used, sending the flames a hundred-and-fifty feet or more into the air. The residents in the surrounding area protested that this was dangerous, but Selznick was allowed to go ahead. A large force of Los Angeles firemen stood by with their equipment to support the studio fire force.

While the main burning of Atlanta was in progress, I made several runthroughs along the smoke-filled streets as flaming debris fell all around me. My principal work came later when various sections of the city had been rebuilt, so that they might be set on fire under controlled conditions for the safety of the stunt men.

My first real stunt in the picture was to drive a one-horse hack at a full run through alleys and narrow streets with burning buildings on either side. We worked until midnight without getting a printable scene. I tried to explain to Mr. Cukor, that it was impossible to run horses through a fire that heavy. "However," I said, "we can get the effect by having an open gap just wide enough to drive the hack through, then add more fire wall to the far side of the gap by running this wall back twenty of thirty feet into the set. With the camera set at the proper angle, the gap in the flames would not be seen. It would look like a complete wall of fire by adding a few burning pieces of wood falling from above and landing around the hack as it went through the opening."

Cukor insisted that the scenes had to be more realistic. He wanted to see the horse-drawn hack come through an actual wall of fire. I kept trying to explain that it couldn't be done the way he wanted it—I had great respect for him as a director but he just didn't seem to understand the action part of films.

We were still thrashing this out when, just after midnight, David Selznick appeared on the set. Seeing the lack of activity, he talked with Mr. Cukor for a few moments, then came over and asked me what the trouble was. I told him.

"Do you know a director who does this kind of work?" he said. I told him Breezy Eason was, in my opinion, the best action director in the business. He asked for his phone number and I gave it to him. Breezy was on the set within the hour. After a little briefing we went to work. We did the runthroughs as I had suggested. They came off well and looked very real on the screen.

Later that night we were set up to do a short sequence in which I turn the one-horse hack off a burning street into a narrow alley where I am attacked by three or four ruffians.

"When the ruffians make the attack," Breezy said, "I want to see the horse rear and paw out at the men who try to stop him, and Yak, you lay the whip on them!"

Tracy Lane, a cowboy who was working with us, owned the horse we were using and he had trained him to rear and paw out with his front legs the way Breezy wanted. To make sure the horse performed at the right moment, Tracy had taken a small "hot shot" and put it under the breast collar. The "hot shot," similar to the battery-powered electric prods used to herd cattle, had been weakened, as it only takes a small shock to cue a horse into action and not hurt him. Tracy had a wire running from the "hot shot" bug to a switch that was under the hack seat and he was to lie on the hackbed covered with a tarpaulin. I was to give him the cue when to hit the switch.

The fires were brought up and on "action" I put the horse into a run. As we turned into the blazing alley, the ruffians attacked me. I touched the horse with the whip and gave Tracy the cue. The horse reared up, pawing like a demon. At the same time I was laying the whip on the renegades who were trying to get me. Tracy hit the switch a second time and the horse reared and slashed furiously. His hind feet must have slipped because he sat down and came over on his back with all four legs sticking straight up between the shafts. I jumped out of the way and hollered, "Cut"! We got the horse up just as Breezy walked over and asked me if I knew what picture I was working on.

"*Gone With the Wind*," I said.

Breezy snorted, "Oh yeah, looks more like a Mack Sennett comedy to me."

Everyone had a good laugh. I had Tracy move the bug from the breast collar to the back britches on the harness and, after replacing a couple of broken straps, we did the scene again. The horse worked well, the ruffians were great, and Breezy was happy.

Following the burning of Atlanta I did a number of run-throughs on the burned-out streets with one horse hitched to a light wagon. I doubled Gable and Elaine Goodman doubled Vivien Leigh. In the back of the wagon, hidden under a tarp, were dummies, to simulate Melanie, her newborn baby, and Prissy, the black servant played by Butterfly McQueen. For one scene I had to learn Gable's dialogue for timing. After speaking his lines to the double girl, I drove on out. The director was going to put in a big closeup of Gable later but in the finished picture, his voice was dubbed in and the scene was left just as we did it. I could hardly believe my eyes when I saw the sequence in the theatre but no one else seemed to notice. Gable and I were about the same size. His tailor-made suits were a perfect fit—although the duplicate double clothes were a lot less costly!

In one runthrough, the right front wheel hit a broken post and flipped the wagon, throwing both Elaine and me out. She got a bad bruise on her hip but was able to continue work. I landed upside down, the back of my neck hit a two-by-four brace, which cooled me out for a few minutes. The wranglers brought the horses and wagon back and we went ahead with the work. For an hour or so I was a little hazy. I couldn't figure out what picture I was working on. After a few runs they started shooting some scenes that I wasn't in, so I relaxed for awhile. The assistant director came to me and asked how I felt.

"Okay," I said, "but would you tell me the name of the picture we're working on?"

He looked at me a little funny, then said, "You must have

got quite a bump! You're working on *Gone With the Wind*." Strange as it seems, the moment he named the picture, my brain cleared up. When you work on as many films at one time as stunt men often do, and get as many bumps on the head, memory jokes become a sort of stock in trade.

Despite all the directors and cameramen working on *Gone With the Wind* the firm, creative hand of David O. Selznick could be seen in all their work. No one looking at the picture could tell where one director or cameraman finished and another took over.

The second unit moved to a location near Big Bear Lake in California, where Breezy Eason began filming a sequence with Elaine Goodman, again doubling Vivien Leigh. She drove through the shanty-town countryside in a one-horse buggy followed by Big Sam, one of her Tara servants. He was some distance behind her on foot, trying to catch up with her. Big Sam, played by the black actor, Everett Brown, was properly named. He was well over six feet tall and weighed at least two hundred and fifty pounds.

One of the setups was on a high piece of ground with a winding road that ran over a ridge and down a fairly steep grade that leveled out very abruptly. At the bottom, the camera was set at a slight angle to one side of the road. The steep part of the grade was about a hundred-and-fifty feet from the top to the bottom.

On the call of "action" Elaine Goodman brought the buggy to a nice trot over the ridge and down the hill and on through the valley. Then Big Sam came into scene on foot, running wide open. Along with doing stunts, I was also cast as a renegade who was to attack Scarlett O'Hara in this sequence, with Big Sam coming in to save her. I was standing alongside Breezy, watching the action, and as Sam went down the sharp incline, he never slackened his speed. I knew what was bound to happen.

"I'll bet you twenty dollars he falls down at the bottom of the hill and knocks himself out," I said to Breezy.

"It's a bet," Breezy said.

Right on cue down went Big Sam, out like a light. Breezy handed me a twenty dollar bill.

"How did you know he was going to do that?" he asked.

I grinned and replied, "That's your basic fall."

Breezy had the cameramen move the camera to the proper position for the long shots of my attack on Scarlett's double.

He had planned two ways to shoot this sequence. The first was to put me in Scarlett's clothes and wreck the buggy on a sharp turn. Then in another cut, as the renegade, I was to catch Elaine near the wrecked buggy for the fight with Big Sam. "If it doesn't look right," Breezy said, "we'll redo it with Elaine driving. You can stop her horse on the bridge."

For the wrecking of the buggy, I had a ramp built out of rocks on the hill side of a narrow, sharp turn in the road. Then, dressed in Scarlett's double's clothes that had been made for me, I put the horse into a run and pulled the buggy close to the ramp. The right front wheel hit it and bounced the buggy into a complete flip. I was thrown over the edge of the roadway and rolled down the hill.

The V.I.P.'s saw the rushes the next day and Selznick said the stunt was spectacular, but Scarlett's double looked more like a man than a woman. So, we changed our schedule and arranged to stage the attack on the bridge that Breezy had picked out as second choice.

When Elaine and I did the scene, I caught the horse's rein and stopped him. Then, looking at her I ask, "Have you got a quarter, lady?" She slashes furiously at me with her buggy whip. I take it away from her, but not without getting a few lashes that left marks on me. I am just in the act of dragging her out of the buggy when Big Sam arrives for the rescue. He jerks me away from her. There we were to stage a short fight.

We shot the scene several times and although Everett Brown was a good actor, he knew nothing about fighting in pictures. I rehearsed the routine repeatedly with him, trying patiently to show him how to deliver a punch which would miss my chin but would look like a solid blow from the camera's angle. Everett didn't seem to like the idea of me telling him how to do the scene. Finally he turned to Breezy and said, "Why don't you get someone to play this scene with me who knows how?" Breezy replied that he was already working with one of the top stunt men in the business and that I was only trying to help him.

Breezy had warned me to be careful of what I said and did around Brown since he had the reputation of being difficult and might walk off the set if crossed. Despite this warning, I was so mad that I told him to quit behaving like a temperamental actor. Stunt work and staging fights was my business. If he'd just listen, we'd get the scene shot in such a way that we could both be proud of it. Brown calmed down, and, after a few more rehearsals, the fight was filmed in one take with two cameras. Big Sam knocked me under the buggy, apparently unconscious, and the rear wheel ran over me when the horse plunged ahead. Then he rolled me off the bridge with his foot and I landed in the stream below.

When Breezy finally called "cut," satisfied with the way the scene had come off, Everett Brown came over to me and apologized for the way he had acted. He admitted that he learned a lot about fighting in pictures from me and thanked me for helping him. We shook hands and the studio car took me back to my lodgings at Big Bear. I had finished my work on *Gone With the Wind*. Or so I thought.

Several days later I went to New Mexico to do stunt work on *The Light That Failed*, a film based on the famous story by Rudyard Kipling. Blue Washington, a black actor who had also been working on *Gone With the Wind*, was with me. William Wellman was shooting the picture in Santa Fe, on the head waters of the Rio Grande. Blue hated to fly and on the plane to New Mexico he sat glued to his seat, looking straight ahead and saying nothing to anyone.

I had been on the picture only a few days when I had a phone call from the casting director for *Gone With the Wind*. He said Selznick had made arrangements with Paramount Studios for me to fly back to Los Angeles. I was needed for closer shots to cut into the scenes where I attacked Scarlett on the bridge. This time it was to be a process shot filmed in the studio and I was to work with Vivien Leigh.

I flew back to Hollywood and reported on the set at RKO-Pathé where I learned Victor Fleming was to direct these scenes. I was amazed at the difference in his appearance and behavior. He was cranky as all get out and seemed to have aged years. The first take on my scene with Scarlett was cut before I had hardly opened my mouth. Fleming stalked over to me and sneered, "All right, ham it up!" He then went back to the camera, leaving me bewildered. Whatever his disposition, it certainly did not affect his talent for making great pictures. He had a nervous breakdown shortly after this incident, but he still stayed with the picture until it was finished.

The pressure of the big leagues took its toll on a good number of talented people in the motion picture industry. I could see that firsthand. But at least at this time the most creative things happening in motion pictures were in the big budget productions—and that's where I wanted to be.

SEVEN

From Yellee to Yeller

"Turn him loose."

The fellow on the snubbing horse let the bronc go and he took off like a rocket. This was no cherry picker—he reared, tossed, jumped and whirled. He was trying every trick that he knew to do his one job—getting me off. With one hand in the air, the other on the reins, and my legs gripping his sides, I was doing one of the jobs I knew best—staying on. Twenty years earlier that would have been my only job, but this spring night I was doubling Clark Gable in the M.G.M. film, *Boom Town*, and the second unit director had given me my instructions. I was to ride the bronc across the arena to where the orchestra was playing, and there I was to have the horse vault me over the fence and through the band's big bass drum for a dramatic finish.

Some directors don't understand why you have to do a stunt a certain way. I had tried to explain to Waters that when you're on a bucking horse you're a passenger—he goes where he wants. This was true when I started riding at thirteen, it was true when I rode to three world championships, and it was sure true that night. I had told him how I wanted to do it. He could get all the bucking footage he needed from a couple of straight rides. Then I wanted to have his workmen put up a V-shaped panel fence. The fence would come to a point from either side of the orchestra platform, just out of the camera side lines. This would keep the bronc in tight quarters and whenever he got close to the orchestra's section of the enclosure I'd make the fall. Of course, making the fall didn't worry me. Using specially designed short stirrups I had by this time perfected some pretty spectacular falls. I could fall to either side, flip over the horse's head or, far more dangerous, back flip over his rump.

But the type of flip didn't matter until we got the horse to the fence. Waters was one of those directors who test stunt men's mettle more than the stunts themselves—one-shot directors. They think that action has to be in one shot in order for it to be authentic. He wanted the ride and the fall all in one shot. So there I was, groggy and punchy, having already put in a full day's shooting at Republic, watching them saddle another bronc.

"Okay, Yak, listen," Waters said. "Let's try it one more time. If it still doesn't work, we'll do it your way. Okay?"

Well, it wasn't really okay. I knew that, but I had to fight my frustration. I was the hired hand, still the stunt man who had to follow someone else's directions even though I knew that there were ways to get the same or better effect in half the time with less than half the risk. I was forty-four and would have been a damn fool if I didn't admit that my reactions weren't as fast as they used to be. My legs were slowing down a bit and, as any stunt man can tell you, your legs are your main equipment. By 1940 I had been stunting for over eleven years, not counting the stunts I did for my own silent serials. I figured that I knew just about all there was to know about horses. Yet here I was biting the bullet and going through with a stunt that I knew was almost impossible as planned.

I was about as angry and distracted as a tired man can be when I climbed onto that last bronc, as it turned out, one of the better-rested and saucier ones. The snubber turned him loose and I raked my spurs over his shoulders. The horse reared up for his first jump and then threw himself straight over backwards. Ordinarily, I would have stepped off in midair and cleared him, but I was too worn out to move quickly enough. He lit square on top of me, his approximately twelve hundred pounds balanced there for what seemed an eternity, then rolled to his side and got up. Pain screamed through my body. I felt as if I was completely torn in two. The saddle horn had hit square in the center of my stomach, gone through and pulled out some of my stuffing on the way out. I doubled up and pulled my knees into my chest. The first-aid man did all he could, but it wasn't exactly an iodine and Band-aid job.

The director ran over, terribly upset, blaming himself and saying over and over that he should have done the scene my way. My thoughts were miles away. I thought I had bought it. While waiting for the ambulance I thought of my wife, pregnant with our third child, and, cloudy as my mind was, I tried to figure out how much insurance I had. Tears were welling up in the director's eyes and I really felt sorry for him. I told him not to blame himself—it was just one of those things that could happen to any stunt man. Certainly, other stunt men had died in sillier stunts. But I also knew that it wasn't Waters's fault—I should have known better. If you've seen *Boom Town*, you may remember that Clark Gable does not go through the band's bass drum. Another double simply falls off the horse.

After a nightmarish ride to the hospital, I found out that two of my intestines were nearly cut in two, my diaphragm was injured badly, the lining covering one kidney was torn off and six ribs were broken. They operated on me that morning and somehow put me back together. When I woke up later in the day and heard Audrea talking to me, I felt that a miracle had happened. I had what you would call a complete overhaul and had to stay flat on my back for three weeks in intensive care. Fortunately, sulfa drugs had been recently discovered and the doctors were able to check the peritonitis that had set in.

Six weeks later I went home to endure a long recuperative period. It was good, though, because it gave me a chance to do a lot of hard thinking, to see my life a little more clearly and to make plans. One thing was certain—I had to phase myself out of stunt work and fast. Some five years earlier I had started the background work to make the transition from stunting to action directing and had several impressive jobs to my credit. Throughout my career I had always worked closely with the writers and helped them inject action into the pictures. I had studied how different directors approached their material and how they used their cameras. I felt that I was ready to tackle bigger stuff and stay behind the camera.

But this wasn't to happen right away. When I first returned to Republic, I took it easy, doing bit parts and supervising the action. Within a few months I was doing stunts again, but I was having trouble with what turned out to be adhesions. After my operation I had been on my back so long that one of my intestines grew back together in a tight "U" and the wrong food would obstruct it. Two or three times a week I had to call the doctor for relief from the pain. Finally I promised the doctor that when the picture I was working on was finished, I would go into the hospital for exploratory surgery.

After lunch the following day I was driving a six-up stagecoach in a fast chase when one of my stomach attacks hit. Driving six runaway horses on a stage takes a lot of strength at any time. As the chase drew to a close I was in such pain that I was having trouble keeping the teams lined out. Stopping them was beyond my power. I managed to turn them off the road into a flat field and was straining to pull them up when a couple of cowboys saw that I was in trouble and came to my rescue. They caught the lead horses and helped me stop them.

While pulling the reins with all my might, I felt a sharp pain in my abdomen. It felt like someone had stabbed me with a red hot knife. The boys helped me off the coach and a friend drove me home.

We had driven only a short way when the pain suddenly ceased. In fact, to my amazement, I felt great. I decided to wait a day or two before calling the doctor. We had guests in for venison dinner that evening and, since I hadn't eaten any solid food for a time, I decided to eat one good meal, stomach be damned. I ate a couple of steaks while my wife's eyes grew large. I might kill myself, she said. Well, I wouldn't die hungry, I replied, and finished with dessert.

After the guests left, I was afraid to go to bed, feeling sure I would have to call the doctor. I sat up and read until around two-thirty but the pain never returned. When I told this to the doctor the next day, he said the pain must have been caused by an adhesion and, when I strained to stop the team, I tore it loose. He was convinced that I would have no more trouble—and he was right. Of course, performing major surgery with a stagecoach is a bit crude and certainly not recommended, but I guess it does show how well suited my body is to my calling.

I was not about to tempt fate, however, by pursuing stunt work much longer. Shortly after my recovery, Sol Siegel called me in for a talk. He had entrusted the action sequences on Republic's first two big-budget pictures to me, and I was now elated to learn that he wanted me to coordinate the stunts on *Dark Command*. This was to be Republic's first big-budget picture to star John Wayne since his great success in

Stagecoach. Wayne was now a box office attraction and the Republic executives were quite disturbed that United Artists had made such a big splash using *their* star. *Dark Command* would team Wayne with his leading lady from *Stagecoach,* Claire Trevor, and Raoul Walsh, the director of *The Big Trail,* Wayne's first big picture back in 1930. Several colorful actors filled out the supporting cast, including Walter Pidgeon, Roy Rogers, George "Gabby" Hayes and Marjorie Main. Initially budgeted at $750,000, the picture finally cost more than twice as much as UA's *Stagecoach.*

Republic had always been known for its action and when Siegel spoke with me he had action on his mind. He wanted a new, spectacular thrill for Wayne and suggested I work it around a sequence in which Wayne and three other men are being chased by Quantrill's raiders and have to make a getaway. I told him I'd kick it around and see what I could come up with. That evening I worked out a stunt I was sure would fill the bill.

It meant changing the end of Quantrill's ambush. Instead of making their escape on horseback, Wayne and the three men would get into a small supply wagon and make a run for it, leaving the roadway and driving the team off a bluff and into a river fifty feet below. I worked the action out in detail and put the scenes on paper.

The jump would run only five or six feet of film, but equipment, construction, and stunt men would cost about five thousand dollars. That's a lot of money for five feet of film! I didn't think that Mr. Siegel would go for it.

The next morning when I explained the sequence to him, the only thing he said was: "Will it work?"

"When I get it rigged," I said, "it can't miss."

"It sounds thrilling," Siegel answered. "Go ahead."

I had the special-effects department make a double wagon, a replica of the wagon we would use in all of the runs up to the jump. The trick wagon was made mostly of light balsa wood and only enough heavy timber was used to carry the weight. Then I had the work crew build a chute at a forty-five degree angle, reaching from the top of the bluff above the river to a shelf below where the ground leveled off for a few yards. Here we built a tilting chute, strong enough and long enough to hold the wagon and team. The floor of this chute, when tripped, would line up with the floor of the long chute that ran to the edge of the bluff above the water. We then built a camera tower that straddled the lower end of the chute. The cameras could shoot straight down, holding the side of the bluff and river in the photographic field. I had breakaway snaps on the tugs and inside reins of the harness. Also, on the neck yoke straps, a small cable measured to the proper length would free each horse from the hook-up during the fall. A small float on the end of each line would give the men standing by in boats a chance to make a quick rescue if a horse got into trouble.

When we were ready to shoot the scene, I had a talk with the three stunt men who were going to ride the wagon down with me. I gave them my opinion of how it would work, and advised them to jump from the wagon as it left the chute and entered the camera range. The other stunt men were Cliff Lyons, like myself an ex-rodeo man, and two brothers, Bill and Joe Yrigoyen. The Yrigoyens were raised near Calabasas, California, and had grown up in the picture business. We took our places in the wagon, two on the seat and two in the back. The two back men had a bit harder jump to clear the wagon, so I changed wardrobe with Cliff who had hurt his hip a few days before and was a little lame. He would double Wayne, so he would have an easier jump. Joe was in the back with me, and Bill on the seat beside Cliff.

When all was ready, the wagon was moved into the top tilting chute. The full length of the entire slide was seventy-five feet and it was a forty-foot drop to the water. It was impossible to know just how fast the team and wagon would slide since it was a bit like doing a shoot-the-chutes.

When the cameras got up speed and the director gave me the signal, I told the effects man to trip the chute. He did, and the tilting chute fell into a forty-five degree angle, emptying us onto the main chute floor. I was amazed at how fast the wagon traveled. Within a second we were really on our way. Everything worked perfectly. Cliff, Joe and I cleared the wagon in mid-air, but Bill didn't jump quite quickly enough. Standing on the platform of the wagon bed, he rode it into the water.

"Bill, you've got to be on your toes getting off of a falling object," I said to him later. "You know, you could get hurt that way."

Bill had both courage and a great sense of humor.

"I was the only one who had guts enough to ride the wagon into the water," he replied with a grin.

"That you did," I said.

On the trip back from the *Dark Command* location, Mr. Siegel complimented me on my work and asked if I was still interested in becoming a second unit director. That was my ambition, I told him, and he said that when the right opportunity came along, he would see that I be considered.

I thanked him for his confidence in me and, if I had any doubts about his sincerity, they were erased forever by his comment to me after screening the location footage of the wagon scene.

"Yak," he said, "if you come up with another gag as thrilling as that one, I'll go for another five grand."

I knew then that I was definitely in line for a second unit job.

My next job was doubling Errol Flynn in the Warner Brothers picture, *Virginia City*. This was the first of four pictures I worked on with Errol, and we always got along better than well. He was a he-man, and the women really went for him. He had a lot of bad publicity about his conduct with the fair sex, but I think that any man who had his appeal for women would have played it just the way he did—a bit wild. In any case, everyone who knew Errol Flynn really liked him.

A couple of years later, when we were doing *Gentleman Jim*, Flynn played the role of Jim Corbett, one of the first heavyweights to really dance around the ring. The director had one of the fastest fighters in boxing, a man named Steele, working with Errol. When I watched them, I thought that Flynn was just about Steele's match in the footwork.

I worked out with Steele in a sequence of a barn fight. This man Steele was very fast with straight jabs. I was doubling the actor who was doing the part of Corbett's brother, an awkward man who worked out with Gentleman Jim. Since I was doubling a clumsy character, I had to keep throwing wild haymakers. For every swing I made I would receive two or three fast jabs. Then Steele would step out and Flynn would dance around me and jab my nose. He seemed to be just as fast as Steele, and by the time we finished, my nose looked like a mashed-up red potato.

Michael Curtiz was the director of *Virginia City*. He had a thick European accent that sometimes made it difficult to understand him. When he got angry, he would come out with dialogue that really got a laugh. Once he sent the prop man after something and was pacing back and forth, waiting, when the man finally arrived with the wrong thing. Mike blew his top:

"Next time I send a damned idiot after something," he exploded, "I go myself."

One morning Curtiz was shooting a sequence where Flynn makes a flying mount, spins his horse alongside a heavy's horse standing nearby, and then puts his horse into a run, leading the other horse. The heavy and his gang see Flynn leaving and start firing. At that point, Mr. Curtiz cut the action and called me over. (He could never pronounce my nickname "Yak"—it always came out "Yucca".)

"Yucca, I have a good gag," he said. "Can you do it?"

"Just tell me what it is," I answered, "and I'll give you a quick 'yes' or 'no'."

"Well, you are doubling for Flynn," he said, "you are riding his horse leading another horse. You are riding like hell to get away—they are shooting at you and your horse gets hit. He does what you call a 'Running W.' When he falls, you catch the saddle horn on the other horse and do a pony express. You know, when your feet hit the ground, you bounce up on the horse and keep going. It must be done in a fast run."

He looked at me for a second and then asked, "Can you do it?"

I was amazed at him. This was a good gag and I wondered why I hadn't thought of it myself.

"For two hundred and fifty dollars I can do it," I told him. "It will take me about an hour to have it ready."

"Good," he said.

While he was shooting some close shots, I took the two horses to a spot where the stunt could be done. I knew that one of the horses had been used for pony express mounts and trick riding. I fastened them together like I would a team for Roman riding, then ran a heavy strap from saddle ring to saddle ring, and riding the horse that was to fall, I worked with them in a trot. After thirty or forty minutes I had them so that they really ran good together. I then rigged a short piece of small, flexible cable with a pelican trip hook so it would trip and free them from each other just as the horse I would be riding in the scene was thrown by a Running W.

When Mr. Curtiz called "action," I put the horses into a run and just as we hit the end of the cable I reached over and grabbed the saddle horn. My horse turned end over end. Hanging to the saddle horn of the other horse, I hit the ground with my feet, vaulted up into the saddle, and raced out of the scene.

When I rode back, Curtiz shook his head and with a broad grin, said, "Yucca, that was good. Thank you."

Before going further, let me explain what a Running W is and how it works. It was something that caused a lot of controversy for stunt men and Western producers. I remember reading an article written by an officer of the Humane Society that stated we were tying wires on the horses' legs and crippling them so badly that they had to be killed after we did the stunt. In my fifty years of handling action in the picture business, I have only lost two horses: one was a runaway who crashed into a tree and broke his neck, and the other broke a leg on the ice in a sleigh chase.

The Running W, used right, would not hurt a horse. To clear up some of the bad feeling, I invited a couple of Humane Society officers to come out to our location and see how the Running W is done. I was to do a couple of them a day or two later at Vasquez Rocks, a short distance out of Los Angeles.

To prepare the Running W, you make up a pair of leather hobbles, lined with sheepskin and with a D-shaped ring extending from the back of each. These hobbles are buckled on each of the horse's front legs between the hoof and the fetlock, with the D-ring at the back.

A stout leather circingle is wrapped over the saddle and around the horse's body, just back of the saddle cinch. Hanging from it under the horse's body is a ring about three-and-a-half inches in diameter, with three smaller rings welded in its lower half—this is the "W" ring.

A piece of flexible 5/32" airplane cable is tied to the lower center ring of the W, run to the D-ring on one of the horse's legs, back to the front W ring, down to the other D-ring and back to the back ring of the W.

The cable is taped to the horse's front legs just below the knee, leaving just enough slack so that the horse can run without getting tangled up. Then the rest of the cable is measured to reach from the starting point to the spot where the horse is to fall, and firmly tied at the starting point.

When the horse hits the end of the run, the cable pulls both front feet up to the W ring, and the two D-rings on the hobbles act as scissors cutting the line. The horse turns over, comes to his feet, and runs on with the other horses.

The two Humane officers came up to our Vasquez Rock location. I had everything set and ready. I first showed the officers the complete W rigging and explained how it worked. They asked questions and I gave them the answers. I showed them the soft ground with some rubber rocks scattered around. They stood by the camera to watch. After doing the W's and letting them look the horses over, they said if they were all done that way they could see nothing wrong with them and gave the picture an O.K.

I have used some horses several times in Running Ws. Once in a while, though, they will quit after a couple of falls. I recall a fall that I was making in John Wayne's picture, *Dark Command*. I was using a horse that I had done a couple of Ws on. I laced the Running W on him and, when they called "action," I put him in a fast lope. When I got within fifteen or twenty feet from the spot of the fall, the horse came to a quick stop and then lay down. He certainly had it all figured out, and that was his last Running W.

I have done some three hundred Running W's and never crippled a horse. It was generally understood in Hollywood that Flynn had reported to the Humane Society about horses being mistreated, but it wasn't on *Virginia City*. I did a couple of Running W's for him in that picture, and he always watched me doing it and all he ever said was, "Now why don't all the fellows do them that way?"

Shortly after this picture, two horses were killed on a major studio location using this device, and it was finally ruled out by a gentlemen's agreement between the Producers Association and the Humane Society. Today, in Western pictures where there is a falling horse, the horse has been trained by the rider to fall on cue.

Falling a horse that is standing still is much simpler. You use what is called a "four-hobble" fall. The equipment is the same kind of hobble that is put on any grazing horse to keep it from running off, plus a cable.

The stunt man gets on the horse, and with the camera turning, the horse's feet are pulled together off scene, and he falls on his side—an easy fall for both horse and rider. When it is filmed, it looks exactly as if the animal has been hit in the heart or brain.

After finishing *Virginia City* I went back to work for Republic Pictures on Roy Rogers's film, *Idaho*, directed by Joe

Kane. I had already worked with Joe on many pictures. He loved action and usually let me handle the stunts in my own way. Of course, I always added some and kept trying to invent new gags.

During the preparation for the shooting, Joe heard me say that the *Stagecoach* gag I did in the John Wayne picture was one of my best stunt creations but it had never been done in its entirety. He said that he would like me to take the script and write in the sequence, using a six-horse team hooked to a covered wagon that is being pursued by a group of outlaws. I routined this gag in full, pleased that at last I would get a chance to do the complete stunt.

On location near Kernville, we worked a couple of days filming bits of action, then began shooting the wagon chase. At the start of the main stunt, one of the outlaws made a transfer onto the lead team and, standing on the lead tongue between the lead horses, tried to bring them to a stop. I started to fire at him, but my gun was empty, so I leaped from the wagon onto the wheel team. From there I leaped to the swing team, then stepped up on a bar that was fastened from hame to hame on the two swing horses. From there, I jumped on the outlaw. We went into a hand-to-hand struggle and, on a given cue, we dropped down onto the lead tongue.

Then Joe cut the scene and changed to a longer lens and I rigged the next part of the stunt. I took a good life-sized dummy and dressed it in the outlaw's clothes. With its hands tied to my ankle, I stood on the lead tongue and, when the camera car and the team got into a good run, I overlapped the drop we had made in the previous scene and ended up on the ground between the lead team, hanging onto the tongue. I dragged for a way with the dummy hanging onto my ankle, then turned loose and let the team and wagon pass over me. In a much closer shot, another stunt man got under the front part of the wagon with me. After getting everything into motion, we dropped to the ground and again I caught hold of a prepared bar which stopped us under the back end of the wagon. After a brief struggle, I kicked the outlaw away from me and made my way up the back of the wagon, across the top and onto the seat.

In doing this gag, I had made a complete circle over and under the wagon and the six-horse team, ending at my starting place in the wagon seat.

At this point a third stunt man took over the driving and I doubled one of the outlaws. I made a transfer from a running horse to the seat of the wagon and engaged the driver in a hand-to-hand struggle. This ended with the driver knocking me off the runaway wagon down an embankment. On the steep side of this spot, I had the effects men put in a net and then cover it in with green bushes so that when I was knocked from the wagon, I would land in the bushes and drop out of sight of the camera. The principal I was doubling was to be in the bushes beneath the net, and, of course, out of the camera view. When I hit the net in the fall, he was to dive out of the bushes and roll on down the embankment toward a camera at the bottom, then get up in the foreground, do a bit of acting, and exit. This would give the effect of the real character coming all the way from the wagon to a closeup in front of the cameras.

We were working fast, trying to clean up that location before lunch and I wanted to have a couple of obstacles placed on the upper side of the embankment to keep the team close enough for me to make the fall safely into the net. However, Kane was hurrying things to keep a tight schedule so I did not force the issue. With a blind driver (a driver hidden under the wagon seat out of view of the camera) handling the team, I figured we had a good chance to make it okay. We got all set to go and the cameras started rolling. On the call of "action" the other stunt man and I began the fight, and I worked myself into position for the fall.

Just as we arrived at the concealed net, the team swung away, and I had to make a desperate leap to get over the embankment. In using so much effort to get distance, I landed wrong. I hooked my boot heels as I turned over, and broke both my legs at the ankles. I actually heard the bones snap. I lay in the net gritting my teeth, while the actor rolled on down and did his two bits' worth of acting in front of the camera. When the director hollered "cut", cold sweat was running from my forehead. One of the special-effects men came to the net to ask if I was all right, and I told him I thought both my legs were broken.

The crew rushed to get into the net to help me, but it shook so much that they couldn't keep their feet. I asked them to get a two-by-twelve plank from the prop truck and shove the end of it down to me. This was quickly done, and I pulled myself onto it and they slid me out. It was around a hundred-and-thirty miles to Hollywood and a good hospital, so I was loaded in the back seat of a sedan with my legs propped up and given a quart of Old Crow to kill the pain.

My left leg had a bad break from about four or five inches above the ankle slantwise into the ankle joint proper, and the right leg was fractured in the same way, but the break was not separated. The doctor put a temporary cast on my left leg, but only taped up my right ankle.

My broken ankles healed rapidly, but I had to use a cane to help me get around. When I went back to work at Republic, they were getting ready to make the picture, *In Old Oklahoma*, starring John Wayne, now their hottest property. They made a deal with me to write in a lot of stunts, to supervise the construction of horse-drawn oil tanks and to ramrod the action during the shooting. I went to Kanab, Utah, with a crew of workmen two or three weeks ahead of the company. I bought wagons from the farmers and the crew built some twenty-five tanks that fit on the running gears. When finished, they looked real. I had quite a time hobbling around with that cast on my left leg and a good bit of tape yardage on the right ankle. However, I managed, with the cane, to get around in a sort of "hop and go fetch it" way.

When everything was ready, Joe Kane brought the company up from the studio and we began work on the picture. The shooting went smoothly but before we finished, I was having trouble with the cast on my left leg. I had gotten burrs and foxtail stickers inside it and when a bit of blood came out of the bottom near my toes, I couldn't take the pain any longer. I asked our first-aid man to take the cast off, but he refused. He said that the doctor had ordered him to leave it on until I got back to Hollywood. I couldn't talk him into changing his mind, so I got the special-effects man and a carpenter to cut the cast off.

The cast had been on six or seven weeks, and I am convinced that if I had not taken the action I did, I would have had a bad case of blood poisoning in that leg. When the cast came off, the odor from the wound was sickening. I had to use crutches for quite a while after we completed the picture.

Both ankles were soon completely mended, and in a short time I was back to stunting. But I did have to choose my jobs for a while since my left ankle would swell to twice its size whenever I made a hard jump on it. I knew my time was up on stunt work and I wasn't about to stay in a field where I would soon be a second-rater. I had quit rodeos when I was at the top and decided to quit this end of the business while I was still in the high brackets.

EIGHT

Animal Adventures

In the next decade, a good deal of work came my way, a lot of it because the producers and directors knew that I could handle animal sequences. It was really gratifying to be hired for my accumulated know-how, rather than for my body's stunting ability.

As far back as 1936 I'd had the privilege of working with the world famous animal trainer, Clyde Beatty. It was on a Republic serial, *Darkest Africa*, directed by Joe Kane. Breezy Eason handled the second unit, and I was the number one stunt man.

A huge African jungle set had been built on the back lot and was completely enclosed by a network of heavy wire fencing twenty-five feet high. It was a big cage and within it, camouflaged by trees and bushes, were two smaller animal cages, set about fifty feet apart. Clyde Beatty had trained a beautifully maned lion to go from one cage to the other on cue for runthrough shots.

After we made a few run-bys back and forth, changing the background trees each time to make it look like different parts of the jungle, the cameras were placed to cover the entire space between the cages and Clyde Beatty was to rope the lion. The director filmed a close shot of Beatty throwing a loop out of the scene, then I got on top of one cage with my lariat to make the actual catch.

"What will happen when I rope him and turn him around?" I asked the trainer who was handling the lion. "What will he do?"

"That lion weighs better than four hundred pounds," he replied with a laugh. "When you try to stop him, he may pull you right off the cage."

"But, just in case I do turn him around, what will he do?"

"He'll probably run back into the cage."

"Let's shoot it," I said.

When Joe Kane called "action," I whirled my loop and the trainer pulled the rope that raised the door and prodded the lion. He came charging out and headed for the other cage, while the trainer made an exit through a barred door. I threw the loop and made a perfect catch around his neck, then set myself, and when the lion hit the end of the rope, it popped him completely around to face me. He stood motionless for a moment, then moved slowly toward me, his teeth bared menacingly. Instead of going into the cage, he halted at the side of it and looked up at me. No question about it. I was in danger. I watched him without moving. The set became ominously quiet, then the trainer called warningly to me.

"Don't make a sudden move, and watch his eyes. I'll ease around and get him away from you."

The trainer moved around the big cage toward a side entrance, while I stared unblinkingly at the lion who stood motionless for what seemed like a couple of minutes. It was actually only thirty seconds or so. I held my breath and zeroed in, eyeball to eyeball. If he got ready to spring before the trainer got to him, I knew one of the other trainers would have to shoot him. He was a valuable animal and I didn't want this to happen. I continued to stare, and finally he turned and went into the cage. I tripped the door shut with a sigh of relief and watched, as the trainer came in and took the lion out to calm him down.

A few days later, we were shooting some scenes with a large Himalayan bear whose name I remember was Himmie. John Haliat, owner and trainer of the bear, was an elderly man who had been with Beatty in circuses for a number of years. On this particular day, the bear had been working before the camera for some time and was beginning to get a bit cranky.

I was sitting outside the arena talking with one of the

animal trainers when all of a sudden we heard Haliat hollering, "Himmie! Himmie!"

I turned to look in the direction of the voice and saw Himmie throw Haliat to the ground and begin mauling the struggling man and chewing on his leg. The trainer and I grabbed a couple of two-by-fours and rushed into the arena. I hit the bear over the head but it didn't faze him. The trainer knew more about animals than I did, so he stepped in front of Himmie and kept him chewing on his two-by-four. All this time, the bear was holding Haliat down and clawing at him.

I yelled for a rope and when it was thrown in to me, I moved in closer and straddled Himmie. I then tied the rope around his neck and yanked him off Haliat. The bear turned toward me and the rope slipped off over his head. He whirled back to Haliat who was struggling to get up and again the bear threw the man down and mauled him some more. The trainer called for someone to get a gun, and hearing this Haliat managed to gasp out, "Don't kill Himmie—don't kill my bear!"

I stepped in, straddled the bear, and again tied the rope around his neck. This time we managed to pull him off Haliat who was able to get up and stumble out of the arena through the gate. The bear stood looking at the trainer and me for a moment, his eyes a fiery red, then all of a sudden he let out a fierce growl and started for us. We ran a dead heat to the narrow gate and both of us went through it together. The trainer knocked his shoulder out when he hit the gate post but I slammed the gate shut just as the bear hit it.

It took some ninety stitches to sew up Haliat. Within a week he was back on the job. I didn't eat lunch that day, and I wrestled Himmie the bear in my sleep for a night or two.

One of the funniest bear sequences that I was ever involved in was during the filming of a Republic picture at Idyllwild in the mountains south of Palm Springs, California. The picture was one of the *Three Mesquiteers* action movies and I was head stunt man and ramrod on the show. We had one scene where the villain got tangled up with a bear. The company hired a man who had a big bear that was trained to wrestle. I had read the script and added a few stunts to the story, but I told the producer that I wanted no part of the wrestling bear as I had seen two or three people chewed up by so-called trained bears. When we got to the location I informed the trainer, who owned the bear, that I was doing the stunt work, but I would not wrestle the bear. He said the bear wouldn't hurt a fly. He had performed all over the states and Europe and had even wrestled with some of the crowned heads.

I said, "That's great, so you won't mind wrestling him yourself."

"Oh no," he replied hastily, "I have to talk to him and cue him."

"If you want him to be in the picture," I said, "you'd better find someone to work with him. We have a bearskin costume we'll use if we have to."

Pappy Kirk, a heavy-set cowboy, was on the picture doubling the man whom the bear was supposed to chew up. Shortly after lunch the director was doing some closeups of the actors. The bear, who was chained to a tree nearby, seemed to be in a bad mood and kept moaning and growling. Right in the middle of one scene he gave out with a loud growl.

The director hollered, "Shut that bear up!"

The trainer went over, stroked the animal's head, then leaned close to his face and said, "Give papa a kiss."

The bear's "kiss" took off the end of his nose. It took several stitches to sew it back in place but it healed perfectly after a few weeks.

That evening I went into the dining room with a couple of the stunt men and, across from us by the wall, the bear trainer was having dinner with Pappy Kirk and was trying to talk him into wrestling the bear. But Pappy wasn't saying a word. He just looked at the bandage and tape on the trainer's nose, and it was easy to see that the injured nose wasn't helping the sales talk. We finally decided to use the bear costume, so Pappy didn't have to make a decision.

I had two or three stunt men on the job. One, by the name of Ken Cooper, was always pulling a gag on someone, so I had one of the other stunt men take the bear costume and open the zipper, which ran the full length of the body, and put it on an ant hill. Believe me, a few red ant stings will really set you on fire. While the director set up for the wrestling scene, Ken rehearsed without the costume. When the routine was right, the director told Ken to get the bear suit on. We put it on him fast and, when the scene began, the ants had started stinging him. He carried on for a moment and then let out with a yell and started rolling on the ground and hollering for help. We unzipped the bear suit and he came out of it in nothing flat.

The director was quite concerned. "What's the trouble?" he asked Ken.

Ken scratched his head sheepishly. "It took me a week to learn those lines," he said. There's nothing like a true prankster who can take a joke in style.

In 1948 I received a call from Aubrey Schenck, a producer who was preparing a picture for Eagle Lion Productions called *Red Stallion of the Rockies*. Aside from considerable straight action involving the rounding up of wild horses, the script had one sequence that particularly intrigued me. A beautiful six-point elk, which had been raised by a woman and her daughter on their ranch, turns one day and attacks the mother and a big red stallion, also on the ranch. A terrific fight ensues between the elk and the horse. This is something that, of course, could never really happen, but if it can be made to look convincing on the screen, the audience will accept it.

I knew that staging a spectacular fight between these two animals would pose some problems, but given time and money, I thought it could be done. Before discussing the script with Schenck I called Lionel Comport, a friend of mine who furnished animals for motion pictures and who, I knew, owned a nice big elk. He gave me the rundown on what the elk could and would do. His animal was tame and well-trained, and he didn't think it would fight a horse.

"I know that," I said. "I also know a horse won't fight an elk, but I think I can work out something that will pull it off."

When I met with Schenck I learned that Breezy Eason had turned the job down, saying the fight could not be done. We discussed the stunt for a while, then Schenck put the question.

"Yak, can you do this horse and elk fight?"

I had to chuckle. "Well, that's an abrupt question, so I'll answer you the same way. Give me time, cooperation, and enough money, and I'll make a mouse fight your horse!"

He laughed. "The job is yours."

The company made a deal with Comport for his work and his elk. We also bought an English red deer that was just about as big as the elk.

We went to Aspen, Colorado, high in the Rocky Mountains. The ranch we used for the family home had corrals and a barn, and the house was surrounded with a parklike lawn. This was where the fight was to be staged. At one side, some fifty or seventy-five feet away, was a gully. We ran an eight-foot fence down this gully, on around the house to the barn and corrals. This gave us a complete enclosure which we figured would hold the animals.

First I put the red deer into the pen and then the horse. I wanted to study their reactions. We drove them together. They both turned to and ran. I tried to turn the red deer and he backed me to the fence and stood with his nose out toward me, chomping his lower jaw against the upper, a characteristic sign that a deer is ready to attack. I was in a spot and knew it.

Comport came in from the side and the red deer turned and charged him. Comport was fast on his feet. He had a very close call, but he took me out of a rough situation. These animals are beautiful creatures, but they can kill a man very quickly. The big deer stopped, looked over all the fencing and made a run for the lowest point, which was at least eight or nine feet high. He went over it with ease and headed across an open field and into the timber of the Rocky Mountains. That was the last we saw of him.

We went to work then with the six-point elk. He had broken off one of his antlers seven inches or so above its base, so each time we worked with him we would have to put him in a portable chute and tape his horn on. We got all of his run-throughs and close shots right up to the fight. This would assure us of enough footage to save the sequence, if by chance something went wrong in the fight scene and he got hurt.

I had worked out a plan that I thought would get the results we wanted. I had the workmen dig a ditch a bit longer than a wooden railroad tie, a foot wide and four or five feet deep. In the center of the ditch were two chains a few inches apart, and to the end of each chain we attached a cable pulley. Then we filled in the ditch with rocks and dirt, just allowing the pulleys to be tight on the surface. This was camouflaged with grass and small green plants. Then we used small flexible cables and two-toned them with dashes of green and brown paint, so they would blend in with the background and also make them invisible to the camera.

We placed the elk chute about one hundred feet to the right of these pulleys. With the elk in the chute, we put a strong band around the base of his antlers. This band was made of doubled leather, with a cable in between the folded leather, and a covering made of tanned fur-covered skin that matched the natural fur on the animal's head and neck. We then attached the small cable to the band, running the other end through the deadman pulley at the point where the two animals would meet. This cable was arranged with what we term a double-speed pull. With a crew of men on this, each with good handholds attached, they could pull the elk at twice the speed they traveled. We then placed a second cable through the other pulley at the meeting point and fastened it to the horse, so he could be led right to the meeting point with the elk. The men were instructed to bring them in as fast as possible.

I had two men standing by ready to cut the cables if it became necessary. When all was ready, we rolled the cameras and the action began. The men at the chute opened the gate, and the crews on both horse and elk started them moving. The elk was bouncing along stiff-legged and swinging his head right and left, fighting the invisible cable. It really looked terrific and very natural. The horse was brought from the opposite direction to the meeting spot. He was frightened and tried to get away. The horse then reared and pawed out with his front legs as the two animals met. The elk tried to go around him, swinging and bouncing. From the camera angle it looked like a real fight. I let them go until I got enough footage, then hollered for the men to cut the cables. When this was done, the two animals separated and took off in opposite directions. We had two cameras on the scene and got some excellent shots. I repeated the action once more using different setups and lenses, which assured us of a good master scene.

I knew that with some good closeup shots cut in the sequence would be successful. At this point in the picture business there were a few trick cameramen who were doing marvelous split screen and traveling matte shots. I had the company contact one of these men and send him out to the set. I explained what I wanted and he then told me what was necessary to effect these shots. We set in a heavy post with a pulley on top of it and had a couple of bales of hay placed on end on either side of the pulley.

We again put the small cable on the elk, and when the matte man rolled his camera, the crew pulled the elk right up to the bales of hay. It reminded me of a prize fighter shadowboxing. He swung his head right and left, tossing it up every once in a while, trying to break the cable. He also kept his body and feet working back and forth.

After we got a lot of footage, we took the elk out and put the horse on the opposite side of the bales. He was well trained and the trainer brought him in and stopped him at the bales and had him rearing and pawing out with his front feet. After some good footage, we put a cue wire on him, the trainer's helper got back out of the scene, and after the horse made a few good rears, the helper pulled his wire, which cued the horse for a fall. He went right over backwards.

The matte man said that he had everything he needed for two or three matte shots, so when he left I had the special-effects man take a mounted elk head and build a set of horns with tubing running through them. He also rigged an air pressure tank, so he could blow artifical blood out of the horns. The neck on the elk's head extended to the shoulders and we mounted this on a bicycle wheel with handles attached so it could be wheeled, turned, and worked up and down. I handled this myself.

We got the horse used to this gimmick and he would rear and strike at it. We used three- or four-inch lenses, shooting nothing but big close-ups of the head and horns raking the underbelly and sides of the horse. These shots were gory, but spectacular. When one of the antlers would rake the horse's side, the blood effect made it look realistic. When the matte shots were finished and cut into the master scenes, the horse and elk were in the same shot and, at one point, the elk flipped the horse over backwards. Over all, the sequence was a great success and the producer was well pleased with it.

I thought I was off M.G.M.'s list after the bad accident I had there in 1940 when I was doubling Clark Gable in *Boom Town*. So I was agreeably surprised when, after finishing *Red Stallion of the Rockies*, I got a call from Nicholas Mayfack, the producer of a film entitled *The Devil's Doorway* for that studio. With Robert Taylor starring and Anthony Mann directing, this was to be an important film, with a twist on the typical Hollywood handling of the Indians. Taylor plays an Indian who fought in the Civil War and returns to his people only to find that he must fight to right the injustices they have endured.

Mann was already shooting with the main cast in Grand Junction, Colorado, and Mayfack assigned me to shoot the second unit. He alerted me that there was one animal sequence he was worried about. At one point in the movie Taylor is raising cattle and the villain runs sheep on his land, ruining the grass. The Indians retaliate by stampeding a huge flock of sheep over a high bluff. The scene was very important to the story and Mayfack was afraid the Hays office, the Motion Picture Association's "policing" agency, would cut it out of the picture if it was handled wrong. I studied the sequence and told him that I could understand his concern, but there was a way to get the gruesome effect desired . . . and do it safely.

I then suggested that I rewrite the sequence, replacing the slaughter of the sheep with a more spectacular scene, which would give the effect of completely destroying the flock. It would also pass the Hays office. Mayfack asked me to put the sequence in shooting form and they would consider it.

I outlined my idea, which was that instead of running the sheep off a bluff, they would be driven into a ravine with a cliff on the far side and a steep low ridge on the near side at the bottom. We could set in high mortars, camouflaged with sagebrush, every twenty-five or thirty feet, completely covering the floor of the ravine. These could be loaded with our regular harmless explosives and covered with plenty of lamp black and Fuller's earth. When the sheep are stampeded into this trap, the horsemen could then ride in on the rim of the low ridge and start heaving dummy sticks of dynamite down among the sheep. Then the explosions would be set off in fast rotation, completely blotting out the ravine, but still showing flames bursting up through the smoke and dust.

Nicky Mayfack okayed my outline and sent me to Grand Junction to work with Tony Mann and find locations for the action. He was to come over later. When I arrived on location, Tony was right on schedule with his work. I did quite a number of action pick-up shots while he was working with his principals, and blocked out some scenes I was to film with a group of Sioux Indians who were coming in from Pine Ridge, South Dakota, to work in the picture.

During the break one day, I was kidding Bob Taylor about playing an Indian with his blue eyes.

"You will be the only blue-eyed Indian in the picture," I told him.

A day or two later the Indians came in and when they arrived at the location, one of them, an old fellow, looked over and saw me.

"Yakima," he exclaimed, "no see for a long time."

I hadn't seen this particular Indian since my early rodeo days and had completely forgotten about him—he really did have blue eyes. Bob Taylor came over to talk with the group and when he saw those blue eyes, he laughed loudly.

"No blue-eyed Indians, eh?" he jeered. "Wait until I tell the producer how much you know about redskins!"

Well, that was the only blue-eyed Indian that I ever saw.

A couple of days before Tony finished his part of the show, Mr. Mayfack arrived on location. He seemed very happy with all the film he had seen so far. When the first unit was getting ready to leave for home, he asked if I had found all my locations and how long I thought it would take to finish my second unit work.

"Seven days of sunshine," I said, "and we'll be on our way home."

"Wait a minute, Yak," he said dubiously. "We're not making a quickie."

"Nicky," I answered, "if the light stays good and the crew works like I'm sure they will, I wouldn't know what to do with more than seven days. However, I won't print anything I don't think is right."

Mayfack shook his head, still doubtful. "This is your first directorial job at M.G.M.," he warned. "Don't muff it."

When he left, the unit man who had heard the conversation turned to me very much annoyed.

"Yak," he said, "you're crazy! You've got three weeks' work here."

"If it takes that long," I replied, "M.G.M. better get a new crew."

I had a good assistant and a fine special-effects man named Bob McDonald. His wife was going to have a baby soon, so I knew that he wanted to get home as quickly as possible, which assured me there would be no holdups in that department. I had everything cleaned up by the sixth day but the pseudo-destruction of the herd of sheep. This was filmed as I had outlined. I've never seen a special-effects job handled any faster. We were all ready to stampede them into our trap when the unit man came out to the location. He was all smiles and handed me a telegram from the producer, which read: "Have seen the biggest part of your action film. Don't know how you're doing it, but it looks great. Good luck, Nicky."

I had three cameras on the big stampede: a full comprehensive shot over the horsemen throwing dynamite as the sheep were driven into the trap, a second camera covering the sheep, and the third getting close shots of the explosions among the panicked animals. It was a beautiful scene and not one sheep was hurt.

Everyone was happy and eager to get home. On these jobs, when you have a crew like I had, you can get it done first class and on schedule. The studio carried me an extra three weeks, which I thought was not only more than fair, but a token of their appreciation for my work.

The year 1950 was my year for Indians. I no sooner finished *The Devil's Doorway* than I went to work for Warner Brothers on *Only the Valiant*, which starred Gregory Peck. Mr. William Cagney, James Cagney's brother, was the producer and Gordon Douglas was the director. The supporting cast included Barbara Payton, Ward Bond, Gig Young, Lon Chaney, Warner Anderson, Jeff Corey and Steve Brodie.

The story had an early Indian background and was to be filmed in and around Gallup, New Mexico. School was out for the summer, so I took my oldest son, Edward Clay, or "Tap" as we have always called him, along for what was supposed to be his vacation. He wasn't quite eighteen, but had been riding horses all of his life and was an excellent horseman. When we were ready to start shooting, he wanted to work in the picture, so I put him in the cavalry and paid him the same money that the local cowboys and Indians received.

The first two or three days, we did straight runthroughs of the cavalry. Then we started setting up a big action scene at an old Spanish mission for the final battle of the picture. This battle would climax with many overwhelming charges in which, although the Indians were stopped with heavy losses, the cavalrymen were to be cut down one by one. The commander had sent out a couple of men to try and get through to the fort for help and had seen one of these men shot from his horse. The success or failure of the other is unknown. The Indians in great numbers make their final attack for the kill. The few cavalrymen try to make a heroic stand, but the odds were so overwhelming that it looked as though all was lost.

But as in all of these cowboy and Indian pictures, the cavalry arrived just in time to save the day. As the fresh reinforcements swung into the flat in front of the mission, they dismounted and lined up their rifles on either side of an equipment-covered wagon. They then took out a Gatling gun and victory seemed assured.

In setting up this scene, I planned for a great number of falls—both horses and men. While I was picking men for the stunts, Tap came up to me.

"Dad," he said, "let me do some of those falls. Your stunt guys are making a hundred bucks a fall."

"You've never made any falls from a horse," I said. "You might break a leg or an arm. Forget it."

"I know how to fall," Tap pleaded, "and the ground is sandy and soft."

I hesitated for a moment, then got what I thought was a bright idea. If I let Tap get a good bump, maybe he would forget the stunt man idea and think a bit more about school. So I had him go to the wardrobe truck and get into an Indian outfit. When we got the scene all set up and ready, I explained to him how and when to start his fall. We had three cameras on the scene: a front master shot over the cavalry, a side angle on Indians only and a three-quarter front angle that would hold many of the falls.

I had given Tap a spot near the side-angle camera. At that point, I could be close enough to see how he handled his fall. Naturally, I was worried. I knew that he was very athletic and the odds were that a good bump would be the worst that would happen to him. If he got hurt though, I would never forgive myself.

Finally all was set and the cameras started grinding. I gave them the go-ahead signal and the Indians came pouring out of the canyon and spread across the flat, charging straight at the cavalry. When they were in the right position, I gave the cavalry the cue to start firing and the Gatling gun joined in. This was the cue for the falls to start. Indians and horses were going down in all directions. My eyes focused on Tap, and when he hit his spot, off he came head first and tumbled end over end.

It was a good fall and looked professional. When the cameras stopped, Tap came over and asked me how he had done.

"I'm sorry to say so," I replied, "but it was very good."

"Boy, and you get paid for doing it," Tap grinned. "How long has this been going on?"

Well, I knew I had made a mistake. I remembered my first bucking horse and my success in riding him. Nothing in the world could have stopped me then from becoming a bronc rider.

Tap made several more falls and went home with a nice little roll of money, telling everybody what a ball he had making it.

After our return to Hollywood, I began to hear stories about all the wild things that he and his younger brother, Joe, had been doing in the way of stunts. I recalled the day a couple of years earlier when he came in with one of his pals, holding a bloody handkerchief over his mouth. He had a terrible cut under his chin and his tongue was cut almost in two. I drove him to our family doctor and it took quite a number of stitches to repair the damage. I never really found out how it happened until he was grown.

It seems he had been practicing stunts and was making a ramp jump with a jeep—and no safety belt on. When the jeep hit the ramp it went into the air, flipping him over backward. His chin hit the tailgate as he came down.

I soon learned that both Tap and Joe had their minds made up to be stunt men. You can only tell your children what to do up to a certain point and they take it from there.

Both my sons and daughter are now grown up, married and have families of their own. Tap and Joe *are* stunt men, well liked and respected, both professionally and personally. Of this I am very proud.

M.G.M. gave me my first shot at filming a picture abroad with *Ivanhoe* (more on that later). They thought enough of my work on that rousing adventure story to call me into the production office in 1952 to discuss what would prove to be an even greater challenge. They were getting ready to make the picture *Mogambo*, a remake of the 1932 Clark Gable film *Red Dust*, this time teaming Gable with Ava Gardner and Grace Kelly. Sam Zimbalist was producing and John Ford directing.

They wanted me to go on what can only be described as a special assignment—I wouldn't be working with the principals or the director. In fact, I wouldn't be within thousands of miles of them. They wanted me to shoot a family of gorillas in their natural habitat. I was to shoot process plates (background shots that would be processed in with shots of the principals) and get all the excitement and pictorial value possible. The key shot, which was a "must", was to be footage of a charging, big, male gorilla. The M.G.M. location manager had made an exploratory trip into French Equatorial Africa, or better known today as the countries of Gabon, Cameroon, and the Republic of the Congo. There he found the gorilla population to be plentiful. We were supposed to go to the district headquarters in Makambo.

There was another meeting the following day to work out plans. I listened to some of the ideas that the studio heads had to offer and could hardly believe my ears. Some of the ideas they proposed were laughable. I had never been on a gorilla hunt but I did know a lot about animals, both domestic and wild.

I said that I thought the best thing for me to do was to go to Africa, look over the situation, then work out a plan. I felt sure that the only way we would get any worthwhile scenes would be to find a way to herd the gorillas into a photographic compound where we would have them under control. Mr. Zimbalist said he had the utmost confidence in my judgment. It was decided that I would leave at once for Brazzaville, where Henry Geddes, a unit man from London, would meet me and help handle the business affairs. I was to use an English crew.

I spent a few days getting my passport in order and taking the necessary inoculations: small pox, yellow fever, tetanus and typhoid. When all was set I was called to Mr. Cohen's office.

"Sit down, Yak," he said as I came in. "I want to have what you might call a 'fatherly' talk with you. The region that you'll be working in, I understand, is one of the most disease-ridden areas in Africa, so be careful and don't take unnecessary chances."

"I've shot in a lot of strange places," I said, "and I'm pretty tough."

"That I can believe," he replied. "But I don't want another *Trader Horn*. If you remember, Edwina Booth contracted a mysterious disease making that movie that eventually killed her. No picture is worth a life and I want you to come back in good health."

"I appreciate your concern," I said, moved by his sincerity, "and I promise to follow your advice."

"Good. Now we'll get down to business. Any time you feel that the gorilla scenes can't be done, wrap it up and come home and we'll never hold it against you. On the other hand, if you think they *can* be done, go ahead and spend whatever money is needed. You'll be on your own and too far away to holler 'Help'."

He then handed me a letter giving me full power to represent the studio in any financial dealings. I was the boss.

After this talk, Joe Cohen went to the top of the list in my book. He is one man of whom I have never heard a bad word spoken. It would be nice if the world was full of people like him.

A few days later, I was flying across the Gulf of Guinea, striking the African Coast again near Libreville and on across to Leopoldville in the Belgian Congo (today known as Zaire). Looking down from the plane at that vast entanglement of vegetation they call a jungle, I began to imagine hunting and corraling a family of gorillas in that kind of terrain. If, by some stroke of magic, I did get them into a pen, the cost of bringing photographic equipment and lights in would be prohibitive. I had to find a spot on the edge of an open savannah where the jungle began to break up.

From the window of the plane, I could now see the beautiful Congo River with Leopoldville on the south side and Brazzaville on the north. We landed in Leopoldville and I stepped out of the air-cooled plane into a torrid atmosphere that transformed me into a very uncomfortable human being. Heat had never bothered me, but this was something else. I hoped that I could cope with it. I got a cab and went to a hotel where I was to stay for a few days and confer with certain people who were known to the studio through the earlier exploratory trip.

I went to the American Consul's office the next morning and was introduced to Mr. Arthur Alberts, the Vice Consul. He was pleasant and gave me quite a bit of time, introducing me to people who could answer many of my questions. He made an appointment for me to meet a Monsieur Blancou in Brazzaville, just across the Congo River. Blancou was the head of the game department in French Equatorial Africa and everything I did had to be cleared through him. Mr. Alberts went with me and before the day was over, I found out how important our consuls and their staffs are in foreign lands. Monsieur Blancou proved to be a very fine person but he spoke only French, so all my talks with him were through an interpreter.

While in Brazzaville, I registered at the Rellias De Maya Hotel for myself and the unit man from London whose arrival I was expecting in a day or two. Mr. Alberts, knowing that I was to use an English crew, introduced me to the British Consul and through that office we received a great deal of help.

A few days later, Henry Geddes arrived, followed soon after by the British crew that had been hired in London for the gorilla capture. The camera crew consisted of four men: Jack Whitehead, chief cameraman, Freddy Cooper, Doug Wolf, Jackson Drury, and Johnny Pallatt, a young Englishman who was to act as my assistant.

I had heard of a Frenchman by the name of Gilles Bonneau who, with Bill Said, an American, had made a business of capturing young gorillas and rare animals for zoos. Bill Said had been killed a year or so earlier in a jeep accident, but Bonneau was available to join our expedition. I had Geddes contact the London studio and they made a deal with him, and also sent us a French doctor experienced with tropical diseases.

After several weeks, we managed to get our outfit organized. I took part of the group on a trip into the gorilla country to find a likely spot to set up a camp for the job of capturing and fencing in the gorillas.

In one of my talks with Monsieur Blancou, I had learned that the heavy forest of the Gabon started breaking up a bit north of Ewo and that it had just been opened for gorilla captures after being closed for a number of years. I also learned that near the village of Opari, Teddy Roosevelt had made camp on his hunting trip into Africa, and it was there that he obtained the gorilla family specimens for the Smithsonian Institution in Washington. I figured if the Ewo section was good enough for Teddy, it was good enough for me.

After many ups and downs, we left for the bush and four days later arrived at Ewo, where the District Commissioner met us with welcoming handshakes. We spent two or three days looking things over and I decided to scout the Makambo district, the place originally picked by the studio on the first exploratory trip. So Henry Geddes and I drove on up to the area. I had never seen such heavy jungle, it was so dense that the light could hardly penetrate. I told Henry we'd go back to Ewo and establish our base camp near there.

We picked a clearing on high ground a few hundred yards from the village of Opari and left Johnny Pallatt with some natives to supervise the construction of the camp. Then we headed for Brazzaville, where I found that our American red tape was duplicated in other parts of the world. Getting guns and equipment into Brazzaville was like pulling teeth. I had brought along a couple of guns from home and these were held in customs. When I went to get them out, I was told that I would have to get a hunting license and gun permit. After a lot of trouble, I finally reached the Governor General, Paul Chavauvet. He was a big, fine-looking man who loved the outdoors and with his help, we had no more trouble.

Our mission of rounding up a family of gorillas and driving them into a photographic compound became a big joke to the citizens of Brazzaville, even though we had the full cooperation of the Game Department. I became known as the American cowboy who was going to rope gorillas. When all was set for the move to our camp, I went to the Game Department in Brazzaville to thank Monsieur Blancou for his help. I told the interpreter to ask him if we should hold any small gorillas for him if we happened to catch any. Blancou smiled and patting me on the shoulder, replied, "If you capture any small ones, I will come in person with a crate to get them."

We left Brazzaville the following morning and arrived at camp on the fourth day. Johnny Pallatt and his native crew had done a great construction job. A long, barrackslike building with sleeping quarters in either end and a mess hall in the center was our headquarters. Another building contained a kitchen and space for storage, and a third long building was for housing our native help.

I felt my chances of success were good, as there were many sightings of gorillas. I had read everything that I could get hold of concerning these animals. I found many conflicting statements. It seems that no two hunters agreed on the animals' habits and what they would do under certain circumstances. All my native help agreed that gorillas could not be driven into a fenced enclosure. They were sure that once men surrounded the gorillas and tried to move them, the big male would charge and either some of the hunters would be killed or we would have to shoot the animals.

I had met and talked, through my interpreter, to several natives who had been mauled and badly scarred by gorillas. Some of the stories told by these natives were quite humorous, but they were so sincere that I had no doubt that they believed what they were saying. One of the stories by a native who had part of his hand chewed off went like this: A gorilla had come into his banana plantation and started tearing up a young tree (any native who owned a plot with one or two of these trees considers it a plantation). This gorilla then ate out the center, or pith, of the tree, which ruins it. The native, armed only with a spear, told the gorilla to get out of his plantation, whereupon the gorilla replied that it was not the native's land, but his, and the native should get out. The native said if the gorilla didn't leave, he would spear him. The gorilla still refused and the native threw the spear and missed. The gorilla caught the native and bit part of his hand off, told him that he was a bad man, and that he was going to leave and wouldn't come back to see him anymore.

Other natives had similar stories, and after listening to them, I made up my mind that there was probably a certain amount of bluff to a gorilla. I decided that if you stood your ground and made plenty of noise, such as firing blanks and hollering, you had a chance to stop and turn him back without killing him. I still knew that the only way I could succeed in photographing a gorilla family was to get them in a controlled area. If I couldn't do this, the trip would be a flop. After a lot of talks and explanations on my part, I finally got my crew and hunters to promise full cooperation on the gorilla drive. However, I was convinced that only a few of them believed it could be successful.

I had worked out my plans on paper, starting with the usual native way of hunting. When they found a family of gorillas, they formed a circle around it about a mile to a mile and a half in circumference. The natives used nets which were about five feet in height and twenty to fifty feet long. These were put up on poles that were sharpened and driven into the ground. The big circle is gradually drawn in and the nets are moved closer and closer.

While this operation was under way, we would build our photographic enclosure, leaving the arena a natural part of the jungle where the foliage was broken up, allowing good sunlight for filming. The arena would be two hundred feet long and a hundred and fifty feet wide. We would complete the arena, leaving one end open for the drive. As we moved the gorillas to the enclosure the nets would be connected to either side of the open end.

Three other hunters and I were to go inside the nets with forty or fifty natives; thirty of them with machetes would cut away all the undergrowth inside the nets, starting at the opposite side of the enclosure area from our arena. Backing them up would be another twenty natives with muzzle-loading guns, loaded with blanks, to try to bluff the male gorilla if he charged. If this failed, he would have to be killed.

The next move was to hire four or five hundred native

hunters. Before hiring them we would have to sell them this new method of hunting. So, with our camp in order and my crew well briefed and ready to carry through once we had the hunters, we—the District Commissioner, myself, and two of my native leaders—started calling on the villages. Paul Nanchen, who spoke both French and the native dialect, but very little English, was our interpreter.

Our first stop was the village of Okalataka. It was the biggest settlement in the district, with a second village nearby. These two villages were very important to us, as they would have to furnish at least half our hunters. We met with the chiefs of these places, and they in turn called in their hunters. Then the powwow began.

I could tell that as Nanchen explained our hunt and drew it on the ground before them, we weren't selling them on the idea. As Nanchen went on to say that we would use blanks instead of bullets, and that we were to drive the gorillas into a pen made of wire netting, they not only gave dirty looks, but they began asking a lot of questions about me. It looked like I was on trial with a pretty hostile jury. Finally, the chiefs said that they wanted no part of the hunt. Anyone who wanted to capture gorillas just to take their pictures and then turn them loose was certainly crazy. The villagers seemed impossible to convince, so we shook hands with the two chiefs and went back to our base camp.

After a couple of gins with grapefruit juice, dinner, a vitamin pill and a quinine tablet, I hit on the only way that I thought these villagers could be brought into the hunt.

The next day Nanchen and I, with a couple of native helpers, loaded our beds and groceries into the power wagon and headed for Okalataka. I took along five five-gallon demijohns of cheap French wine.

We arrived in the village that afternoon, and after dinner, the natives of the two villages gathered and put on a dance. I established a kitty in the center of the dance ring and threw in a handful of franc notes. I also had the interpreter let them know that this was a friendly call before we left for some other part of the country on our gorilla hunt. I thought this tack might help bring them over to our side, since I knew these natives weren't too friendly with the pygmies in another district whom we might hire to help us.

Finally I took one of the five jugs of wine and put it into the circle along with the kitty. An intermission was called immediately and they drank for awhile, then resumed their dance. I could notice a big difference in the tempo—it really picked up. The natives were also a little more friendly and some of them actually smiled at me. I had Nanchen talk to the two chiefs again and arrange for them, with eight porters, to go with us the next day on a buffalo hunt. They agreed and went back to the dance and the wine.

Early the next morning, accompanied by the two chiefs and porters, we headed for buffalo country, which was about fifteen miles through swamp, jungle and some open plains. The younger chief carried a single–barrel, French-made shotgun that was the only one I had ever seen of its kind. On this trip I took my heavy rifle. During the afternoon we saw a guinea hen running through the grass in front of us. The young chief handed me his shotgun and pointed to the hen which was about fifty yards away. I took the gun and walked toward the bird and the chief started making quite a fuss, trying to tell me to shoot it. But I flushed the bird into the air and shot it on the wing. This made quite a hit with the natives as they were not used to seeing things shot out of the air.

Later on in the day, the older chief, who was walking in the lead, stopped and motioned everybody down. There were two bull buffaloes visible in the bush about two hundred yards ahead of us.

Nanchen and I took our heavy rifles and started to move downwind from the animals. As we sneaked toward the animals, I noticed that the natives' eyes were all on me. They seemed to watch every move I made. We got around to a good vantage point and I shot the biggest bull. The other immediately headed back toward some scrub. For some unknown reason he didn't charge. I walked closer to him while the chiefs chattered in their dialect, trying to tell me that I was getting into a bad spot. I motioned to them to be quiet and fired another shot, which killed the bull. He proved to be of record size for that part of the country.

After the natives finished dressing the bulls, we went on for a mile or so to a spot where we were to camp for the night. On the way, I killed a running waterbuck at a distance of about a hundred and fifty yards. This thrilled the natives, who judged a man by his hunting ability. By this time they were thoroughly convinced that I was a good shot and knew how to hunt. We made camp and during the night these natives cut up the meat of the waterbuck and seared it over a campfire, the way they cured all their meat.

All of us were up before daybreak the next morning and the chiefs started one bearer back to the village to tell of the buffalo kill. The native men can run all day or night, so before we got back to the village, we passed a crew of women coming out to get the buffalo meat.

On our arrival the two chiefs gathered the hunters of the two villages together and they went into a powwow. This time the attitude was markedly different and when they finished, they came over to Nanchen and one chief explained that they had decided I was a great hunter and they wanted to hunt gorillas with me, even if I was doing it in a crazy way.

My problem of getting hunters was now solved. The only thing left to do was to start our trackers out to locate a gorilla family.

Before the hunt was to begin, the natives insisted on a hunt ceremony. The ceremony took place at night in the jungle away from the village. All the chiefs, the witch doctors, and the choice hunters formed a circle around a fire and all the weapons to be used in the hunt were brought in and stacked in this circle. Chickens and a goat were killed as sacrifices to make sure that the hunt was a success. I had to pay them four or five dollars for the animals. After the ceremony, I discovered that they were taken home and eaten. The natives weren't so dumb.

At daylight we started trackers out in three different points with instructions not to go farther than a kilometer and a half off the road the first day. I was trying to locate a gorilla family, if possible, at a spot where we could get our heavy equipment in without too long a safari. If any of the trackers located the gorillas, they were to return to camp at once. One of the men reported that he found a family bedded down about five miles or so from our camp. He was brought in and through an interpreter, I questioned him.

Gorillas build their beds with branches, ferns, leaves and grass. Once they bed down they stay there until sunup the next day. The native said that there were thirteen gorillas in this family, one big male, a small male, three or four big females, and then, of course, the others ranging in size. I had the interpreter ask him if he had seen them. He said he hadn't, so I asked how he knew that there were thirteen gorillas with a big

156

Yakima Canutt "doubles" a gorilla in
Circle of Death in 1932.

Here special-effects man Bert Monk is the gorilla, clowning with Yak on location in Africa for *Mogambo*. (Photo courtesy of MGM)

The real thing: gorillas photographed for *Mogambo* in French Equatorial Africa. (Photo courtesy of MGM)

Yak and a native hunter with the slain "Big Garcon."
Native superstitions made the killing of
the big gorilla obligatory.
(Photo courtesy of MGM)

Westward Ho, the Wagons. The wagon train heads into
the pass and a surprise attack by Indians.
(By courtesy of Disney Studios)

Yakima Canutt (in upper right corner) directing the scene in *The Swiss
Family Robinson* where James MacArthur as Fritz fights a huge snake.
The man with the pole is the snake handler; the cameraman is
seated below Yak. (By courtesy of Disney Studios)

one in the family. A big male, or Garcon, was very necessary for the picture.

The interpreter answered that it did not matter whether the native had seen them or not. If he said there were thirteen gorillas, I would find that there were thirteen gorillas. And if he said a big one was in the family, I could bet there was a big one.

I decided to take the native's word about where this family was located. I started out our trucks that night for the different villages to gather the hunters. By midnight, we had five hundred native hunters and their nets at a point in the jungle near where the native said the gorilla family was bedded.

Shortly before daylight the natives split into two groups and began cutting paths into the jungle in different directions. This was one of the slickest operations that I had ever seen. Twenty or thirty machete men lined up in the lead of each group, followed by other men with poles which they had cut to hang the nets on. The men with the nets trailed behind tying them on the poles. Other men carrying shotguns loaded with blanks were stationed in the more open places. By midmorning the circle that we had laid out was complete to the point where the nets came together. I went around the entire area, which was about a mile in circumference, looking for a spot for the photographic arena. As I was doing this, I passed a witch doctor who was carrying a big basket with the lid closed under his arm.

After he had motioned for my attention a few times, I finally asked the interpreter what the man wanted. He talked to him, then came back to me.

"Witch doctor has gorillas in the basket," he reported.

"Tell him to put them in the pen," I said, going along with the gag. "That's where we want them."

The interpreter laughed loudly. "Is not that easy, Mister Yak. If witch doctor opens the basket and the gorillas get away, the hunters will all quit and go home."

I realized that I was being conned by the interpreter and the witch doctor, who were in cahoots, so I took the hint.

"How much does he want to keep the lid closed?" I asked.

Again the witch doctor and interpreter jabbered.

"Two hundred francs," he said, trying to conceal his satisfaction.

I gave the witch doctor the two hundred francs, which was then equal to one U.S. dollar. This kept the gorillas in the basket that day. Of course, he was back the next morning for another couple hundred francs. I don't know what he did with the gorillas during the night, but I learned that I had to at least pretend to take these funny whims seriously or I might end up by myself on a gorilla hunt.

By noon our trucks moved in with the fencing equipment, tents, and supplies. We kept cutting through the jungles —moving the nets amd making our circle smaller. By sundown I had the nets secured for the night. This was as far as we would carry the hunt until I got the photographic arena finished.

By nightfall, we had our gorillas, still unseen, within the net circle, so I hoped, and guarded by something like twelve hundred natives, women and children included. Fires were built every fifty or sixty feet outside the circle of nets and hurricane lanterns hung between the fires on the net poles. The natives were given plenty of black gunpowder for shooting and making noise, the women sang and danced, and my assistant passed out Brazza cigarettes and wine. This was one of the most colorful operations that I had ever seen.

By morning our photographic arena was completed. The gorillas now could be driven into the enclosure. Fifty men were to go in to cut the underbrush and vines, twenty with blanks in their guns. Three other men and I stood by with loaded guns in case of trouble.

Before the natives would enter the arena they wanted to know what we would do if a gorilla charged out of the bush at one of them. I said that if the animal got close enough to become a danger, we would kill it. All that we asked the men to do if a gorilla charged was to fire their blanks and then get back out of the way. This satisfied them and we all went into the circle.

Within the first half hour of cutting vines and brush, I was convinced for the first time that we had plenty of gorillas. They had been two nights and one day without water, and the circle was getting small enough for them to realize they were surrounded. Abruptly, the cutters all stopped work, looked and listened for a moment, then the leader pointed into the bush and motioned for me to join them. I moved warily over as they went ahead with their cutting.

In less than a minute, I heard a terrific gutteral sound and the vines in front of me started shaking. I could hear the animal and although I couldn't see him, I knew that he was charging straight toward us. Just as he came through the shaking vines, the natives fired blanks right at the spot where he emerged. The blue smoke from the black gunpowder concealed him for a moment. When the smoke cleared, the gorilla was eighteen or twenty feet in front of me. I raised my gun to shoot, but he came to a stop, snorting and whoofing menacingly. I held my ground and started to "whoof" back at him, but when I opened my mouth no sound came out. In a moment, he turned and went back into the bush.

The next few minutes were quiet, other than the native songs and the sound of the machetes. Then again we heard the loud "whoof" of the gorilla, the vines started shaking and I soon found myself the focal point of another charge. The same procedure was repeated and the gorilla retreated. I was confident now they could be stopped and driven into our trap.

This gorilla later proved to be about five feet seven, weighed over four hundred pounds, and had an arm spread of eight feet four inches. Since this was the first time that I ever had a gorilla charge me, he had looked a great deal bigger than he was. However, he had made his first charge and my notion that a gorilla had a certain amount of bluff in his make-up was proven.

As the day went on, the ring of nets got smaller and the natives worked faster. I was really amazed at the marvelous way they carried out the operation from the few briefings we had given them. At the point where the gorillas were to enter our trap, we had cleared a trail across the entrance between the posts, minus the wire, and I had put a man in a tree to signal when he saw the gorillas crossing into the arena.

The natives with the machetes continued working as fast as they could and the hunters kept firing blanks as fast as they could reload their guns. Soon gorillas were running every which way, but moving gradually toward our arena. I finally got a signal from the man in the tree that one gorilla had gone in, then another, until the thirteen gorillas that made up the family were all inside.

At this point, the natives went wild. As I gave orders for the crew to put up the wire across the entrance, they were joined by their wives and children. They swarmed across the trail so that we could hardly force them back to make room for the fence. Had the gorillas turned and charged, there would have been no way to keep some of them from being killed. However, the trained fence builders put up the wire and made it secure on sixty-five yards of post in ten minutes.

The second day after the capture, I got several glimpses of gorillas, including the big one, and I could see that they were suffering from lack of water. The hunters said that they would never eat or drink around humans, but I've always been convinced that if any living things get hungry and thirsty enough, they will eat and drink wherever they are. I had the natives bring over a couple of gunny sacks filled with pineapples and also put canvas troughs of water into the arena. I hoped it would rain—and it did.

The next morning, I was out early in the rain and found the gorillas yawning and getting up. They moved curiously around to peek out through the vines and bushes at us. I also discovered that the pineapples we had thrown into the compound were mostly gone. The gorillas that I could see seemed to be in good shape.

It continued raining for four days and nights and we were not able to do any photographing. On the fifth day the sun came out and we got our camera set up. The tough job was to get some charges out of the big Garcon. I had the crew fix up a dummy, using men's clothing, stuffing it with ferns and leaves. We attached this to a line on a long pole so it could be dropped into the arena alongside the camera and then raised up the same fashion which you would use to pull a fish out of water. We threw sticks, fired blanks, and herded the gorillas to one corner of the jungle arena. I then got everyone quiet and out of sight. The first time that we saw a big male peering out of the bush, I pulled the dummy up alongside the camouflaged camera outside the fence and hollered "boo" at him. To my great surprise, the gorilla charged clear across the arena to within a few feet of the camera, then stopped and made faces, trying to bluff the dummy. We yelled at him and he went back among the trees and vines, only to charge again when the dummy was let down. At one time, both he and the young Garcon charged to within a few feet of the camera and gave us some very fine shots. We got other excellent shots with as many as seven or eight of the gorillas in one scene.

We also needed scenes with gorillas in trees, so we built a second small arena around two beautiful trees. I had the trees trimmed so that once the gorillas climbed to the high limbs, we would be able to photograph them with no obstructions.

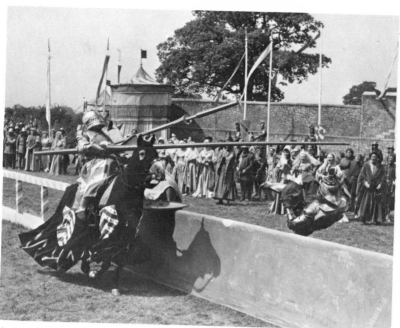

A joust by English stunt men recruited by Canutt
for *Knights of the Round Table*. (From the MGM release
Knights of the Round Table © 1953 Loew's Incorporated)

Kirk Douglas in one of the action shots staged by Yak for *Spartacus*.
(From the motion picture *Spartacus*, Courtesy of Universal Pictures)

The British stunter Paddy Ryan performing his breathtaking
sixty-foot fall into a shallow moat in *Ivanhoe*.
(From the M.G.M. release *Ivanhoe* © 1952)

In their father's footsteps: Yak's sons Tap (with spear) and
Joe collaborate in a horse fall in *Khartoum*. (Copyright © 1966,
United Artists Corporation.)

Joe Canutt in a spectacular saddle fall as a dervish in *Khartoum*.
(Copyright © 1966, United Artists Corporation.)

Lee Marvin as the tipsy Kid Shelleen in *Cat Ballou*.
(Copyright © 1963, Columbia
Pictures Corp., courtesy of Columbia Pictures Corporation)

This arena, of course, joined the main one. After it was completed, we cut a gate to join the two arenas and tried to drive the gorillas in. No matter how much noise we made, shooting, hollering, throwing sticks, they wouldn't budge.

The following morning, we cut a larger section out of the arena fence, took our Dodge power wagon and drove it into the arena. We ran it at the gorillas, honking the horn and keeping the engine in low gear. That, plus the noise from the natives, seemed to spook them and we were able to get eleven gorillas into the small arena; four of them climbed the trees. However, in the excitement of forcing them to move into the little arena, one of the small ones began squealing and making a big fuss, so I roped him and took him out of the arena and put him into a crate. He was later taken to the Brazzaville Zoo. I asked the Game Commissioner to name him "Cowboy." He said, "No, we will name him 'Yak'."

With the four gorillas in the trees, we secured some very fine scenes of them going from limb to limb, standing up, and beating their chests. It was after these scenes were shot that the natives, who were very superstitious and considered gorillas to be human beings, not animals, and that they were fighting a war, instead of carrying on a hunt, insisted that I kill the big Garcon. They said if I didn't, they would. This was confirmed by the District Commissioner, who also said that they might kill more once they started shooting. I decided to make a scene out of it. I turned the rest of the troop loose and they went back into the jungle.

The natives had started the hunt with a big ceremony, and so they ended it the same way. I supplied the wine and they supplied the song and dance. I had grown quite fond of them during my stay in Africa and felt a bit sad about leaving them when the time came to go home. *Mogambo* was a picture I will never forget.

NINE

Live Action for Mr. Disney

Until his death in December 1966, Walt Disney was literally a one-man institution. He parlayed the character of a mouse into a multi-million dollar film company—a mouse that most of the smart producers and distributers in Hollywood said would never make it as a leading cartoon character.

One producer, however, saw possibilities in the quaint little mouse that Disney called "Mickey," and worked out a deal for Columbia Pictures to distribute the cartoon series.

Mickey Mouse hit like gangbusters! He and Minnie soon became world famous and Walt Disney went on to bigger and even more creative animated pictures. He was without peer in the entertainment business. His *Sleeping Beauty* and *Fantasia* are still classics, and who doesn't remember his *Three Little Pigs* or *Ferdinand the Bull.*

He changed his distribution from Columbia to R.K.O. A few years later he formed his own distribution company, Buena Vista Film Distributing Co., and built a fine studio on the outskirts of Burbank, California.

Along with his love of fantasy, Disney had a great affection for the American past. He was a deep student of the Old West and when, in 1955, he finally decided to produce live action films, his first selection was a large-scale Western, *Westward Ho, the Wagons.*

It was to be in Cinemascope and Technicolor and the cast was headed by Fess Parker, Kathleen Crowley, Jeff York,

Davis Stollery, Sebastian Cabot and George Reeves. William Beaudine, a veteran of the silent era and the director of hundreds of fine features, was to direct the film which was written for the screen by Tom Blackburn, based on a novel by Mary Jane Carr.

I was very happy and proud when I was asked to shoot the second unit of Disney's first live-action feature. I had been directing for eleven years and, with my many years as a stunt man, I always felt at home doing action. The script was entertaining and well written, but there was one sequence that really bothered me. It involved a skirmish between a wagon train and a large band of Indians in a narrow pass. As the wagon get into the pass the men jump off, duck behind rocks and start firing, while the Indians ride in a big circle, firing arrows and throwing spears. A rip-roaring battle—but no one gets hurt! I didn't see how the audience would believe that.

I figured that the writer, Tom Blackburn, needed a little help on the action of the fight, so I went to his office and had a talk with him. He finally agreed that I could go ahead and rewrite the fight sequence and he would look it over. After reading my changes, he said it was fine and then sent it to Mr. Disney.

The next day I had a call to come to Mr. Disney's office and when I arrived, he greeted me with a friendly handshake and motioned me to a seat.

"Yak," he said, "this is your first work with us, isn't it?"

"Yes, it is," I said.

"We make pictures for families—no blood and thunder —so what do you say if we shoot it like the script describes it."

I shrugged and said, "O.K. I'll do the best I can with it."

After weeks of preparation with Bill Walsh producing under Disney's executive reins, filming got under way in January, 1956.

Our location was on the Conejo Ranch, a 26,000 acre spread of pasture land in Ventura County, an hour or so drive from the studio.

My first day's work was shooting long shots of the wagon train as it came across the valley and headed toward a rocky pass. Then I had the camera operator pan around to a ridge where a long line of Indians were sitting on their ponies, watching the wagon train.

I moved to the far side of the wagon train. Then, as an outrider pulled up to the foreground, he looked up and saw the Indians and shouted a warning for the wagons to make a run for the pass. After some close shots of different wagons on the run and the Indians coming to and by the camera, I did a full shot from the rocky pass, shooting the lead wagon careening through the entrance. Women take over the reins as the men leap out and take cover, keeping up a rapid fire with their rifles. Other men fire from wagons, and as the last wagon goes through into the pass, the Indians form a circle in front of the opening, firing arrows from their bows while some get closer and throw spears.

The scenes were well photographed and looked beautiful, but no one was being hit. To me it just wasn't right. The next evening we watched the rushes in the studio projection room and when they finished and the lights came on, there was complete silence. After a moment Mr. Disney turned to me:

"The circling Indians looked like sitting ducks, Yak," he remarked thoughtfully.

"I agree," I said.

"I am not blaming you," he answered. "I can be wrong in thinking that we could make a wagon train and Indian fight interesting without anyone getting hurt. After all, in the days of the covered wagons, both Indians and whites were killed during the battles. You'd better make it authentic."

I thanked him and left for home, thinking about my eleven years as a second unit director and recalling some action sequences where the producer or first unit director had told me how they wanted them done. If the scenes turned out good, it was great, but if they were bad, it was usually thrown in my lap. But when Mr. Disney saw the rushes and realized they were not right and said, "I'm not blaming you, I could be wrong," believe me, those words put him at the top of my list.

The next day I made a number of close shots to cut into the race for the pass. I had special effects fix the canvas on a couple of wagons so that they could be pulled up like curtains. A number of stunt men were dressed as Indians, some riding trained falling horses. When the Indians got close to the wagons, the side canvas would go up, then men would start firing, a couple of horses would go down, and other Indians would fall from their mounts. These shots looked very effective. I did a number of close shots of men firing from the wagons. I also made two or three shots with a two-camera setup in which the Indians ride straight to the camera and make falls in the foreground. The picture finished smoothly and on schedule, and William Beaudine expressed his satisfaction with my work. Mr. Disney personally thanked me and said that I would soon be working for him again.

That was no idle remark. I was called to work on the Disney picture *Old Yeller* within the year.

Disney's love for the old American frontier, demonstrated throughout his career as a showman, was never brought out more beautifully or realistically than in the film *Old Yeller*. It was directed by one of Hollywood's finest motion picture directors, Robert Stevenson, and was filmed with fun, laughter, love, adventure, and tears. To say I was pleased to get the second unit assignment would be an understatement.

Old Yeller was based on a novel by Fred Gipson, who collaborated with William Tunberg on the screenplay. The stars were Dorothy McGuire and Fess Parker, supported by Tommy Kirk, age fifteen, as Travis, and Kevin Corcoran, seven, as Arliss. Both youngsters were in Disney's "Mickey Mouse" television series.

The story begins with Jim Coats (Fess Parker) leaving his home in frontier Texas to join a cattle drive to Kansas. In a touching scene he tells his son Travis that he will have to assume responsibility as head of the house while his father is away.

"So take care of your mother and Arliss," he says soberly, "and remember to gather the corn when it is ripe, or there'll be no bread this winter. Also earmark some of the young wild hogs."

With a farewell embrace from his wife Katie, and a pat on the heads of the two boys, he rides off to catch up with the drive.

My first scenes in the picture were with Travis, who had his mule Jumper hooked to a walking plow and was plowing a strip along a split-rail fence that enclosed one side of a corn patch. The far side was a portion of the yard fence near the house.

While plowing a furrow along the rail fence, Travis is turning the plow at the end of the row when Jumper suddenly throws up his head, pointing his ears at an off-scene jack rabbit being chased by a barking dog.

I stopped the action to change angles and shoot a scene of Old Yeller chasing a rabbit at and past the camera toward the fence. This was the stray dog's introduction into the story. Then, with weeds camouflaging a "V" fence which would bring the rabbit to a hole in the rail fence, I fastened a "hot shot" under the mule's bellyband. Let me explain again that a "hot shot" is a weak, electrical charge, usually used in long cattle prods to force the animals into loading chutes or trucks.

When everything was set and the mule and Travis were in

their places, the rabbit and dog ran through the hole in the fence and under the mule's belly. As the dog went under him, I pressed the "hot shot" and the mule jumped into the air and ran toward the house, kicking and dragging the plow with Travis hanging onto it desperately. He finally freed himself from the reins which were around his shoulders.

I then had a stout ring welded on the point of the plowshare, tied a flexible cable on a solid anchor and ran the cable through the ring on the plowshare, under the fence and through an anchored pelican hook which could be tripped as soon as the plowshare was in position to start the destruction. We had weakened the fence posts so that they would break easily.

Just before the camera rolled, Tommy Kirk's double secured lines to the mule's collar so that the mule could drag Travis behind the plow and he could free himself just before the plow hit the fence. With two camera setups, we were ready. Frank Weatherwax, the trainer, held Old Yeller's double and when I hollered "Action," the wranglers turned Jumper loose and the dog ran after him. They went around the corner of the house and the cable swung the plowshare through the fence. The pelican hook was tripped, and with the ring on the share keeping it on the opposite side of the posts, that fence was really torn up and flattened from the corner of the house to the corral gate.

The studio had made a deal with a man who had a tame, beautiful four-point buck, which was to be used in a scene where Travis is hunting deer. Before we started filming, I went to see the buck at the studio where he had been taken. The owner had him out of the truck—several people were there and they were all petting him. He was completely loose and friendly. When I got within twenty-five or thirty feet of the group, the buck lowered his head and ran straight at me. I grabbed his antlers and held him until his owner put his lead rope on him and got him back in the truck.

"I don't know what got into him," the man apologized. "He's mostly friendly with everybody."

"You must have told him I was a deer hunter," I replied with a grin.

We had fenced in an acre of Sherwood Forest, a beautiful wooded area near the Ventura County line, and had built a nice water hole in it, which we also fenced in. The buck deer and several others were kept in this enclosure for a few days ahead of the filming and this got them used to the water hole.

We built another small corral and kept them in it for a couple of days so that they would be thirsty and go to the water hole for the scenes we needed. We did a shot where a doe and her faun come down and drink, as Travis watches them and smiles.

I took over from the first unit, and filmed the buck as he stalked out of the bushes and stopped. We drove him to the pool, but he just would not drink. I sent for Doc Reed, a veterinarian whom I had used several times to make horses drink. He said that if I could hold the buck, he would give him a shot that he'd guarantee would make him drink.

We got the deer into the corral and Doc gave him a shot, telling us to get ready. With Travis in the foreground, grinning and watching a couple of squirrels playing, the camera turned, the buck trotted into view, went straight to the water hole, waded in and drank his fill. Then, as he started to leave I made a close shot of Travis, who began to slowly raise his rifle. I changed angles, shooting toward the waterhole. A second gunshot, out of the scene, caused the buck to wheel in sudden flight. I then made a close shot of Travis as he fires, then runs toward the off-scene buck.

My next action sequence was a scene where Arliss captures a bear cub. In a gully near the ranch house, Arliss is throwing small bits of corn bread to a bear cub which seems to be alone. Each bite brings the cub closer, until the boy grabs him. The cub starts squealing and fighting to get away.

Travis and his mother are trimming fence posts when they hear the commotion and hurry to the gully. They see Arliss hanging onto the cub, which was really yelling and fighting to get loose.

Travis hollers at Arliss, "Turn that cub loose!"

He starts to run toward Arliss when he sees the mother bear coming on the run to rescue her cub. Just before she gets to Arliss, Old Yeller's double, commanded by Frank Weatherwax, charges out of the bushes and leaps onto the bear, practically turning a flip over her head. The enraged mother bear turns on the dog, but the dog out-maneuvers her on every move. When the bear tries to run, the dog nips her on the rear, turning her around.

I cut this action and had the trainer bring in another bear that was trained to wrestle. When the dog ran at her, she stood up on her hind feet. I guess she thought that she was going to wrestle with the dog. The bear would turn with her paws extended and always kept the dog in front of her. The dog would jump and try to get hold of the paws, but the bear would swing them away from him. All in all we got some good footage, which when cut and put together, made a really exciting fight.

I had to make a process plate of the bear charging down the gully. The first unit director, Mr. Stevenson, was going to use the scene to process Arliss holding the squawling, fighting cub in the foreground. In the plate, the bear had to run straight over the camera, which was to be in a covered pit with an opening for the lens. We made a lane with two brush-camouflaged fences running on either side of the path, from where the bear would start her run down and over the hidden camera.

In all my experience with animals, I think that the bear has proven to be the most unpredictable of all and this one was no exception. When everything was ready, the trainer gave the bear a bite of unstrained wax honey, then ran down the gully and over the pit—the operator rolled the camera and the bear was turned loose. She looked around, and in a slow walk started down the lane. The trainer hollered, "Come on, baby," but the bear was obviously in no hurry.

I hollered "cut," and told the trainers that I thought the bear would run if she was prodded with a "hot shot" when they turned her loose. They agreed, but when the slight shock hit her, she let out a mad roar and cleared that set in nothing flat! Some of the crew went up trees, and others ran to jump the fences. The bear settled for the head wrangler, George Guessford, who was a tall man, six feet four or better. She took after him and it was a close race until George stumbled and fell. He rolled over on his back, kicked the bear in the snout with both feet, and at the same time he let out a yell that would have made the scream of a panther sound like Mickey Mouse. The bear turned and ran back into the pen.

The following day, without any undue persuasion, the bear gave us a good run down the lane and over the camera pit.

In one of the sequences I filmed, Travis had discovered that racoons were eating their corn. The workmen had hauled dirt into one of the big stages at the studio, and set in rows of corn. Travis, with Old Yeller, now his pal, is sleeping in the corn patch to scare off the marauders if they show up. While they were asleep, we got several close shots of racoons coming through the fence. Then we opened some of the corn husks and smeared the corn with fish oil. Those coons climbed the stalks which would bend over and let them at the corn. We got a real close shot of a couple of coons fighting.

Each time we finished a scene, we would have to catch the racoons and put them back in their cages. The animal trainers were having a hard time getting one of the little rascals back in the cage, so I had to get into the act. I grabbed him by the back of the neck and as I took him to the cage, I made a motion with my right hand toward the cage door and told one of the workers to open it. I had pointed too close to the coon's head and he grabbed hold of my index finger and one of his teeth went in between the bone joint. He hung on like a bulldog. When I released my hold on his neck, he turned loose. The blood was really spurting so I had first-aid give me a tetanus shot and Lionel Comport, who furnished the racoons, said that they better give the coon a shot, too.

In one scene, Old Yeller chases a coon into an old, dead oak tree that had an opening at the bottom and was hollow for about five or six feet up to a second opening. He starts digging and scratching, trying to get inside. The coon looks out of the top hole, sees the old dog, and jumps down on his back. Old Yeller whirls and twists trying to get the coon off.

I had special effects make a fur-covered belt to put on the dog. Then I fastened the coon with a small trip, with a fishline to trip it loose. The cameras rolled and the dog whirled by the fence. I tripped the racoon loose and he jumped off the dog, scooted through the fence and dashed away.

In another scene, we had to show Travis, with Old Yeller, trying to take a newborn calf from its mother. We did some good shots with the cow chasing Travis and I did one shot where the cow was real close to him as he ran out of scene.

Then we put the cow in a chute and put a halter on her, made out of small cable with a ring on its side. Another small, flexible cable was placed inside a dummy dog made to look like Old Yeller. The cable extended out of its mouth and through the ring on the halter. One man held the dummy dog and the other man held a larger cable that was fastened to hobbles on the cow's front ankles. As the cow charged out of the chute the man threw the dummy dog, making it look as though it leapt at the cow's head. The man on the cable pulled the dummy dog tight against the cow's jaw, and the man on the hobble cable pulled the cow's legs from under her. She did a perfect fall. The action was well coordinated and fast, and the scene was very authentic.

My next action sequence was of Travis earmarking wild Havoline hogs. With a lasso around his shoulder and his sharpened knife in his pocket, he follows Old Yeller who had picked up the scent and was on the trail of the herd.

Before starting the picture I had gone to Santa Ynez, which is a beautiful, mountainous section some forty miles north of Santa Barbara, where a very good friend, Sigard Hansen, had a ranch. Wild hogs were plentiful in that section of the country, and I had him arrange to trap twenty-five or thirty head and truck them to Lionel Comport. He kept them in our rocky, oak tree location. When we were set to start filming, Weatherwax had old Yeller really working like a sheep dog.

The set was cleared of everything but the hogs and when the cameras started turning, Travis and Old Yeller came into the scene. Old Yeller went to work on the hogs, keeping them bunched in an "L" formation in an area with high rocks and a huge oak tree in the center, its limbs spread over the bunched hogs. When one would try to break out, Old Yeller would bring him back, barking and snapping at his heels.

In closer shots, I showed Travis out on the tree's limb where he makes a loop in his rope and drops it down and over a shoat. He pulls the squealing pig up and clamping it between his legs, takes his pocket knife and cuts a notch in its right ear and a slit in its left.

"All right, pig," Travis says with satisfaction, "you are now wearing the Coates's mark."

In a longer shot, Travis drops the pig back into the milling and squealing herd being held at the tree by Old Yeller, and making a loop, snares another hog. Just as the rope is tightened, one of the larger hogs launches a charge at Old Yeller and slams into the rope. Travis is almost jerked out of the tree. He slides further out onto the limb, which starts to crack. I was using a double for the boy in this scene. The limb broke and the double fell down among the squealing pigs. He scrambled to his feet and, keeping his back to the camera, ran to a big rock and tried to climb up on it.

I changed camera angles and I had a good, stout leather band tied on the double's leg under his trousers just above the knee with a small, stout trip on it. We tied shut the mouth of a big hog with a small, flexible cable and used black tape, the color of his hair, to cover it.

With Travis's double standing against the rock, we set the camera in a tight, close shot showing his legs up to his belt line, and fixed a heavy-duty brace out of the scene for him to hang onto with his hands. The camera was to be back cranked, so that the finished scene would show in reverse. We fastened the hog with his jaws tight against the double's leg. I held the trip wire and when the hog was shaking his head and pulling back, I tripped him loose and he went out of the scene backwards. When projected it would show the hog as he came into the scene, grabbed the double's leg and started shaking it. We again tied the hog to his leg and, grinding the camera at normal forward speed, I held a small wire fastened to the trip while the trainer held Old Yeller. The hog dragged the double, shaking and whirling him around. With enough footage, I had the trainer send Old Yeller in. As he got to the boy, I tripped the hog loose.

In all motion pictures where children are used, you must have a teacher. In the middle of the scene with the hog, the woman teacher on this picture came around a big rock just in time to see the pig dragging and shaking the boy doubling Travis. She screamed and fainted.

When she was revived, and we knew she was okay, I couldn't help feeling some satisfaction as a director that the scene looked so realistic.

We resumed filming and after we had enough footage of the boy's double and the pig, I had Old Yeller sent in. As he grabbed the hog by an ear, I pulled the trip which released the double's leg from the cable. He got to his feet, while the dog worried the hog out of the scene by continuing to pull on his ear.

Old Yeller was perhaps one of the best trained dogs that I ever worked with. For a scene with a sick cow who is supposed to have hydrophobia, I had the veterinarian, Doc Reed, give the cow a shot and put suds on her nose and mouth. She did a good job of staggering and then falling to the ground. I made an over-the-shoulder shot of Travis's double firing his rifle; then a dissolve from Travis's face showed that the cow had been killed.

Travis returns to the house and hears his mother frantically calling him. He grabs his gun again and rushes out to find Old Yeller locked in deadly combat with a huge loafer wolf.

We had a German Shepherd doubling the wolf, and he was to battle Old Yeller's double. We tied both their mouths shut, which didn't seem to bother them. They wrestled and rolled on the ground, going all through the motions of a fierce fight. With the camera shooting over Travis's shoulder, I showed how difficult it would be for him to get a bead on the wolf without hitting Old Yeller. In one of the scenes the wolf's double threw Old Yeller to the ground and stood over him trying to get to his throat. I changed angles to a front shot of Travis as he finally fired at the off-scene wolf.

We had rented a big pet wolf from a lady living near Lionel Comport. We wanted him to zoom in to a close-up, so we had Doc Reed ready to give him a shot to put him to sleep. The wolf was very gentle but the minute we tried to hold him he would snarl and let us know it was hands off. We phoned the woman who owned him. When she came out, she walked over to a seat and called him over. He obeyed, lying quietly in her lap as she petted him. The Doc gave him the shot and when he was out we balanced him over Old Yeller and with the camera grinding, we tripped a prop from beneath him and got the effect of finishing the fall. Old Yeller wiggled out from under him and the camera trucked into a big close-up of the real wolf, who was frothing at the mouth. When the film was put together, it looked very real.

At this point Robert Stevenson, the first unit director, took over and finished the picture. The story ends movingly, in a scene showing Travis forced to shoot the beloved dog that had saved his life, because the wolf had infected Old Yeller with hydrophobia.

Working on a Disney picture was always a privilege and a pleasure. I was very happy to get a call from the Disney Studios in 1964 to do the second unit direction on a film version of Johann Wyss's classic, *The Swiss Family Robinson*—the well-loved story of a family shipwrecked on an island in the West Indies in the time of Napoleon.

Disney combed the tropics carefully before choosing the beautiful palm-studded island of Tobago, in the West Indies, as the setting for his picture. He was also careful in picking his cast, which starred John Mills, Dorothy McGuire, James MacArthur, Janet Munro, Tommy Kirk, Kevin Corcoran, Cecil Parker (like Mills, a British actor) and Sessue Hayakawa, the Japanese star. Bill Anderson was the producer and it was directed by Ken Annakin.

One of my first assignments was to shoot scenes of the father and the two sons bringing equipment and animals to the island from the wreck. I had three lines of three-quarter-inch hemp rope, each a hundred feet long, tied to the raft. The two outside lines were held apart with a forty-foot under water rod. This gave them a narrow "V" formation. The third line was in the middle and was also tied to the underwater rod, and the animals, a big hog, a donkey, cows, goats, ducks and geese, had small, empty barrels harnessed to their sides. I had a flatboat constructed to use as a camera boat. The raft was tied to the flatboat and the complete outfit was pulled on an underwater cable.

We got the small, barrel lifesavers on the animals, then got them off the wreck, into the water, and tied to the tow lines from the raft. I had a makeshift sail put up, but there was not enough wind to move the raft along so we had to depend on a small outboard motor to propel the flatboat which pulled the raft.

In the story, Fritz, one of the sons, was to rope a huge turtle and use it to tow the raft. Naturally, this had to be staged to look real, so I had a couple of divers capture a big turtle. Special effects drilled a hole on the right front side of his shell and connected a metal plate to it with a hook sticking out an inch and a half from the shell.

Earlier I had an underwater shaft constructed that could be fastened onto the front of the flatboat. It stuck out twelve feet from the boat and then turned straight up. A pan made to fit the underside of the turtle's shell was welded to the shaft. With the turtle fastened to the pan and the camera on a small barge, we shoved the turtle near Fritz but out of camera range.

I did a close shot of Fritz throwing a loop from the offscene raft toward the turtle. In another take, with the camera shooting close on the turtle, I threw a loop out and made a perfect catch on the swimming reptile. As the front of the loop sank beneath the turtle, I tightened the rope quickly. It caught the hook as planned, and we had our turtle secure. I then had the camera crew set their cameras shooting straight on the turtle going toward shore. The turtle stuck his head up and paddled hard with what you might call a breast stroke. With the rope tied to the raft it looked like he was really pulling the outfit.

The only trouble was that after a couple of takes the turtle discovered that he could move along without paddling. To fix that, I got a native from the crew, who was an excellent water man, to stand on the shaft just back of the turtle, four feet under water. When the raft began moving, with the camera rolling, he submerged and prodded the turtle's rear end with a stick. This maneuver worked beautifully and the animal really paddled for all he was worth.

I filmed a number of scenes of the turtle from different

angles, and made his swimming look faster with a slower camera speed. As they head for shore, Fritz settles back with an air of pampered luxury and grins happily.

During this sequence, I did individual scenes of the cow, the mule, and especially the big, gentle pig, which stood perfectly still when the wranglers tied the barrels to his sides. When they led him into the water, he went right along with the other animals and seemed perfectly content. I shot some very close scenes of his swimming and he actually seemed to enjoy it. After we finished with the raft scene, we discovered that the pig was completely blind.

Before we left Los Angeles, the company had bought a tiger to double our well-trained one, which was to be used in two or three sequences in the picture. We had a vet put him to sleep and declaw him. While he was asleep, I had the crew make a cast of his mouth and teeth. From this cast, a metal mouthpiece was made with rings that would slip over his eyeteeth on the top, and a lower part that would fit under his tongue. When this was tied solidly under his jaw, he could not get it off and he looked like he was snarling.

The first scenes with the tiger were where Francis has snared a young elephant by the front leg and tied him to a tree trunk. Our trained tiger walks out in the opening, and comes slowly toward the baby elephant, growling ferociously. Francis is terrified and picking up a rock, hurls it at the tiger, who snarls viciously as the rock lands near him.

The mother, who is looking for Francis with the two dogs, hears the growling tiger and sends the dogs in. For the next scene, the trainer put the big, trained tiger back in his cage and brought out the clawless tiger in a smaller cage, with straps holding him tight against the side bars. The mouth plate was fastened on him; his fangs showed, but he couldn't bite. We tied the dogs' mouths shut and all was ready. The vicious-looking tiger came out into the scene to face Francis, who stood in the foreground. The two dogs ran in and when they caught him, they were really trying to fight. This made the scene look good and the tiger finally was put to flight. We put the tiger back in his cage, where we took his mouthpiece out. Neither he nor the dogs ever received a scratch.

According to the script, Fritz and Ernst were to make an exploratory trip in an outrigger canoe to find out if they are on an island or a continent. On the second day they round a headland and in the distance, through their telescope, see two ships anchored out past the entrance to a rock-strewn bay. They lower their small, makeshift sail and paddle their outrigger among the rocks to get in close enough for a better look. At this point, the canoe is to be wrecked.

With two doubles in the outrigger, I had special effects tie a cable on a big rock and fasten a ring on the cable, about four feet from the rock, and a pelican trip on the lower, central part of the outrigger. This cable was coiled and secured on the outrigger and was just long enough to let the rock land on the bottom when released. I told Loren James and Chuck Courtney, the two stunt men who were doubling the boys, to bring the boat by a certain big rock, turn it broadside to the camera and when I hollered, "Now," to trip the rock loose.

Courtney asked, "And then what?"

"Just let nature take its course!"

The stunt men got the boat in position, the cameras rolled and I waved for them to start the action. They paddled by the big rock and turned the boat broadside to the cameras. A giant breaker started rolling in and I hollered, "Now." They pulled the trip and from the way it looked, that big anchor rock hit the bottom just about the same time the breaker smashed into the boat, flipping it upside down. The two boys had a rough swim in, but it looked like a real wreck. They managed to get to shore with the bed rolls and compass—everything else was lost.

The boys rescue a young captive from the pirates who were in the anchored ships, but are forced to abandon a second prisoner and flee. I filmed the chase as the three run through the woods. As one big pirate runs toward them, Fritz tells Ernst to dive for his legs while Fritz catches the man higher. They both dive, and Ernst locks onto the pirate's legs as Fritz crashes into his shoulders. The pirate spins half around and topples to the ground. The kris he has been holding falls from his hand and Fritz seizes it. The pirate, shaking his head groggily, gets to his knees, but goes down and out as Fritz brings the handle of the kris crashing down on his skull.

One of the most interesting scenes I filmed was in a jungle quagmire where the three children were wading in waist-deep water. Ernst steps into a hole and goes under, but manages to grab a limb and pull himself up, sputtering. Roberta, the young girl the boys have rescued, screams at the sight of a large anaconda snake.

The company had hired a snake handler named Wes, who

had one arm that was pretty well shriveled up from a bite of one of his poisonous creatures. The man knew his snakes, and along with a variety of smaller reptiles, he had an anaconda that was a little over twenty feet long. I had the cameraman set up for Roberta's point of view of the anaconda and said to Wes:

"Okay, bring on the worm."

"If you ever call that beautiful creature a worm again," he snorted angrily, glaring at me, "I'll take him and go home!"

We made shots of the anaconda coming straight to the camera and of Roberta screaming with terror as she sees it slipping into the water, then submerging. Ernst's double gets hold of the girl and helps her out of the water just as Fritz's double falls down as if his legs had been jerked from under him. Turning and spinning, he surfaces, as he holds the snake just behind the head.

Right in the middle of this sequence, the anaconda got sick. Wes gave him a shot of penicillin, but the snake was unable to continue working. Wes then got in touch with some outfit somewhere near the Amazon jungle, which was not too far from Tobago. It only took four or five days for the capture and delivery of another anaconda, but this one was wild and even larger, well over twenty-five feet long. When he arrived, he struck at everything that got near him. But in three days, Wes had him gentle as a lamb. Fritz's double, Loren James, would get hold of the snake just behind the head, then Wes would wrap two or three coils around him. He did a beautiful job keeping the snake's head close as though it was really trying to get hold of him. He would spin around, fall and go under the water and then surface. Between scenes, Wes would wade in and the anaconda would run his head under his elbow and up over his arm and relax, seemingly very content.

At the end of the snake fight, Chuck Courtney, Ernst's double, went into the water to help Loren. We had the snake wrapped over his shoulder and around his body. When Chuck got hold of the snake and tried to pull him off, the snake tightened up on Loren. Luckily, it was not enough to really hurt him. After editing, this sequence was very exciting.

My next action sequence was where the three, after getting out of the jungle and into a more hilly area, come over a ridge and find a zebra mired in a bog with four or five hyenas closing in on him.

I had set the camera in a suitable place to photograph the hyenas when the kids drove them off. I didn't want to wait for the crew to build a fence around the camera area, so I got a limb from a tree, trimmed it to about four feet, then told the crew that if the hyenas came toward us, I would keep them away from the cameras.

When the cameras turned, the doubles came over the ridge and saw the helpless zebra in the bog with the hyenas getting closer and closer. They hollered and threw rocks as they ran toward the bog. All but one of the hyenas ran out in the right place, and that one headed straight at the cameras. I jumped out in front of the cameras and whacked him with the shillalah. It was lucky for me that I landed a good one, as my feet slipped out from under me and I lit flat on my back.

To celebrate the safe return of Fritz and Ernst with the rescued Roberta, the Swiss Family holds a celebration and stages the most unorthodox race I ever helped to film. The race is to be between all their pet animals, and even includes the ostrich.

Francis is to ride his young elephant, Ernest is astride the ostrich, Roberta is on the zebra, and Fritz aboard the donkey. Francis's monkey, Nips, dressed in holiday garb, sits on the back of Duke, the dog. The other big dog, Turk, is fastened to the table with a leash.

After shooting a number of pickup shots, I located a good place for travel shots near a small, fenced-in area where the animals were kept. They were put there a week or so before the shooting commenced. I had my native driver drive the camera car and in preparing to make some runs with the ostrich, I gave him strict orders that if the bird turned in front of the car, he was to hit the brake hard and turn it sharply so as not to hit anyone. I also told the camera crew to be ready to find good handholds in case this happened.

The first run with the big bird was fine, but an ostrich is unpredictable. On the second run, he was going fine when all of a sudden, he speeded up and turned to cross in front of the camera car. When he turned, he fell and threw Ernst right in front of the vehicle. The driver was on the ball and swung the car sharply off the course before Ernst hit the ground. The camera crew got a good jolt, but they patted the driver on the back and congratulated him.

The young elephant would run for food any time so we had no trouble with him. He made a couple of beautiful runs. The zebra, like the donkey, ran okay but slowly. The monkey, riding the dog, was fast and I'm sure it got some big laughs, not only from us, but from audiences throughout the world.

The zebra didn't rein too well, so I had a trail made around a steep hillside about forty-five or fifty feet above the valley floor. At a point where the hill was the steepest, I had the crew dig in a roadway, six or seven inches deep and four or five feet wide, from the trail to where the valley leveled off below. Then cross-timber planking was nailed down making a solid floor with a railing of two-by-fours nailed to the planks six or eight inches from the sides from top to bottom. I had a coating of axle grease put on the slide, blocked the trail with an old dead timber stump and covered the boards with sand and dirt. Bushes were then placed along the slide so that it would blend in with the natural landscape. I used a two-camera setup and had Fez Reynolds, a small man who owned the zebra, double for Roberta. I told Fez to move the zebra along at a good gait, then turn him straight down the slide. "When the animal starts to slide," I told him, "just pull both reins straight back and enjoy the ride."

When we were ready, Fez managed to get the zebra into a trot and turned him down the slide. The zebra just stiffened his front legs and sat half down, as he was sliding very fast. In fact, I thought for a moment he was going to fall but he held his feet to the bottom and ran on out of the scene.

Ernst came past the second pylon but couldn't make the ostrich turn. With his hand over the bird's eye, he finally got the big bird to turn down the back stretch. Roberta was on the zebra with Duke in hot pursuit at the zebra's heels, the monkey still clinging to the dog's back. The ostrich and the zebra passed, going in different directions. The zebra ran through a stream, bolted onto the beach and making an abrupt turn threw Roberta in a flip to the sand just as Duke, with the monkey on his back sailed past in pursuit of the zebra. Roberta gets up laughing but reacts with fearful amazement as she looks off and sees the pirate ships in the bay and the long boats pulling toward the shore, each filled with men. She turns and hurries back to inform the family of the pirates' return.

The family has made preparations to protect themselves as best they could in the event of a pirate attack. Deep pits have been dug all around the bottom of the hill and concealed by bushes, logs have been piled in strategic high places to be cut loose should the pirates come up that section of the hill.

A huge pile of boulders is stacked on the top of a wooden platform, under which explosives have been placed in such a manner that when they are set off, the boulders will be blown outward and down the hill. Fuses are placed so that the defenders can light them at the proper time. Many crude bombs have been constructed out of coconut shells, and other protective devices are hidden near the bridge and on the trails leading up the hill.

All of this had been done under the supervision of the special-effects crew, although I had figured out many of the gags and was to shoot the action scenes when they were filmed during the fight.

I had cameras covering all the action as the pirates, led by Kuala, land on the beach and rush toward the hilltop fortress.

From a place of concealment in the foreground, Fritz and Ernst watch, both holding lines which are hidden beneath moss and earth. When the first group of pirates reach the bridge Fritz suddenly tightens his rope and the booby trap bridge breaks apart, dumping the pirates into the water. Fritz grins with satisfaction, and motions to Ernst, who pulls another rope that trips several cocked and pre-aimed crossbows—each crossbow ingeniously fires a whole quiver at a time. The pirates in the water, plagued by the descending arrows duck for cover. During this confusion Fritz and Ernst rush up the hill and leap over the parapet to help their father, Roberta, and their mother, who are loading muskets. Francis ties the two dogs to a heavy stake near the log pile. As Kuala and his pirates charge across the lowland toward the hill, a tied-down tree branch springs up and knocks one of the pirates backwards into a bed of cactus. Another is caught around the ankle by a concealed noose which whips him into the air. Kuala halts long enough to have the man cut down, then they continue on toward the hill. One man slips down out of sight with a scream, then two or three others disappear only to come bounding out of the pit, their clothes torn to shreds and bleeding from the mauling they have received from the tiger in the pit.

Kuala moves over and looks down into a pit and the big cat leaps up at him. He jumps backwards and turns a complete somersault, then gets up and rallies his men about him, pointing dramatically up the hill. As the pirates move forward, the father uses a little positive thinking, addressing the pirates in a low voice he says, "Over this way . . . over this way . . . just a bit more." Kuala takes a pistol from Auban, a huge pirate, and orders his men to go a little up the hill. The father smiles, hands Frances the torch and says, "Number three." The pirates rush to take refuge behind the rock pile—number three. Then the air is literally filled with rock boulders and pirates. Kuala rallies his men and sends them up toward the log pile. The father runs with the axe to the back of the log pile and cuts the logs loose. They roll and tumble over the pirates. One log bounces at the bottom of the hill and into a pit, taking a pirate with it. The pirate comes out of the pit on the log, with a tiger in pursuit, chasing him into the bushes. All the other pirates run for the beach, shouting and screaming.

I did one very effective shot. Three pirates have somehow managed to climb a cliff on the seaside of the fort and in the skirmish, Fritz becomes tangled in a hand-to-hand fight with one of the pirates on the very edge.

At this spot, the height of the cliff was a good hundred feet or more. About twenty feet or so below the top, there was a seven- or eight-foot-wide ledge, and on it was a good-sized tree with strong limbs. I had the crew build an eight-by-ten-foot platform in the tree, with good stout braces to support the platform. Twenty-five feet or so to one side and a bit lower than the platform, I had them tie a parallel platform to set the camera on. The platform was well covered with bushes so that special effects could stand under it and bounce a dummy out as the stunt man playing the pirate falls onto the platform, which was covered with a layer of empty pasteboard boxes and falling pads on it. With the camera shooting up we showed Fritz and the stunt man pirate in a hand-to-hand fight. Fritz spun the pirate around and knocked him off the cliff. The operator panned the camera as he fell to the platform and was concealed by the shaking foliage of the tree. The camera continued panning, picking up the dummy as it bounced from the foliage, and staying right on it until it landed on the rocky shore and bounced into the sea a hundred feet below.

I moved everything from the ledge on the cliff and placed the cameras at various points to cover the mass action around the fortress.

The struggle gets increasingly desperate as more pirates head up the bluff. Turk and Duke, the two dogs, are barking furiously and straining at their leashes, and Ernst and Fritz are barely holding their own in a hand-to-hand struggle. The mother and Roberta are inside the fortress loading muskets for the father. Francis sneaks to the dogs and unties them.

With a camera shooting from the fortress roof, I showed Kuala and the huge pirate creeping out on the roof to get in an advantageous position above the defenders who don't see them. Fritz and Ernst are fighting with other pirates and are screened from view by the fortress. Kuala and the other pirate reach a position above the father. Kuala fires hastily as the father sees him and starts to grab a loaded musket. He is wounded in the shoulder and the huge pirate leaps down on him. At this moment, Duke and Turk, who have been released by Francis, come hurtling through the air, knocking the pirate back. He stumbles on the edge of the bluff and tumbles off into space.

In a close shot, Roberta fires and kills a pirate who is trying to take a loaded musket from the mother. Then, seeing Kuala and his men moving along the steep side of the bluff, with Kuala shouting in Malaysian for them to charge the fortress, she decides there was no chance for the family if she stays with them. She is the one the pirates want.

Looking warily toward Fritz and Ernst, she suddenly dashes to the ridge and clears it in one leap, calling to Kuala as she runs. Fritz springs into action almost before Roberta is over the ledge. He overtakes her and seizing her roughly, hurls her behind a big rock. She struggles to get loose, as a bullet whines off the rock. Then they hear cannons and think that the pirates are shelling them from the ship, but when they look in that direction, they can't believe their eyes. The pirates are screaming fearfully and scrambling madly down the bluff to leap into the sea. Others run for the long boats.

I wish there were more men like Walt Disney in the industry. He was not only a fine man, but surrounded himself with good people, and to this date, the Disney Studio has some of the finest personnel in the industry. Walt Disney's death was not only a severe loss to the film industry, but to his many friends throughout the world. I worked in several pictures for him and he was always the same—a friendly man. He will long be remembered.

TEN

Big Battles Abroad

Until 1952, the year I signed with M.G.M. to do the action on their production of *Ivanhoe*, most of my work had been on Westerns. That picture established me as someone who could handle action on spectaculars—big costume pictures with battle scenes involving hordes of extras and lots of unusual stunt shots.

I had done a little of that kind of work before, mostly because of my reputation as a horseman. I remember getting a call to do a scene with a team and chariot in an RKO picture entitled *The Last Days of Pompeii*. The year was 1935, Preston Foster was one of the leading characters in the picture, and it was directed by Ernest Schoedsack. The scene was to be a narrow street in the city of Pompeii, a set built on the back lot at R.K.O. The buildings were made of a light material so that parts of them could break up in the filming.

At the eruption of Mt. Vesuvius, the whole set was to be smoked in, with buildings and debris falling everywhere. This spectacular action, plus the tremendous sound of the volcano erupting and the screams of women and children fleeing for their lives, was the type of scene that can spook horses until they become unmanageable.

Ernest Schoedsack, knowing this and aware of my ability to handle horses, had asked for me. When I showed up on the set, he was sitting in a seat mounted next to the camera, which was on a boom. He explained the scene he wanted. On "action" I was to start out of scene around a corner of the set, drive the team on a run straight at the camera, then swing the team to the right and stop them at the curb. As he told me this, he pointed to an object sitting on the sidewalk.

"That is a marker," he said. "If the chariot wheel stops there it will be fine. But as you swing the horses, I want their heads to cross in front of the camera, or as close as you can without hitting it. If their mouths are open, it will be a great effect. We will start moving the camera back just as you make the turn."

"With the pull it will take to bring them to a quick stop," I told him, "their mouths will be open without a doubt!"

"Good," he said. "Now, we will make a rehearsal run."

I nodded in agreement. "I would like to hear whatever sound effect you are using," I said, "as well as the noise of the people. I want to see what the team's reaction will be." (Of course a team that has been used in a number of pictures is less likely to be upset by anything.)

I took the team around the corner and had them place a man out of camera range to give me my signal. All was ready and the thunderous noises started. I got the signal, popped the whip over the team, and away we went. As I was nearing the camera, I could see the crew was not starting to pull the camera back quickly enough. I pulled with all my might, mostly on the right rein. The horses' heads cleared the camera and went practically across the director's lap. With their mouths open, it must have looked a bit scary to him, because he reared back and fell off the boom seat backwards. However, I had stopped the horses right on the spot.

Schoedsack got to his feet and walked over to me, a bit irritated.

"Did you have that team under control?" he asked angrily.

"Yes, sir," I said. "Right on the nose."

Schoedsack walked over and looked at the chariot wheel. It was right on the marker. Then with a weak grin he said, "okay, do it just that way again and we'll move back a little quicker this time."

When we did the scene with all the smoke, debris, plus wails and screams, it was actually pretty terrifying. It seemed to be all in a day's work though to the horses. After finishing the chariot run, Mr. Schoedsack was very pleased and thanked me. I might add that in the rehearsal, he did a fall that I would have charged a couple hundred dollars to do, and he seemed to have had no ill effects from it.

Ivanhoe, though, was a picture where I had full charge of the action shots, and it was the first picture work I did outside the United States.

Before I went to England as second-unit director of this film, the usual practice for a Hollywood studio making an action film overseas was to shoot everything but the action on the foreign location, and do all the rough stunts after they came back to America. *Ivanhoe* was to set a new precedent.

The M.G.M. adaptation of Sir Walter Scott's classic novel had Pandro Berman as producer. The director was Richard Thorpe, a very competent craftsman who could make the invested dollar show on the screen and who always brought a good picture in on schedule. He had come up from the ranks of the "quickies," and before joining M.G.M. was known as the best B-movie director in the business.

I found him to be a man who would listen to ideas from anyone working with him, and would give fair consideration to the suggestions. To a second-unit director, this meant a lot.

Ivanhoe had an exceptional cast. The male star was Robert Taylor, with whom I had worked several times, and the leading feminine role was played by Elizabeth Taylor, who at that stage of her very successful career was, in my estimation, the most beautiful actress on the screen. Other fine actors in the film were George Sanders, Guy Rolf, Findlay Currie, Francis DeWolf, and several other English performers.

M.G.M. had a big, well equipped studio at Elstree, a suburb of London. For the picture they built a beautiful castle among the large oaks on their large back lot. A moat surrounded the castle and a field in front had been fenced off and planted with grass as a green meadow for the opening scenes, especially the siege of the castle.

It was early spring, 1952, when I arrived in London. The shrubs and trees were still barren, and the weather very crisp. You can hardly compare the London weather with that of Southern California, but it was nice to see the spring and early summer transform the countryside into a green and beautiful parklike setting. I am sincere when I say that the countryside in England is something to be proud of. You see no debris scattered along the roadways; each and every Englishman takes pride in keeping the landscape free of litter.

In London, Mr. Thorpe had preparations pretty well

under way when I arrived. I soon discovered that horsemanship in England was the same as in the eastern part of the United States—the riders use both hands on the reins. When roping and handling cattle, our western horses are broken to a neck rein, a one-hand job. The rider holds both reins in one hand and as they are pulled across the horse's neck, the horse is taught to follow the movement of the hand to the right or left. With this system, one hand is free to use a rope, or, for picture work, a gun, a sword, lance or whatever the scene calls for. I knew that for the action sequence it would be necessary to buy twenty-five or thirty good horses, set up a training school, hire a group of riders, and teach them how to use a neck rein.

Mrs. Dora Wright, who was head of production at Elstree, hired a man named Younghusband to help me in buying the horses and finding good riders. He was a riding master and had a private riding school. We soon had our horses and riders, and went to work on the training. I was out every day with them and was pleasantly surprised at the way both men and horses accepted the changeover from the gee-haw system to a neck rein.

I got quite a few laughs the first few days, especially when we started training for the jousting sequence. The crew had set up a training field so that I could rehearse the riders who were to take part in the jousting matches. Tommy Howard, head of special effects (and, I might add, a man worth his weight in gold to any company), helped me design lances that would telescope a few feet on the handle end. The forward part of the shaft was made of heavy rolled paper, as a safety precaution.

I got some of the men mounted and handed each a shield and lance. One of the men had the reins in his left hand and the shield in his right. When I handed the lance up to him, he looked at me for a second and said, "You know, Governor, I've only got two hands."

The training really paid off and when all was ready, we started shooting. The men were a willing group, but when they clashed head on during the jousting matches, they just couldn't fall from their horses quick enough to make it look convincing.

Back in my stunt days, I had been roped and pulled off horses backwards many times. I had a wide leather belt made that fit under my shirt across my chest, with a metal ring in the back, just between the shoulder blades. I had done gags with it, where I would tie one end of a light flexible cable to a strong limb of a tree and the other end to the ring in the wide belt. We would measure this off and prepare the ground for the fall. Around this spot we would have a battle raging with both ground men and riders. I would ride in, sword in hand, and one of the ground men with a balsa wood rifle would swing it with all his might across my chest just as I hit the end of the cable. Over the rear end of the horse I would go. I knew that to get the effect I wanted in the jousting sequence, I would have to use this pull-off system.

I explained what I wanted to Tommy Howard, and he had the wide belts made. He also built a spring ratchet machine that I had figured out in my later days of stunt work, but just hadn't had a chance to try out. Tommy was great on this kind of machine, and we came up with a good one. When the equipment was ready I explained to the men that by putting the machine up in the small towers at either end of the lists, the spring would absorb the shock as the rider was pulled abruptly off his horse backwards. This prevented a snap back, and thus eliminated any chance of his landing on his head. Of course, landing in the foot-deep bed of peat moss that we had put on the field would be like falling into a feather bed.

The men did not like the idea of being pulled off their mounts by mechanical means. I gave them a pep talk, telling them that I had great hopes of being the first to bring a complete, finished picture to the United States with the rough action all shot. I added that if they did not want to do the jousts the way I planned they should say so and I would have a few cowboys sent over from the United States to do the job.

"Governor," one of the men said, "let me try it once more my way, and if I don't do it right, I'll try your machine."

"That's fair enough," I agreed.

I had two of them mount up and stand their horses on either side of the list rail, facing each other at the point where they would clash.

"You will be hit by the lance here," I said to the man who was to make the fall. "Now where will you land on the ground?"

He pointed down to a spot only a few feet ahead. I asked the grip to mark the spot. I then stepped off ten or fifteen yards down the list lane, and made another mark.

"From observing the way you fellows make falls," I said,

"you will end up near this spot. Remember you're not falling off your horse, you're being knocked off. Therefore, on contact with your opponent's lance, you must throw yourself backward and a little to one side. This can only be accomplished by a fast shove with your feet against the stirrups." I knew that it would be very hard for him to land on his spot.

The two jousters took their places at either end of the list and waved that they were ready. I ordered the cameras to roll and gave them "action." Both riders started well and were riding fast. They met in the center of the run right on the mark and made a perfect clash, but instead of a fast shove with his feet, the man I had talked to about the fall just fell backwards over the horse's rump was carried on down the lists, where he landed a few feet beyond my mark.

When he saw where he had hit the ground, he looked at me rather sheepishly. "All right, Governor," he said, "I'll try it your way."

We laced the vest on him beneath the phony flexible armor made for the purpose. We then hooked the ring in the back and fastened the other end of the airplane cable to the spring ratchet machine in the small tower at the end of the field. With this job of rigging, I had been very careful about every little detail. I knew that one miscalculation on my part would shake their confidence and I would be in trouble all the way.

When all the preliminary preparations were made, the camera rolled and the horsemen started forward as though they meant business. After a good run, they made a spectacular head-on clash. The man being hit was snatched off backwards by the unseen cable, his lance went into the air, and he hit the ground in perfect form. It was really a scary-looking event.

When I hollered, "cut," all the riders ran to him to see if he was okay. He got up and took off his helmet with a delighted grin.

"Old boy," he said to me, "that machine is all right!"

The only trouble I had with the men from then on was timing. It took two or three runs to get each joust. One of my best horsemen was a good looking young man named Jeremy Taylor. He had played a lot of polo and I used him as a key man on a great number of gags. On one of the jousts I paired Jeremy with a big fellow by the name of Tommy Clegg. Clegg was a former wrestler and very strong, but not too good as a horseman, which was bad for timing. I figured that maybe

Jeremy could make up for this deficiency. We had Tommy tied off with the cable and I explained that if the timing was off, and he didn't reach Jeremy at the right moment for the fall, I would holler and he could stop his horse before he hit the end of the cable.

The scene started and both riders put their horses into a run. I could see Tommy was moving too fast, and I knew Jeremy would never meet him in the right spot, so I let out a loud "Hold it!" Tommy dropped his lance, grabbed the reins with both hands and began pulling with all his might. He couldn't stop in time, and when the cable tightened, it yanked him back. He was so strong that he pulled the horse right over backward on top of him. The horse jumped up, dashed on down the lane, and as I ran over to Tommy, he got up and took his helmet off.

"I stopped him, Governor," he said laughing.

"You sure as hell did," I replied. If I could have gotten that kind of a gag with good timing it would have been one for the books.

We finally got the jousting sequence filmed with great falls and effects. I think it was probably the first picture where the jousting was really effective.

I next prepared to shoot the siege of the castle. This was a very exciting sequence and called for real stunt men. There were high falls from the castle walls into the moat, ladders loaded with men being shoved over from the top of the walls to land in the water, other falls on the inner side of the walls to thick pads, and one fall from the very top of the castle tower into the moat.

The moat was cemented, and, at the point where the man would hit, was only about five and a half feet deep. The top of the tower was a little over sixty feet from the water. The production manager had hired a man touted to be the number one English stunt man. His name was Waddum (not to be confused with another excellent stunt man by the same name). Waddum was to hire a stunt crew of fifteen or twenty men and was to do the fall from the tower himself. I had a meeting with him and he just didn't talk as though he knew much about stunt work.

I took him to the top of the tower where the fall was to be made to see what his reaction would be. He just stood there in silence, looking at the moat below.

"What do you think of it?" I asked.

"I'll do it," he replied in a rather unconvincing voice. "They'll probably carry me away, but I'll make the fall."

We had a couple of days before we were to go to work on the siege, so I told Dick Thorpe about this fellow who had been introduced as England's greatest stunt man.

"If he is," I said, "I think we're in trouble."

"Then you had better get someone else," Thorpe said.

Before I left Hollywood I had heard from a director friend about an English stunt man by the name of Powell. My friend said Powell was top-rated and had worked for him in a European film a year ago. I called Powell and he told me that he had had some trouble with the production head at Elstree Studio and could not work there. However, he recommended a little Irishman named Paddy Ryan and said Paddy was the best high man in London. Powell also told me that Waddum could not do anything right and that the men he had hired had practically no stunt experience. Some of them were fine blokes, but that wouldn't help my action scenes. As it turned out, I did get Paddy and he proved worthy of Powell's recommendation.

When we went to work on the siege, our first setup had the cameras shooting from the high castle wall out over the moat and across the beautiful meadow of knee-high, green, wavy grass. This was the meadow that I mentioned earlier. Six hundred bowmen were concealed in the trees and bushes on the far side of this meadow, and a hundred or so other foot soldiers armed with lances or swords would be carrying tall ladders, grappling hooks, ropes and sections of a floating bridge for crossing the moat.

We rehearsed all of these scenes away from the meadow so that it would be green and fresh for the charge scene across it. When all was ready we started the cameras and gave the soldiers the signal. As the entire group charged out from the trees and started across the meadow it was a beautiful sight. When they were about halfway across, a couple of Chinese ringneck pheasants took flight from the grass and all the bowmen near the birds stopped and started firing arrows at them. I couldn't believe my eyes! Hours of tedious preparation were wasted by a few unthinking extras. Their actions spoiled most of the scene.

After giving the archers some sharp words of criticism, I resumed filming. I overlapped the scene just before the men shot at the birds. We finished the charge, then made a few close-ups to cut in and take care of the overlap. Everyone had a good laugh over the pheasant incident and we started to work on scenes at the wall.

With several cameras covering the action, men rushed the floating bridges into place across the moat, while others with the scaling ladders crossed them and worked under an umbrella of arrows being fired at the top of the wall. This kept the enemy down. As ladders were placed, men with swords climbed up to do battle. Soldiers on the wall used forked poles to shove the ladders over into the moat with as many as five to seven men on them. These scenes were very spectacular.

They finally established a breakthrough and the fight raged on the wall, where a good number of men were pitched over and into the water below. When this work started, I quickly learned who could do stunts and who couldn't. I was impressed with a number of husky young fellows who were working as extras, and learned that some had been commandos during World War II, while others had athletic backgrounds. I picked out a group of them and asked whether they would like to do a bit of stunting in the picture. They all gladly accepted the offer and in two or three days I had twenty men who could work very well. They certainly didn't lack for courage, were very handy with swords, and all did good falls from the barbican and castle wall.

I didn't realize how many falls into the moat I had the men doing until we were looking at daily rushes of the castle scenes. They looked real good, but I soon was convinced that I had gone a little overboard on the number of men that fell with the ladders and the number thrown from the top of the wall into the moat.

When the rushes were finished, and the lights went on in the studio projection room, Mr. Thorpe looked at me and smiled good humoredly.

"Yak," he said, "I don't believe there is room in the moat for any more bodies." I got the message—I had certainly overshot. He added that the action scenes were fine.

Richard Thorpe was at all times a kind and considerate man. He knew how to correct mistakes without making his subordinates look bad. Most directors never pass up an opportunity to chew someone out. *Ivanhoe* was my first picture abroad and my first work with a foreign crew. I certainly appreciated Mr. Thorpe's confidence in my second-unit filming.

We prepared to shoot Paddy Ryan's high fall from the

castle tower and I knew the water in the moat was too shallow for a safe landing. I had the special effects crew build a latticelike platform fifteen by fifteen feet square, then cover it over with sponge rubber twelve to fourteen inches thick. Four-inch holes were then cut through this material fourteen or fifteen inches apart, and an inflated inner-tube was fastened under each of the four corners. I had the moat drained and placed the padded mat where Paddy would light when he fell. We tied each corner to a ring sunk securely into the cement floor of the moat, leaving slack enough to float it three or four inches from the bottom. When the moat was again filled with water, we tied a thread to the center of the pad connected to a small white cork that floated on the surface as a marker for Paddy. The water over this submerged mat was less than four feet deep. Paddy asked me why I had all the holes in the pad and I told him that when he hit the big floating "floor," the holes would allow the water to come up through the pad, as well as around the sides, and would soften the fall.

We got everything set and ready. I cautioned Paddy to be sure not to hit the water head or feet first, and if he went out of control in the fall, to pull himself into a ball and tighten every muscle.

My main camera was on a raft at the edge of the moat, as low as we could get it and shooting up. Others were in position to cover all closer angles. We turned the cameras and Paddy, who was struggling with Ivanhoe on the top of the tower, took an arrow, spun half around, and off the tower he came, making a beautiful fall, a layout with his side down. He said later the surface water stung him pretty hard but my submerged pad made it feel like hitting a big bowl of nervous porridge.

Everything continued along fine until there was only one very important sequence left to do. It was a fight to the death between Ivanhoe, played by Robert Taylor, and Sir De Bois Guilbert, played by George Sanders. This was to be the last action sequence in the picture; the producer, Pandro Berman, wanted it to top all previous thrills. I told him that I would do my best but the jousting sequence was going to be hard to beat. Mr. Thorpe was taking Robert Taylor to Austria to shoot scenes of Ivanhoe searching old castles for Richard, his imprisoned King. While he was in Austria, I was to do the complete fight with doubles. We would do the close-ups of Sanders and Taylor on his return.

The fight was to be on horses, with maces and axes as weapons. We had replicas of both weapons made of solid rubber and edged with pliable soft material. The type of mace we used was a round, heavy ball with a short chain fastened to a wooden handle a couple of feet long. I had two sets of doubles, both men and horses, and spent three days doing the fight. I kept them moving at all times—clashes, spins, and chaselike scenes, but always swinging and fighting.

At the end, Ivanhoe is dehorsed by a heavy blow of the mace, and Sir De Bois Guilbert charges at him swinging the mace with all his might. Ivanhoe takes the blow on his shield but the force of it turns him in a somersault on the ground.

Sir De Bois Guilbert charges again with such force that it knocks Ivanhoe's shield completely out of the scene. Guilbert then rides in for the kill, but as he swings the mace, Ivanhoe, now on his feet, stretches his arms out at full length, with an end of his axe handle in either hand. The ball of the mace goes over the axe handle between Ivanhoe's arms, and the chain winds on around, locking onto the axe. Ivanhoe pulls his foe from his horse and finishes him with the axe.

Mr. Thorpe and many other people at the studio thought this scene topped even the mass battle sequence. *Ivanhoe* as a whole turned out to be a very fine picture and one of M.G.M's top moneymakers of the time.

My work on *Ivanhoe* was followed by *Ben Hur*, and that led to my next assignment. Universal asked me to do the close battle shots for the film *Spartacus*. Universal's 1960 blockbuster starred Kirk Douglas, who was also the executive producer, and almost unlimited time and money were lavished on it.

I had never met the director, Stanley Kubrick, so I was sent to his office for a get-acquainted talk. One of the first things he said that he thought my work in *Ben Hur* was great, but even though it was claimed that no one had been hurt making it, the man who was run over by the chariot in the film had to have been killed.

That tickled me, and I grinned at him. "I see I fooled you too," I told him. "And you're a director!"

I told him how I had staged the stunt, using a mechanical dummy. It had fooled the audience, and now I found that it had fooled the experienced Stanley Kubrick, too. I knew it would fool an audience—even to the naked eye it looked real.

The Spartacus company gave me three scenes to do as my

first assignment. In one scene a man's arm is cut off just above the wrist. They used a man who had his right arm severed about midway between his hand and elbow, and they fastened a hand holding a sword to his handless arm. He practiced until he could handle the shield well. Special effects ran tubes filled with fake blood under his clothing and down his arm so that they would be cut when the dummy arm was severed.

I had a man working with him who was a professional swordsman. When the cameras turned and the background action of the battle got under way, I gave the two stunt men in the foreground their cue. They moved around very professionally, the swordsman glancing his sword off his opponent's shield, bringing it down. When the one-armed man raised his sword, the swordsman took a mighty swing and cut the dummy arm off just above the wrist. The hand holding the sword sailed out of the scene and blood from the pressure tube filled the air. The "wounded" man let out a convincing scream and fell to the ground.

The second scene that I was to do was to show a man's leg cut off in battle. A man who had lost a leg at the knee was hired and special effects created a trick leg, trained him in a few days to fight with a sword, and laced his leg with the blood tube. We had a good-sized log brought into the foreground, and the two swordsmen fought in and near the log. The professional crowded his opponent against the log, causing him to fall backwards on it with his leg sticking straight up. The swordsman cut the false leg off and blood from the pressure tube flew every which way.

Finally, we arranged a scene where a third man was to have his head cut off. I took the smallest stunt man I could find and had the effects crew build pads to bring false shoulders above the level of his head. We cut holes in his clothing so that he could see. Effects gave him the blood tubes. We had other combatants work around him close to cover the most gruesome part of the effect.

When all was set, we started the scene. Right in front of the camera, off went his head. Immediately another fighter went between the camera and the head being severed. It did look gruesome!

I saw the picture after its release, but I don't remember seeing the man lose his head. I think the Hays office got that one. I know that I protested to the company about filming such gruesome scenes, but I was ignored.

At one point in the battle, the Spartans have lined up some huge logs and banked them in a fire. When they are burning, they roll them down the sloping hill. The Roman soldiers are advancing, and a number of them are knocked down and bowled over by the blazing logs. The burning logs open their line, and the Spartans break through. From there on it becomes a hand-to-hand fight with swords, spears, and arrows.

During my work on the battle, the director sent Tony Curtis to our location so that I could do his scenes in the fighting. Tony was a fine actor and very cooperative, and we got some good scenes.

I also did a number of scenes with John Ireland, who was also very cooperative. I did moving shots with him in the battle, and he handled his sword well, and his death scene was excellent.

One day the star, Kirk Douglas, came out to do some close fighting shots. I had worked out what I thought was a good routine for him and had his personal stunt man run through the scene for him. When the routine finished, Kirk shook his head in disapproval.

"Naw, naw," he said, "here is what we'll do."

Then he started showing the stunt man another routine. I knew, or at least had heard, that Kirk had a lot of his own money in the picture, so all I did was holler "action" and "cut." When he finished and left the set I started doing another sequence.

After work the following day we saw the rushes in the studio projection room. When they finished Kirk turned to me. "Those scenes of mine are not too good," he said. "I should have had scenes like the ones you shot with Curtis and Ireland. They looked great."

"Curtis and Ireland took direction," I replied pointedly, and that ended the conversation. I might add, I never worked for Kirk again. But there is one thing that I have to admit about Kirk Douglas. He is really a fine actor.

Mr. Kubrick seemed pleased with my work, and I understand that *Spartacus* made barrels of money.

Ten years before, I had handled the second unit direction with Anthony Mann on *The Devil's Doorway* for M.G.M. Tony was now getting ready to direct *El Cid*, the story of Rodrigo de Bivar, Spain's legendary hero. *El Cid* (which means "The Leader") was to be shot in authentic settings in

Spain. It was to have a lot of spectacular action, and I guess the three previous pictures that I had worked on were reason enough for Tony to ask Samuel Bronston, the producer, to get me to direct the second unit.

Charlton Heston was to play El Cid, and the rest of the great cast included Sophia Loren, Raf Vallone and Genevieve Page, with Herbert Lom portraying the cruel and fanatical leader of the Moors, Ben Yussuf.

When I arrived in Madrid and got settled in a nice apartment at the Torre de Madrid, I went to the studio to meet with Tony, Mr. Bronston, and the other heads of production. Tony gave me a script and a general rundown on what had been done so far.

After reading the script I was really happy with my assignment. It was not only a great human interest story, but was loaded with action. Rodrigo de Bivar, known as "El Cid", was the legendary hero who, in the eleventh century, organized a vast army and conquered the Moorish and Moslem invaders, and thus created a new, Christian country to be known, from then on, as Spain.

The following day, I talked with Tony about the action sequences in the picture and especially the jousting between El Cid (Charlton Heston) and Don Martin (Christopher Rhodes). In the script they fight with lances, and as they charge at each other to meet in the center of the field, El Cid is knocked from his horse. Don Martin whirls his mount and charges back at El Cid, who pulls his sword and throws it, spear fashion, striking Martin in the breast. He falls from his horse, dead. Then as El Cid bows to the Crown, the King says, "I have never seen a man fight so valiantly."

"That line is a cinch to get a laugh," I told Tony. "Let *me* rewrite those scenes and really make the action and the King's statement sound real."

"I don't see anything wrong with the sequence," Tony replied. "But if you want to rewrite it, I'll consider the changes." I rewrote the sequence and when I finished Tony read it and thought it a great improvement.

My first work after looking at the script was to set up a training school. I had five stunt men flown in from Hollywood—my two sons, Tap and Joe, Jackie Williams, Jerry Brown and Buff Brady.

I was next introduced to Commandant Jesus Luque of the Madrid Mounted Police Force, who was not only a good horseman, but very influential throughout Spain. The city had stables, a nice workout track, and a fine arena. Through Mr. Luque, I made a deal for one of the stables and the arena. I then had several big truckloads of sawdust put on the arena ground for horses and men to fall on during training, which soon got underway.

I had been buying horses but was having trouble finding two big, white animals—one for Heston's lead horse and the second to be used as a double. These horses had to be fairly large, like the proverbial war horse. Mr. Luque advised going to Portugal, assuring us that we could find them there.

We left the next morning and got into Lisbon in the late afternoon. The next day, the officers of the Portuguese army had a great number of horses brought out for us to see, finally showing us a big, beautiful white gelding. I looked him over, had his rider gallop and turn him, and then bought him. I asked where I could get a double and within an hour, they found a perfect match, which I also bought.

My son, Joe, was to double Heston, so he took charge of the two white horses, and by the time we started shooting, they were working very well, as were my American and Spanish stunt men.

My first action sequence was a bit complicated. Thirteen enemy knights had captured King Alfonso and were taking him in chains to an enemy dungeon. El Cid follows, and with only a little help from the king, manages to subdue all thirteen opponents, ramming their horses, thrusting with his lance until it breaks, and swinging his mace. Finally, the last of the enemy is knocked from his horse in a back somersault.

For this scene, I had a couple of strong leather vests made and metal plates riveted to the back of each one, even with the shoulder blades. To this plate we welded a stout, round metal post three inches long and sticking straight up, with a stout ring to slide down on it. A small flexible cable was fastened to the ring at one end; the other was made fast to the saddletree under the back of the cantle.

With the stunt man leaning back in the saddle, his helper slipped the ring onto the peg. When the man is hit with a lance or mace as his horse charges, he turns over backwards onto the horse's rump and when he is completely turned over, the ring comes off the peg. The rider falls to the ground face down. Without this vest, he would have stood a good chance of landing on his head.

After shooting this sequence, I lay around waiting for another assignment. Two weeks passed and I began to wonder if Tony Mann was beginning to doubt my ability. I asked him why my unit wasn't working and he said that he wanted to wait until the cutter put together my film of El Cid's fight to rescue the King, so he could see how it looked.

"Tony," I said hotly, "if you haven't any faith in what I can do, why in hell did you ask for me? I want to work or go home!"

"Take it easy," Tony replied unruffled. "The cutter will have the scenes put together in a couple of days—enjoy yourself. You've got nothing to worry about."

He was right. When he saw the sequence cut, he was quite elated and loud in praising my direction of the action. My unit went back to work and did a lot of pick-up shots and I began laying out the action sequences for the final attack on Valencia which, according to legend, had been under siege for months.

We had the combined forces of El Cid and his Moorish friend, Emir Moutamin, stand ready for the climactic attempt to take the walled city. On the call of "action" squadrons of knights are seen preparing for battle. Rodrigo (El Cid), Moutamin, Fanez, Bermudez and other leaders of El Cid's forces are directing the activity. War machines are being lined up to move toward the wall and catapults are moved into place. El Cid looks about to make sure all is ready; then he mounts, gives a signal and moves to the front. Fanez, Bermudez, and Urdonez ride behind him and behind them come squadrons of knights, legions of foot soldiers, and companies of bowmen.

On the battlements of Valencia, Moorish knights and soldiers are manning the walls, waiting tensely as El Cid and his army move forward. Suddenly, El Cid stops and his army comes to a halt. The guards on top of the walls prepare for action.

There is no reply.

We moved the cameras back to show the entire action as the catapults were moved up into position and the soldiers and knights on both sides began taking cover. The townspeople panic as the catapults hurl their charges over the walls. The heavy missiles plummet down, and burst with devastating force on roof tops, streets, and the town's squares. The special-effects crew really did a fine job and the scenes were very effective.

With one of my stunt men dressed in Al Kadir's clothes, we showed him being seized by the mob and tossed off the wall, where he lighted on a camouflaged pad and rolled down into the sea.

I had a talk with Tony about the way I would like to stage the big battle after the fight for Valencia was finished, and I outlined some of the gags that I figured on doing. He let the wind out of my sails by telling me that he was going to stage the battle himself and I could make the action shots to cut in.

"Tony," I said patiently, "if you will just bring the two armies together, I would like to take it from there."

"Yak," he said rather coldly, "I know how to stage battles. Don't worry about it."

"Okay, Tony," I shrugged, "you're the boss."

I had been through a number of situations like this in the past with Tony and couldn't always figure out why he kept asking for me as the second unit director on his big pictures. I never took any guff from him, so that might be one of the reasons he liked me and put up with me.

When everything was set to start the big battle, I watched from the sidelines as the cameras rolled. El Cid wheeled his horse before the closed gates to face his army gathered inside the city.

Tony had the labor crew set up a bridge eleven or twelve feet high, with cameras mounted on it so that the army could ride by or under it. Pictorially, this was an excellent setup. El Cid's army was to drive a wedge between Ben Yussuf's Moslem army and the Africans, thus splitting the enemy in two. During a pause in the action, Tony asked me to put two or three horse falls in among the tightly grouped riders.

"Tony," I said, "if we put falling horses in among that large group they'll never be seen and you know there is a set price for each fall."

He ignored my words and spent most of the day doing runs under the bridge while I staged horse falls with my best stunt men. I got on the bridge and watched over the charging army as they rode through and under the bridge. If I hadn't been looking at the spot where the horses fell, I never could have seen them. I told Tony that he was not getting anything out of the horse falls, but he kept asking for more of them.

The stunt men had a field day and my sons, Tap and Joe, made a bundle while Tony Mann was shooting the battle. I picked up a few close shots and kept out of Tony's way.

We had word that the heads of the studio were coming to the Valencia location the next day. They arrived on the set just about at lunch time and went into a huddle. After a few minutes' talk Tony called me over and he seemed really upset.

"Your boys are a couple of robbers," he said accusingly.

"You'd better break that down for me, Tony," I retorted. "What have they done?"

"They're asking for a couple of thousand dollars for horse falls."

"Tony, you know as well as I do that stunt men have a set price on horse falls. The setups you shot from the parallel bridge was filmed several times and each time you asked for horse falls!"

"I didn't tell them to make the horses fall," he replied curtly.

"Tony, that's a damn lie!" I said angrily. "You had me put two or three in every scene. I kept telling you it was not only dangerous but the falls would never be seen on the screen!"

Tony just glared at me, turned and walked away.

I went back to my hotel, because I figured that he would fire me. The next day was Sunday and I lounged around the hotel while the executives and Tony spent most of the day looking at the exposed film. I didn't attend, as I felt sure Tony would have me taken off the job. Late in the afternoon I had a call from him asking me to come to his hotel. He greeted me in a friendly manner and told me the company was getting low on money and had set a finish date. He was going to Madrid to do interior shots with the principals and wanted me to finish the battle.

I said, "Tony, if you'll leave the equipment and the actors who are involved in the scenes that I have to shoot, I can clean up their scenes in three days and send them on to you in Madrid. But, Tony, I'm going to change a couple of sequences to make it look right."

"It's all yours," he said. "Good luck."

He went to Madrid and I went to work with the principals. They were very cooperative and we finished in the three days and I sent them on to Madrid as I had promised. Then I started to reshoot some of the big battle scenes.

I used the long, master shots Tony had filmed and shot new scenes to overlap them, bringing the armies together in a good, mass action clash. I then moved in for close shots to cut into the fight. I took long shots of El Cid's troops driving the

African army into the sea and to their boats, apparently killing many of them. I also made a number of close action shots in the water and had a couple of men pinned to the hull of their ships with spears. I also took close shots of a soldier with a mace knocking a horseman in a back somersault off his horse.

It is in these close action scenes that good stunt men are priceless. I had two of them ride together in a head-on clash and both horses fell, throwing their riders into the sea. In the close background, other stunt men were being knocked from their horses. The pro stunt men are the ones who make these scenes realistic.

I finished the battle scenes and went back to Madrid where Tony was working at and around the Castle of Delmonte. Tents and pavilions of all colors had been put up outside the walls of Calahorra, while colorful pennants flew from the ridgepoles of King Ferdinand's camp at the south wall. Across the field, King Ramiro's camp at the north wall was also dressed like a rainbow. The whole atmosphere was gala for the jousting match between El Cid and Don Martin.

Let me explain that we had not been filming the picture in continuity. Thus we had shot the end of the picture and El Cid's death before we moved to Calahorra to film the jousting. Everything would be in its proper place when the exposed film was assembled.

Tony had shot the ceremonial ritual preceding the joust and said that we would start the jousting the next day.

"What do you mean 'we', Tony?" I asked.

"I thought we would shoot it together," he answered.

"That won't work," I said. "You're the boss, so if you want to do it, go ahead. I'll pack and go home."

"No, I want you to shoot it," he said, rather reluctantly.

"Okay," I replied. "But you'll have to stay completely out of it."

He grinned and I realized that my fights with him had not been taken to heart. I was glad because, despite our clashes, I really liked him.

"All right," he said, "go to it."

The next morning my first scenes were close travel shots of El Cid on his horse, charging across the field at his opponent, Don Martin.

After that, I made three set shots of each knight charging close by the camera with the lances just missing the top. I had the lances made so they would telescope three feet into the handle. Part of the lance and three feet of the point were made of balsa wood, which shatters easily on contact. The two stunt doubles were my boys, Tap and Joe, each wearing a thick pad on his chest and stomach.

In each end of the field, in front of where the King sat, I had a lance rack built where, if a lance was broken in a clash, the knight could gallop on, take one of them on the move, then whirl back into the fight. With a two-camera setup, one stationary and the other to pan, I knew I would get good coverage.

We got set and the doubles, Tap and Joe, were in their starting positions. Having been a top stunt man for a good many years and knowing what could happen, and also knowing that my sons would always go all out, I swallowed my Adam's apple, then told the cameraman to roll 'em, and the action started.

The two rode in a full gallop at each other three times. In the second clash, Tap's lance missed Joe's shield and hit him in the chest. He told me afterwards that he couldn't get his breath for a minute, but all three clashes were really terrific on the screen.

The rest of the day I did close shots of each knight riding to the lance racks, tossing the broken lances away, grabbing a good one and exiting out of scene—good cut-in shots that could save many a sequence.

The next day I planned a scene where El Cid is to be knocked off his horse taking saddle and blanket with him, leaving only the bridle on the animal. When we did this scene I used the pull-off vest on Joe. He got on the horse and moved to a spot where the ground had been dug up and smoothed. When the small cable had been tied off and measured, we put the horse back to his starting place. I tied a stout strap to the front of the saddle and to his belt. We walked Tap and Joe through this scene a time or two, and then the cameras rolled. I have never seen better timing. Tap's lance struck Joe just as he hit the end of the cable which took him, saddle, blanket and all off his horse backwards. Tap's lance shattered, so he threw it down, took his mace and charged at the downed El Cid. I had the special effects man put a looped wire on Joe's shield and when Tap charged by him and swung his mace with all his might, it turned Joe in a complete somersault and his shield flew completely out of the scene. As Tap started to charge again, Joe dove for his saddle, got to his knees and jammed the saddle into the front legs of Tap's horse. The horse went to his knees and threw Tap to the ground.

This was on the third and last day of the picture and I had quite a number of scenes left. Tony, who had been watching, came over during a new camera setup.

"Are you going to make it?" he asked.

"Tony," I replied, grimly. "It's a rat race!"

He said, "Is there anything I can do to help you?"

"You sure can! While I'm using the doubles, you can shoot the closeup of El Cid picking up the saddle and lunging straight to the camera. Also, you'll need a couple of close-ups of Don Martin after he's unhorsed." Tony chuckled and we resumed filming. He worked with the stars, while I used the doubles.

That wasn't the only argument I had with Tony Mann on that picture. At one point we were standing on the beach going at it hot and heavy and I threatened to throw him into the ocean. So I was really surprised to receive a wire from the Bronston Company in Spain saying they would like to make a deal with me to direct the second unit on the film *The Fall of the Roman Empire*, which was to be another blockbuster. After all, I had called Tony a damn liar, and threatened to throw him into the Mediterranean. I couldn't understand him, but I had to respect him as a man who could take it as well as dish it out.

When I arrived in Spain and reported to the studio, Tony was out scouting locations, so I went to Samuel Bronston's office to say hello. When I opened the door and he saw me, he leaned back in his chair and broke into a hearty laugh.

I looked at him, surprised and a little annoyed.

"I don't look that funny, do I?" I inquired.

"Yak, this will make you laugh, too," he answered. "When Tony Mann signed a contract to direct *Fall of the Roman Empire*, the first thing he said was, 'Get Yak to do the second unit.'"

That afternoon Tony came back and was glad to see me. Working on that picture was one of the most pleasant jobs I ever did.

One of my first assignments was a fight in and around a high bridge that crossed a canyon stream in the mountains. Stephen Boyd, head of the Roman army, had sentenced some of his soldiers and gladiators to death for cowardice. He had a number of the men lined up on the edge of the bridge and every third man was shoved off to fall to their deaths below. My son, Tap, did some of the falls, landing on thick pads camouflaged with trees and bushes. These were falls of around thirty to forty feet, and in full shots we used dummies. I would set the camera so that when the dummy fell, he would go out of sight into the water, which splashed up into the scene. The camera panned down with the dummy and got the splash, then I shot a real man close by floating in the stream.

At this point Caesar's son (Christopher Plummer) drives his chariot alongside Stephen Boyd's. In the story, Christopher's character had worked out with many of the gladiators, and was in fact the illegitimate son of one of them. Boyd and Plummer enter into a terrific fight using their chariots as weapons. They slam the wildly careening vehicles against each other trying to crowd each other off the road. I found a place where the lower side of the road had a rock riprap at least two hundred feet long and twelve to fifteen feet high. At the bottom of this irregular stone wall the ground was very steep for thirty to forty feet. I had special effects weld a hub nut on each chariot together with a heavy swivel, and also had the gooseneck tongues offset so that one of the chariots could have one wheel go off the riprap. The underside of the chariot and axles were covered with a metal plate with the front end bent up like a ski. We fixed the reins so that the man whose chariot stayed on the road could drive both teams while the other man's chariot was off the edge of the riprap. The man in the off-road chariot had dummy reins to hang onto. Along the side of the riprap was a large pine tree with a limb that projected out far enough to hit the man in the near chariot. This limb was cut nearly in two so it would break easily.

Jack Williams was doubling Christopher Plummer and my eldest son Tap was doubling Boyd. They did a walk-through so I could see how it was going to work. It looked safe. I told the doubles that Jack should crowd Tap's team close to the edge as they came around a turn on the road fighting and hitting each other with their whips. This would put the far wheel off the wall. The road had been made foolproof right to the edge of the riprap. In stunts like these everything must be right or someone gets hurt. Both boys were happy with it and it had my O.K.

We got the doubles out of sight and set up one camera for a set shot and the other for a pan. I gave the cue for cameras and action, the drivers came around the turn fighting and Jack crowded Tap's team to the edge of the road. Tap's wheel went off the road, skimming and bouncing along. As they passed the pine tree the limb hit Tap and he fell to the floor of the chariot. He made it look good. They raced on, Tap's chariot wheel came back up on the road and the fight continued.

I cut the scene and moved to a spot that I couldn't resist when I saw it. Well up the mountainside, where the road came around a ridge and into a canyon, there was a big drain pipe and a curved riprap wall about thirty feet high. Below it the rocky canyon sloped off very steeply for a couple of hundred yards. I planned that on the curve Jack's chariot would have a wheel off the wall for a hundred and fifty feet or so, tearing the protective railing completely out. I also had special effects put balsa wood railings on the riprap wall along the road. These railings were about three and a half feet high and extended well over a hundred feet. On action the drivers were to put their horses in a run and continue fighting.

The chariots took off and when they got within a few yards of the railing, Tap reached out and threw Jack's cape over his head, blinding him for the moment. Then he crowded Jack's chariot off the road and through the protective railings, which started flying in all directions. Right in the middle of the riprap, Jack got the cape off his head and as he looked down and then ahead, I'll never forget the way his eyes really opened wide. As he said afterwards, it was pretty damn scary. It was a beautiful scene and looked dangerous. However, I had it as near foolproof as you could make it.

Our next setup was a rigged spot where we were to turn the horses off the road and down the hill through timber country. I had special effects put up a fairly tall tree and cut through most of it. We then fastened a chain from one chariot's hitch bar to the other. As the teams turned off the road and went on either side of the tree, the chain snapped the cut tree. It fell back between the chariots which sped on wildly before coming onto the lower road around the top of a bluff, by a beautiful waterfall. The road had protective rails along the deep gorge below the falls.

I had the crew build a one-wheel ramp that would flip Tap's chariot into and through the road railing. The men would then go out of the scene fighting. When all was set we rolled the cameras and the two teams came around the road above the bluff. When they were within a couple of feet of the ramp, Tap jumped. As he landed in Jack's chariot, his own hit the ramp and flipped over, knocking railings down and tumbling into the river below. Still fighting, the two whirled off the road in Jack's chariot and down through a steep, timbered mountainside. As they got to the bottom the team leaped over a downed log, which broke the chariot loose and turned it in an upside down roll. Tap and Jack dragged behind the team for a few feet, then got up and continued their fight.

After two or three ambush fights we went to work setting up the big battle. I had picked a sandy piece of ground about two hundred and fifty feet wide, walled on either side with big rocks. I then had the man who handled the bulldozer bring in several huge boulders and space them far enough apart so war chariots could go between them. The front row of spearmen and swordsmen could use the rocks as cover if there was a war chariot charge. Thirty feet or so behind the first line of soldiers were a double line of bowmen. The front bowmen were on their knees and the second row standing, all set and ready to rain arrows on the enemy. I had a couple of shallow pits dug between the rocks for horse falls.

On the call of "action" a trumpet sounds beyond the ridge. Over the rise comes the charge, led by war chariots. When they get close enough to throw their spears, arrows rain on them by the hundreds. A few horses fall and many men are hit with arrows and spears shot from spear guns. A chariot or two gets through the first line, but others pile up in gaps between the big boulders. It looked really scary.

In doing scenes of this kind we always had a first-aid crew and an ambulance standing by. The first-aid unit rushed in as soon as we cut the cameras. After a thorough check, the head of the first-aid crew came to me and congratulated me on the way the battle had worked. No one was so much as scratched. After the major clash you are home free. From then on the scene is staged in close, spectacular cuts.

After finishing this fight I had another section of the battle to do. In a narrow, rocked-in ravine, with good ground to work on, a large group was to attack a smaller body defending the ravine. I had the workmen bring loads of dry grass and brush and stack it in a long row across the battleground. The defenders had bowmen stationed on high rocks on either side behind the wall of brush. Bowmen and swordsmen were ready. The cameras rolled and the brush was lit. The enemy charged, but was halted by the fire. However, they took a toll of defenders on the high rocks. I got some nice high falls with my stunt men.

After a given amount of time the fire burns low in one spot and the enemy rides through. We went into close shots of falls and bulldogging men from their horses. Some of the men on the rocks leaped down onto the riders, knocking them from their horses. I then did scenes of the enemy starting to break off the fight and fall back. This soon became a rout and the enemy was soon in full retreat.

In this picture we did just about everything in the book and I am happy to say that no one was badly hurt. Naturally there were a few band-aid and iodine jobs.

At the finish of the picture I received a warm thank you from Tony and the producer, Mr. Bronston.

After *Ben Hur*, *Spartacus*, *El Cid*, and *The Fall of the Roman Empire* my next job was a real change of pace. It was the very humorous *Cat Ballou*, featuring Jane Fonda and Lee Marvin. As soon as it was over, I found myself back in the world of epic battles and blood-and-thunder. *Khartoum* took me to Egypt, to work as second unit director on this story of "Chinese" Gordon.

Charles Gordon, who had earned his nickname for his service in China, was the great British general sent by his government to the Egyptian Sudan in 1884 to help the Egyptians put down an uprising under the religious zealot Mahdi, a self-proclaimed Moslem prophet.

Although Gordon had proven himself to be a skilled and fearless warrior, he had insufficient forces to hold out against the hordes of dervishes, the Mahdi's fanatical Moslem followers, and he was killed by a spear in the battle for Khartoum on January 26, 1885.

Robert Ardrey, a noted screen writer, made the epic story of Khartoum into a screenplay for United Artists. Julian Blaustein was to produce and Basil Deardon, a splendid English film maker, was to direct. The cast was headed by Charlton Heston as General Gordon, Richard Johnson as Colonel Stewart, and Laurence Olivier as the fanatical Mahdi.

Before he left for Europe to line up a crew and scout locations in Egypt, Mr. Blaustein had talked to me about working on the film as second unit director. He was in England when the United Artists production head called and asked me to leave immediately for London. I signed a contract and was soon flying over the North Pole.

Mr. Blaustein was headquartered at the Pinewood Studios. On my arrival, I was given an office and told to beef up the action in the script, make a list of the equipment I would need, and pick a group of stunt men.

I was busy working out details of the action sequences when I was summoned to Basil Dearden's office. He was pacing nervously back and forth when I walked in.

"Yak, I'm really in a bind," he said soberly. "In fact, I haven't slept for a couple of nights worrying about Laurence Olivier. We're paying him big money and his deal calls for all of his scenes to be done in England. I don't know how we can tie him into the picture but I thought that you, being a second unit director, shoot a lot with doubles and put the principals in the scenes at the studio. Can you do this with Olivier?"

I told him not to worry about it. I would break down all of Olivier's scenes into shooting form for process plates and trick angles. Dearden thanked me and I went back to my office and started to work. A couple of days later, I gave the new pages to him. After reading them, he said that he now saw how the Olivier problem could be handled and thanked me again for helping him out of a tough spot. Dearden had only made a few small pictures at that time, but he did a marvelous job on *Khartoum*.

We made a trip to Cairo and looked the locations over. I checked out a place on the Nile where we could build a camp and set up a training school for men, falling horses, and the camel corps. Dearden had a large construction crew nearby duplicating the city of Khartoum as it looked in 1880.

When we returned to London I had my two sons, Tap and Joe, fly over. They, along with the English group, went back with me to Cairo to get the training started.

A man by the name of Ala Gabry was hired to work with my unit. He was very influential and could really get things done. He owned several trading posts and one of his nephews told me, "Nasser has the government, but Uncle has all the money!"

Anything we needed, Gabry got—horses, camels, and cattle. We used a number of mounted police and their horses, as well as the Egyptian army—as many as eight thousand men at one time. I asked him to get me a group of good riders who could work closely with our stunt men. When he got them together, I watched them workout and was quite impressed with their riding ability, but one fellow looked too old for our action scenes.

"Gabry," I said, "that skinny fellow is pretty old to ride in our battle scenes, isn't he?"

Gabry led a horse out, turned him sideways, and told the old fellow to mount up. The man ran and leaped on the horse with a beautiful scissors mount, picked up the reins, and spun the horse around taking off in a run. Some distance away, he turned, ran straight back at me, then slid the horse to a stop and dismounted while in motion. This Arab was well into his seventies but he handled himself like a young man. He stayed on the job, working all through the picture.

By the time the main company arrived, I had plenty of good falling horses and a troop of number one stunt men.

My first assignment was the filming of Colonel Hicks and his ten thousand untrained Egyptian troops being followed and harassed by large groups of Moslem warriors led by the Mahdi, the fanatical religious leader. In the sun-scorched wastes of the Sudan, I shot scenes of Hicks and his troops as they traversed narrow roadways through hills, rocks, and burning desert sands. In these scenes, we shot close-ups of horses and heavy-loaded pack camels who stumbled and fell and then were left behind.

When I first mentioned the camel falls, all the owners objected. I finally made a deal with one for twenty-five dollars. If the camel was hurt in the fall, we'd buy the camel. I had the wranglers roll up a couple of mattresses which were then tied to either side of the animal to look like a normal pack. I put a hobble on all four feet and fastened the end of a small, flexible cable to one of the rings on the hind leg. The cable was then threaded through the front hobble rings, back through the two hobbles on the hind legs, then pulled up and taped to a heavy, stout strap under the camel's belly. With a rope tied to the far end of the cable, three or four men could follow behind the photographic field, and on cue, pull the slack out of the cable. As it tightened, the camel stumbled a few feet, then his four feet were pulled together, and he fell to his side on the mattress pack. When the owners saw how well it worked, they all wanted me to use their camels. However, I only did three camel falls in the picture.

For the final battle and destruction of Hicks and his men, I selected a beautiful location of colored earth and reddish rock formations in a series of huge stone quarries that had been dug in the days of the Pharaohs. The floor of one quarry was ten or fifteen acres in size and sand hills and rocks separated it from a far-reaching desert of hot sun and sand. The other side was a sheer rock wall and crags. I used three cameras on the scenes of Hicks and his officers leading the bedraggled army through a rocky opening only to face burning sands as far as the eye could see. The army comes to a stop, worn and exhausted. Hicks decides to turn back and gives the order to retreat, but regrouping so many tired men throws them into confusion. Then the Mahdi and his followers swarm in by the thousands from all sides. From the high cliffs of the quarry, they rain spears and arrows down on the trapped army. The spears and arrows were made of balsa wood, an almost weightless material, and could hit a man or animal without injury.

I had instructed all of the fighting units to stand still when I yelled "cut" over the loud speaker system, to allow the crew to pick up the spears and arrows. If the animals should happen to step on them they would break. We had a limited supply and we had to use them again.

Following the battle scene the crew finished picking up the balsa wood weapons and one of the men showed me two spears that he had found which had razor sharp metal blades. How they missed hitting a man or an animal I'll never know, and how they got into the battle is still a mystery.

From the desert side of the quarry, I filmed scenes of other Mahdi hordes charging into the rocky opening to cut off Hicks' retreat. In this battle I really made use of our trained falling horses. There were plenty of good sandy spots, and both men and horses had soft places to fall.

The outcome of this battle, which I shot according to historical research, saw the army of Colonel Hicks cut to pieces and virtually destroyed. The Colonel, highly trained in military strategy, was out maneuvered at every turn by the un-military Mahdi. This sequence, when edited, was very spectacular.

The next battle that I filmed was between General Wolsley's crack camel corps and another contingent of the Mahdi's followers. England's Prime Minister, Gladstone, has finally and reluctantly ordered him to cross the desert to the village of Metema, take his men and camels on steamers to Khartoum, and rescue Gordon. In the desert crossing they are attacked by the Mahdi's fanatical troops.

This was a picturesque engagement and fiercely fought. I had Wolsley's front line troops lay their camels down, shielding themselves behind the animals and firing over them. Among the Mahdi's men were some of my top stunt men, experts in riding, jumping and falling horses. In the charge some of them jumped their mounts over the camels, battling the soldiers with swords. Other horsemen jumped over the camels cueing their horses for a fall as they hit the ground. For yet another stunt I put the camera in a pit, shooting out and up. We rigged a camel for a fall—mattress pads and all—with the fight going on in the foreground. The rider on the rigged camel turned him broadside to the camera as they neared the pit and the animal's feet were pulled together. Down he went right in front of the lens. It was a beautiful scene.

The battle ended with the defeat of the Mahdi's disciples, but precious time had been lost by Wolsley and his camel corps. Reaching the river, they began the race to Khartoum to save Gordon.

In Khartoum, Gordon is informed that the telegraph wires to Cairo have been cut and five thousand people have been massacred at Berber, a village down the river. Knowing a siege was inevitable and that the city was doomed if help did not arrive, Gordon leads a detachment of troops to the countryside to gather up cattle, grain, and other supplies. On the way back they are ambushed by the Mahdi's dervishes.

This was to be a hand-to-hand fight, so I picked a location where Gordon and his troopers could dismount, conceal themselves behind large rocks, and let the attackers ride through. These scenes were shot just before sun-up, and I had the camera set so that when the dervishes regrouped and charged back to the rocks the sun would be up and directly in their eyes.

Charlton Heston, who was playing General Gordon, was instructed to ride in behind a big rock, where his stunt double (my son Joe) would take over and in a longer shot lay the horse down. We would then cut in a close-up of Heston as the foe rode through.

"Yak," he said, "why don't you let me lay the horse down in a close shot so an audience will know it's no double."

"That's a little risky, Chuck," I replied. "You could get hurt."

"I don't think so," Heston said, "seeing as how Joe took me out yesterday and taught me how to do it."

I looked sternly over at Joe, who grinned and walked away. I turned to Heston with a shrug of agreement.

"Okay, Chuck," I said, "I'll bet on you. I have nothing but my job to lose."

I had the cameras moved in closer to the big rock, and on "action" Heston rode his horse in close to the rock and ordered his troops to get down out of sight. He then laid his horse down and held him as the Mahdi hordes rode through. Then, as the horse started to get up, he stepped astride him, reined the animal around and ordered his men to form a battle line and be ready to fire at my order.

I then set up for a long shot, shooting one camera over the Gordon men in the foreground and the reassembling enemy. Now the sun was up over the horizon and shining directly in the dervishes' eyes as they charged in a double line. The spot that I picked for the fight was really made to order for horse falls. The sand was deep, so I put in a few shallow pits and used all of our falling horses. This line was marked and in the charge when the Mahdi's men were really close, Chuck, as Gordon, gave the order to fire. At least twenty horses went down and many men fell from their horses. With three cameras on the scene, it gave me a lot of good footage. Gordon, with his small number of troops in comparison to the Mahdi's hundreds, puts up a terrific fight but it looks as though he and his men are doomed. As in all motion pictures though, the day is saved. Stewart, with his Egyptian cavalry, comes to Gordon's aid. I might add that in this picture there were no injuries to a single horse in our work. However, two of the mounted police, during the lunch hour, were playing the game "Chicken." They rode at a full run toward each other and neither one would turn his horse. A head-on collision occurred that crippled two good horses. I stopped that game, but quick, and fired the men responsible.

After we finished the Gordon battle in the mountains, we went to work lining up for the climax of the picture, the siege of Khartoum. The high city walls were built like a fort, the gates of the wall were very strong, and a moat had been dug by hand fifty or sixty feet out from the building. The sand from the moat was carried out in buckets by hundreds of natives. (Believe it or not, that is the way the Suez Canal was constructed.) When the moat was finished, the crew built a good, strong bridge across it at the fortress gate. Several hundred yards from the moat there was a sloping, sandy ridge. I shot scenes of handmade bombs being planted all over the near end of the slope and fuses were buried that ran to the city wall, where they could be set off in rotation.

When the Mahdi's hordes of cavalry and foot soldiers poured across the skyline ridge by the thousands, they pulled a cannon over the near end of the ridge and set it up to batter down the wall gate. When the horsemen hit the mine field, and the explosions started going off, I made good use of the falling horses and men. The effect looked as though the explosions were knocking them down.

I had three cameras working and after a couple of master shots, I moved the cameras in for close shots of the men and horses being knocked to the ground. In one scene, several stunt men charge through the mine field, led by Tap and Joe, who were to fall their horses in the close foreground. When I called "action" someone jumped the gun and Tap's horse whirled around. By the time he got the animal straightened out, he was almost over a mine, which went off. These explosions look dangerous but are actually harmless. His horse took the fall and threw Tap fifteen or twenty feet through the air to the ground. He landed hard, and if it hadn't been for the deep sand, he would have been badly hurt. He was lucky and only had the breath knocked out of him.

In another scene Joe and one of the English stunt men, Joe Powell, were making a couple of horse falls in the mine field. Joe was practically on top of a mine when special effects jumped the gun, setting it off too soon. Joe threw his horse but his eyes were so filled with sand he couldn't see. The first-aid crew washed them out but they were bloodshot and sore for several days.

I did close shots of the gun crew loading and firing the cannon that was set up to batter the gate down. I made cut-in shots of cannon balls hitting the gate and block houses. Then I did a shot of the gun blowing up along with its crew.

The fight progressed over the moat and to the walls of the city. The Mahdi fanatics were prepared to take Khartoum or die. They had brought in tall ladders to scale the wall, but the defending soldiers had forked poles, and as the invaders climbed up the ladders, they were pushed over backwards, apparently to the death of many of them. I had several cameras covering the action as the invaders concentrated on the huge gate, finally getting a huge bomb placed under the bottom, blowing it up. The triumphant Mahdi forces pour into the city and Gordon is killed.

When *Khartoum* was edited, there was no way anyone could tell that Lawrence Olivier, as the Mahdi, had never set foot on location in Egypt where his character played such a prominent part in the action shots.

In the early fall of 1967 I signed a contract to do the action on a spectacular modern-day picture that presented new challenges. I would be filming in the Bavarian Alps, working with parachutists instead of horses, and shooting some big fight scenes and other stunts on a moving Alpine cable car—quite different from my previous experience with freight trains, stagecoaches and chariots.

The picture was *Where Eagles Dare*, an Elliott Kastner-Jerry Gershwin production of a World War II spy adventure. The cast of over twenty-five was headed by Richard Burton, Clint Eastwood and Mary Ure.

My first stop was London, where I hired a group of key stunt men—Joe Powell, Eddie Powell (who doubled Eastwood), Peter Brace, Jimmy Thong, Jackie Cooper, Doug Robison and Terry York—all men I had worked with many times and considered tops. There was also Alf Joint, one of the world's great high fallers, and Gillian Aldam, the British stunt woman who would double Mary Ure.

We went on to the Alps, where our first assignment was to shoot scenes of an Allied team parachuting behind the enemy lines during the war. The objective was an impregnable Nazi fortress—a castle high in the mountains. We had found a picturesque cabin in a beautiful clearing above and near the village of Ebensee, where a cable car was the only route to the castle we were using. We had brought a team of parachutists from France to double our group making the jumps into the clearing. Special effects had organized everything to come to the rescue in case something went wrong.

My first setup was at the end of the clearing so that we could cover the group and later make individual shots of some of the jumpers. We got the cameras rolling, and the plane came across, high over the far end of the clearing. At our signal the men started jumping. It was beautiful the way they worked, but suddenly a sharp wind hit. Some of them made landings on their spots but a couple were carried over us and one fellow's chute hung in the limbs of a tall pine tree. He really looked pathetic dangling fifty feet above ground, and he couldn't get hold of a limb or the main trunk.

Special effects had a man with climbing gear on the way up the tree in a hurry. When he got even with the jumper he belted himself to the tree trunk and tied a pulley to the tree, ran a rope through it and tossed it to the jumper who grabbed it and tied it to himself. Then the special effects man pulled him in to the tree trunk, loosened him from the chute and lowered him to the ground. Special effects did a beautiful job, and *fast*!

When the jumper got to the ground he was laughing. To him it was all in a day's work.

I got several good jumps, and then we moved the camera to pick up one of the jumpers as he bailed out, planning to land as close to the cabin as possible. As he neared the ground he pulled the ring to throw his chute out but it failed to open. He worked desperately for a moment but gave up and threw his emergency chute out. It tangled with the unopened chute.

I watched him as he worked to get the chute untangled and I found myself holding my breath. At the last second or two, the chute partially opened and he just barely missed the cabin and lit in a snow bank. We ran to him but he was up and laughing as he gathered his tangled chute.

I had one shot that I figured would make a nice scene, but it ended up scaring the hell out of us. We put the camera in a helicopter, and rigged Joe Powell, the stunt man, to hang underneath it from chute cords. The camera would shoot straight down, as though it were under the chute, showing the cords and the jumper swinging below. This would have been a good effect shot but as the copter left the ground, the wind started really blowing, Joe started spinning, and the helicopter with our camera crew started spinning and wobbling and came close to hanging the stunt man in a tree. The pilot finally landed, and Joe was about the only one who didn't seem bothered. Anyway, I scrapped the scene. During the other landings we had three incidents that could have been disasters. I was happy to finish the sequence.

I next shot scenes with Richard Burton and Clint Eastwood's doubles climbing on top of the cable car to get to the castle. I had special effects fix a couple of good handholds on either side of the pulley housing. When the men heard the car start, they squatted low, grabbed a good hold on the housing, and in turn came down to the top of the cable car where they lay flat.

The following scenes on the ice-covered roof of the car and in the castle were done at the studio in London by Brian Hutton, and I might add, he did a beautiful job on them.

I did a three-man fight on top of the moving cable car. For my best angles I had thought of using a helicopter traveling alongside the car, but with wind currents as they were, the copter pilot wanted no part of the deal. On top of that, the cable car company would not allow planes or helicopters near the cables. Special effects had built a duplicate car to be blown up later. I had them put a platform on top of the duplicate car that projected approximately fifteen feet or more on either side. With the camera set up and secured on the platform, the same amount of weight was put on the opposite side to balance it. Tying this car to the regular car, we got some good three-quarter angles on the fight. Fine, flexible airplane cable concealed the safety belts on the stunt men. One of them was to slip and fall off, hanging with one hand, and fight his way back. Another man slipped over the side and we doubled him with a dummy that fell to the canyon floor. Finally the last two men got back into the car.

I also had one of the camera operators straddle the trolley housing and, with a wide-angle lens on his camera, shoot straight down to the snow-covered ground twelve hundred feet below. With the wind blowing and the cars bouncing and swinging, the scenes were thrilling. I was certainly very proud of my camera crew and stunt men.

We shot three more good action scenes in the Alps. One was where Burton's double blows up the cable car. Just before the blast the four principals' doubles make a seventy-foot jump to the icy water below.

For the second, I had the crew dam a beautiful mountain stream that ran directly under the cables, making a pool about ten or twelve feet deep. The leads, in a school bus, are fighting a running battle with the pursuing Germans. The fight ends on a bridge we built over the pool. We ran a jeep on grooved tracks over the bridge, manned by three mechanical dummies firing machine guns. When the jeep reached the middle, we blew up the bridge. It exploded in a fiery inferno, bringing the pursuing Germans to a complete stop.

At the airport, I filmed one of the most exciting sequences

in the picture. The leads, doubled by stunt men, are in the school bus coming into the airport, followed by a German jeep. The stunt man driving the bus suddenly turns the wheel and tears through a high fence around the airfield. A guard fires at it as another man runs for the phone. The bus races by the hangars. Two German jeeps fall in behind it.

I had the special effects crew put a small cable on one of the jeeps so that it could be towed and guided by the effects man from an out-of-scene truck. Dummy soldiers and a machine gun were set to fire just before the cable was tripped loose. A shock cord spun the steering wheel, cramping the front wheels into a sharp turn as the cable flipped the jeep into a roll. It exploded in flames.

I was really pleased to be able to work on *Where Eagles Dare.* I'd done a lot of big battles and scenes of that kind, and of course a lot of animal and Western action, but that picture was a chance to try my hand at aerial shots. It was a picture that was all action and thrills, and not only for the audiences that saw the finished film.

ELEVEN

The New "Old West"

Although my work on *Where Eagles Dare* and the big costume spectaculars had me shuttling back and forth over the ocean during most of the 1950s and 1960s, I was still able to keep my hand in the kind of pictures that had made my reputation as a stunt man and action director—the Westerns. One of my most enjoyable films was the hilarious *Cat Ballou*, with Jane Fonda and Lee Marvin—the picture that won Lee an Academy Award for his comic performance as a washed-up, drunken gunfighter who in his early days had been "the fastest gun in the West."

I was assigned by Columbia Pictures to direct the second unit. One sequence that still makes me laugh was when I had to stage a scene that had Kid Shelleen (Marvin) trying to prove to Jane Fonda, as Cat, that he was still as fast and accurate with a gun as an article in an old Western magazine had claimed. Having read the magazine story, Cat had sent for the Kid to help her fight Sir Harry Strawn and his henchman, who were trying to take over her ranch.

The Kid could shoot with some accuracy, but only when he was loaded. In the scene that I set up, the Kid was to shoot bottles and cans as they were thrown into the air. This was done in cuts, first showing the Kid firing drunkenly toward the off-scene objects. I had hired an expert marksman to hit the sailing cans and bottles.

The marksman, however, proved to be not much more of a

sharpshooter than Kid Shelleen. He kept missing the cans and bottles and I finally took the shotgun from him and managed to make several good hits. I had done a lot of hunting and shooting in my time, so it wasn't much of a challenge. When this sequence was cut and put together with close shots of the tipsy Kid Shelleen firing from all directions and all positions, it was really funny.

As the filming continued under the smooth direction of Elliot Silverstein, I had the wranglers train Lee Marvin's old horse to stand with his front legs crossed for the now famous scene where Marvin, in a drunken stupor, is seated on the animal, who leans cross-legged against the side of a store building. The gunfire from the town, and the sound of a hearse in which the leads are escaping, arouses both the Kid and the old horse. Pulling his gun, the Kid charges into the street, firing in all directions. He nearly collides with the speeding hearse, but manages to stay in the saddle and continue on.

For this gun battle I had special effects arrange a lot of breakaway signs, banners, and other objects, which fell to the street as Shelleen kept firing, scaring a team hitched to a brewery wagon. I had a ramp constructed at the edge of the sidewalk and the front wheel of the runaway wagon hit it. The team came loose and the wagon turned over, throwing beer barrels all over the street. The special-effects crew had rigged the barrels so that when they hit the ground, the bungs popped out, shooting geysers of beer into the air.

I filmed the comedy chase between the heavies and the leads after Cat Ballou was saved from hanging in one day. I had several discussions with the cameraman and production heads as to the camera speeds. I finally shot tests using three different speeds and found the speed that I had originally insisted on (16 frames per second) was the one that was eventually used when the sequence was cut.

Basically *Cat Ballou* was filmed with very few problems and the results, as everyone knows now, were the best.

Blue, a Paramount picture starring Terence Stamp and Joanne Pette, was a story about the Mexican border during bandit days. It was shot in Moab, Utah, on the Colorado River. The most important action scene was to be a river crossing.

After meeting the director, Silvio Narizzano, and studying the script, I found an ideal spot where the Colorado was deep enough for the horses to wade. I had the crossing site bulldozed so that the horses could get across the river fast and into a trap that the leads were to spring on a group of Mexican bandits.

While I was supervising the preparation, a driver from the first unit drove up and told me the first unit director, Narizzano, had gone to the hospital in Moab to see a close friend who had been badly hurt in a head-on car collision. He wanted me to take over his unit. I gave my crew a fast rundown on what I wanted done with the trap preparations, then went to the first unit location. I finished shooting the day's work in four hours.

The next morning I was having breakfast when the director came in very much annoyed. "They tell me that you finished the sequence," he said, sourly.

I shrugged noncommitally. "Yes, we finished it."

"What are you trying to do," Narizzano growled, "make me look bad?"

"Silvio," I said placatingly, "you had everything worked out. All I had to do was holler "action" and "cut." He grinned, and had his breakfast.

I went back to my trap location, which was coming along in good shape. The embankment had been cleaned up. There was plenty of sand on it and it was dressed with bushes to look old and used. We had good places on either side of the trap to hide the villagers who were to attack the bandits, and a flexible group could come in on call to the top of the now sandy bank. A huge boulder, six or eight feet high, sat on top and to the side, in a good place for the lookout.

The following morning I was to start the battle. I had the camera crew set their cameras on the far side of the river and shoot scenes of the Mexicans, led by Ricardo Montalban, as they come around a ridge and follow a winding dirt road to the place which we had set up for the crossing. Montalban sends one of his men across the river to be sure there is no trap. The bandit crosses the river and rides through the trap. On the top of the high bank, he waves back that all is clear and the leader brings his men into the river. The Mexican who crosses to make a check sits his horse peering about. Suddenly Terence Stamp steps out from behind the rock. As the bandit pulls his gun, Stamp fires, the horse rears and goes over backwards, rolling over the bandit and on down to the level ground. Bandits then charge to the shore line and the settlers start firing.

Some of the bandits are knocked from their horses with gun barrels and finally the bandits retreat back across the river. I staged some spectacular horse falls, many of them in the river.

I did a great many pickup scenes and was within a day of finishing my action when some of the brass from Paramount came to the location to find out how much longer it would take for the first unit to finish. Narizzano told them it would take him three weeks. The brass said that he would have to finish in one week. He said that he couldn't do it. They then came to me and asked how close I was to wrapping things up. I said that I had only a short day left. They then informed me that I was going to take the picture over and complete the shooting in a week.

I said, "Wait a minute, I belong to the same Guild your director does. I'll talk with him and give you my answer tonight."

That evening I talked with Silvio and told him what had happened. "I wish you would take over," he said wearily. "I can't shoot fast the way you do."

"Why don't we work it together?" I answered. "I'll set the scenes up and you handle the dialogue. We'll finish in a week and both get out clean."

He agreed, and we worked as a team and finished in a week. It got Silvio out of a bad situation into a good one. I had nothing to lose.

A Man Called Horse is, in my opinion, one of the most authentic Indian pictures ever filmed. We shot much of it in Durango, Mexico.

When I signed to be the second unit director and found out that the director was to be Elliott Silverstein, I knew that I was home free. We had worked together on Cat Ballou, and we got along great.

A Man Called Horse starred Richard Harris and Dame Judith Anderson, and a cast that included a number of American Indians. My first week on location was mainly spent looking for good spots and having bows and arrows, along with a couple of arrow-throwing mortars, made up.

The company had a great number of Sioux Indians brought in from Pine Ridge, South Dakota, and several of them were Indians I had known back in my rodeo days. When they brought the Indians out to the location and I was looking them over, one old Indian came over, peered at me, and broke into a broad grin.

"Yakima, long time no see you," he said, holding out his hand. The minute he grinned and started talking, I knew him. It was Richard Fool's Bull, who had been a pretty good friend of mine. He was an ex-rodeo man and a fair bronc rider, with one bad habit—he loved to fight.

"Richard Fool's Bull," I answered as we shook hands. "You look good. Do you still ride bucking horses?"

He shrugged good humoredly. "Ugh—some time ride 'em, some time buck off."

I said that we would talk later, and went about picking out the Indians I would need for close work.

We had only worked a couple of days when my assistant came in the restaurant while I was having breakfast and told me, "Your friend, Fool's Bull, is in jail."

"Was he in a fight?"

"Yes—with a couple of policemen."

"Get him out as cheap as you can," I said, giving him a hundred dollars, "but get him out."

Fifty dollars got him out of jail. I saw the first-aid crew putting a couple of stitches on his cheek and walked over to make sure he was O.K. As the first-aid man finished tying a stitch Richard looked at me and with a grin, doubled up his fist and shook it menacingly. "I got him pretty good," he grinned.

"Now, Richard," I said sternly, "no more fighting while you are on the picture."

"O.K." he said, "anything you say."

I had to admire him. He must have been around seventy years old but was as active as a man of forty. He finished the picture without any more fights.

In the picture Richard Harris plays an English gentleman who is captured by Indians and decides that he wants to live as one of them.

For a fight scene between tribes I filmed close shots of stunt men, made up as Indians, doing some great horse falls, and showed other Indians being knocked off their horses with war clubs. I had one shot set up close to a teepee. As Indians ran inside they went on through an opening in the rear and into a place of safety. Then I had my prop men put a few Indian dummies on the floor of the teepee. The stampeding horses ran into the teepee and tore it down. When the herd got through, the dummies made it look real.

I made a master shot of the village with loose horses running every which way, and Indians on horseback and on foot fighting for their lives. Then I started shooting close shots of their struggle. One shot was with my elder son, Tap, dressed as an Indian with a camouflaged pull-off vest. A small airplane cable was tied to a ring in its back, and the other end of the cable was fastened to a ratchet shock machine tied to a tree about twenty-five feet above ground. At the end of the cable, where Tap is to be knocked from his horse, I had special effects set up a teepee and use breakaway poles on the side he was to hit. Inside the teepee we put a couple of falling pads and another stunt man with a balsa wood war club took his position in front of the tent, leaving room for Tap's horse to go between him and the teepee. Tap was to ride through at an angle that would pull him off and send him crashing into the tent. When the camera rolled, I gave Tap "action" and he rode in, firing his bow. The stunt man swung his war club. As it slammed across Tap's chest, the wire snapped him off his horse and hurtled him through the tent onto the unseen pads. Scenes like this are vicious looking, but if done right, they are "easy money."

I had one location that was at the outer edge of the village in a sandy wash with a sandy embankment. I had several stunt men made up as Indians, with four of them on trained falling horses. I worked out a good routine where some of the men are leaped on and knocked from their mounts; a couple of them were to throw their horses. One Indian on top of the embankment in the foreground was to be bulldogged by another stunt man and the horse was to fall, throwing both men ahead and down the bank as the horse falls and rolls over, just missing them. It was a scary scene but everything worked well. I made several very good scenes that we cut into the picture very effectively.

I also did a couple of fight sequences with Richard Harris, and I was really amazed and pleased at the way he worked.

A sequence where Harris undergoes a tough Indian ritual was really realistic. I worked with the first director on it, helping to plan the action. I had the makeup department make a belt to go around Harris's chest—ten feet away you couldn't tell it from his real skin. In the ritual they shoved sharpened horn spikes through each breast and tied them to a line braided of skins. He is pulled up six or seven feet off the ground and spun like a top for some time. The first time up he spun for a short time and then the rope broke. He got a bad fall, but went right back up and finished the scene in good form. He seemed to be fearless, was a congenial man to work with, and very professional.

Rio Lobo was another picture shot in Mexico—a John Wayne movie directed by Howard Hawks, who had many fine films to his credit. Hawks was a director who appreciated the help of a good second unit man, and I thoroughly enjoyed working with him on this Wayne show.

A big part of the picture was made in Cuernavaca, about forty miles southwest of Mexico City. The one spectacular stunt in the picture, laid in Civil War days, was the high-jacking of a train carrying a shipment of gold from the North. In the story, it is a very elaborate plan, well worked out by the Confederates.

The railway leaves the valley and ascends a somewhat steep grade for several miles up a timbered mountain. I filmed a group of Rebel troopers plastering the rails with heavy axle grease. A few miles down the grade I showed a second Rebel group pulling into a timbered section alongside the railway. Their wagons and horses were hidden among the trees and they had several coils of heavy hawser rope cut long enough to stretch well across the railway clearing. The ropes were tied to several large trees on the high side of the road. Keeping out of sight, the troopers wait for the train to show up. After the train has pulled through, headed up the grade, they drag the heavy hawser ropes across the railway and tie them to other large trees on the other side.

When the group at the top of the grade hears the train coming, they get close to the track and stay low. As the engine hits the greased rails, it comes to a spinning stop, and before the crew realizes what has happened, the engineer has been killed. Knowing that the gold would be in the caboose, the Rebels cut the freight car and caboose loose and climb onto the open freight car, which was partly loaded with equipment. As the two cars gain speed, a couple of Rebs, each carrying a hornet's nest, climb to the top of the caboose, shove one of the lookout windows open and throw the hornet's nests in. The nests fall apart as they hit the floor and the hornets really go to work on the men inside, stinging everyone they can get to.

We found a nice sandy embankment where we could get some good jumps of the Yanks leaving the car. I had a two-camera setup to catch the stunt men in action. Terry Leonard was to make his jump from the top platform railing. Tap

Canutt and a couple of other stunt men were to jump from the steps, and a couple out the side door.

I had special effects trim an old, dead tree snag that was ten or twelve feet high and then cut it so that when Joe Canutt hit the tree it would break up. When all the stunt men had their spots marked and set, the cars were taken back up the grade far enough to get up speed. I also had an out-of-sight man handling the brake to assure the men of the correct speed. When all was set the cars were turned loose. Just before they came around a turn in the background, the cameras rolled and as the men got to their spots they leaped. Terry Leonard made a beautiful long leap to the ground and went into a fast roll. Tap Canutt also made a beautiful leap and roll. Joe jumped and hit the old tree but it didn't break. He glanced off and did a fast roll. As he hit the ground we cut the scene. He was jarred up a bit but nothing to worry about, and Terry Leonard had a lame knee for a couple of days.

We then shot the two runaway cars as they gained speed, both with the cameras on the cars and a couple of good set shots.

Then I moved my crew to the trap. We only used two hawser ropes on the first take. As the runaway cars came into the trap they hit the first rope. (We had cut the tree so it would fall toward the car.) I then had special effects set the tree on a stout platform low on the back right-hand corner of the caboose, and tie it off with a trip so it would fall cater-cornered the full length of the car. As we ran the car at good speed, the tree was tripped and fell on the open car. The high-jackers dove under some heavy boxes of equipment to safety.

We cut the scene and rerigged the master shot, putting the heavy hawser ropes from tree to tree across the railway. These ropes were set up to stop the runaway caboose and freight car.

The following day Mr. Hawks, the first unit director, brought his crew and actors to the train location, which gave us five cameras on the scene, with one on the railroad within fifty feet of the supposed stopping place. When all was ready, we got in touch with the driver and brakeman of the train by walkie-talkie. They were both out of sight in the caboose and some distance above the trap. At the first turn we had a flagman, who could see the runaway cars far enough up the track, signal and give us time to get all cameras turning before it came into sight. When the flagman gave us the signal, all cameras turned and the caboose and open freight car came round the bend really traveling and picking up more speed all the time. When it hit the ropes, it was really something to watch—trees falling in all directions and being dragged. But the brakeman used a bit too much brake and the cars came to a stop a hundred feet or so short. It was spectacular but I felt it could have been better had the driver not used his brakes so hard. The dragging trees did a lot to help stop the cars. Mr. Hawks and I talked it over and he seemed satisfied.

"With five cameras on it," he said, "the cutter should be able to make a good scene out of it. I'm sure it will be all right."

And it would have been all right, but I had the feeling that it could be improved. Mr. Hawks looked at me seeming to read my thoughts. "You figure it could be better?" he inquired.

"Yes, I really do," I said.

"O.K." he replied, "you can have three cameras and good luck."

I set the scene up again the next day, but added one thing to it. I had the crew dig all around a big tree, exposing the root system, and cut the big center root nearly through, just leaving enough of it to hold the tree up. Then all the dirt was shoveled loosely back in the hole around the roots and dressed to look as though it had never been touched. I put one camera near the tree so that we could pan with the oncoming cars and film how the cars actually pull the huge tree down and drag it away. When we had everything set, I told the driver where we were setting the number one camera on the track for a head-on shot, and told him not to worry, as we could pull it out quick if he overshot the mark. I added that I'd like to see the cars come as fast as possible and do a skidding stop close to the camera. He brought the cars around the turn and when they hit the ropes and came to a skidding stop, trees were really flying. It was a beautiful scene. When Mr. Hawks saw it he was well pleased and told John Wayne that I was right on that retake. The cars no sooner came to a stop than the Rebels removed the gold to their hidden wagon and moved out.

Wayne trails the wagon and a couple of Rebs set a trap for him. One reveals himself and as Wayne moved toward him, we cut and reset the camera with Wayne's double on the horse and Terry Leonard doubling one of the Rebs. As John's double faced the man who revealed himself, Leonard leaped onto John's double, knocking him off the horse into the river, which was a very nice shot. Wayne is captured, dressed as a Federal soldier and forced to lead the group, keeping them clear of any Union camp. At one point he rides around a tree with a heavy limb, pulls it back as far as possible, then releases it and it whips back, hitting one of the stunt men. The stunt man's horse made a beautiful fall and Wayne makes a getaway.

Mr. Hawks finished his work in Mexico and moved his crew into Arizona. I finished my last few scenes in Mexico and came home. Mr. Hawks was well pleased with my work, especially the runaway train sequence.

My agent, Harry Fredman, had made a deal for me to shoot the second unit on the United Artists picture, *Breakheart Pass*, being produced by Elliott Kastner and Jerry Gershwin. The story, written by Alistair MacLean, was to be directed by the late Tom Gries and the cast was headed by one of Hollywood's top stars, Charles Bronson. His beautiful wife, Jill Ireland, was the leading lady and among the other players were Ben Johnson, Charles Durning, Richard Crenna, Ed Lauter and Archie Moore.

The script was action packed and was to be filmed mostly aboard an old train from the 1880s. The train was carrying Federal prisoners through an isolated western wilderness to Fort Humbolt. There was an Indian attack on the train, and some of the cars were wrecked.

A location hunt took us to Utah, the Black Hills of South Dakota, and finally into the Lewiston, Idaho, area, where the company decided to shoot the exteriors. The railway ran alongside the beautiful Clearwater River and on into the lower regions of the Bitterroot Mountains. Other railway tracks ran across the Camas prairie, which was a part of the Nez Percé Indian Reservation.

The Nez Percé braves are wonderful horsemen and we made arrangements to use a good number of them in the picture. The train was brought in from Colorado and I was pleasantly surprised to find out that it was the same one I had used in *Cat Ballou*, with the same engineer.

My first sequence was a fight between Bronson and Archie Moore on top of the train. I had the special-effects man put safety rods on each side of the roof which ran the full length of the car. Ringed posts solidly bolted to the roof held them secure. I then plotted the fight with the doubles. Howard Curtis doubled Bronson and Tony Brubaker, a top black stunt man, doubled Archie. We worked out a couple of scenes where they fought into a clinch and rolled off the roof, each grabbing the safety bar and hanging on with one hand while they struggled and tried to kick each other loose. We worked out a lot of good gags and for the end of the fight, as the train is crossing a high trestle, they go into a clinch and Curtis spins around and throws Tony off the car into space. Curtis was to grab the safety rod and save himself.

We were getting close to our starting time and the company hadn't as yet given me a second unit crew. I began to feel that the director did not intend for me to shoot on my own, but was letting me set the action up for him. In other words, I would be a ramrod.

This was not a new situation. I had been through the same problem several times before. Most first unit directors welcome a good second unit man, but some resent having one on their pictures. I suppose that they feel it is a reflection on their own ability if they do not handle the action as well as the drama. Anthony Mann was a prime example. He hindered me in every way he could on the first picture I made with him, then asked for me on the next action film he directed. We still fought and I would threaten to walk off. He would grudgingly give in, but the resentment was still there. It was not until I had worked on several pictures with him (and he always asked for me) that he finally recognized my ability to stage action sequences and let me film things my own way without interference.

I realized that Tom Gries was another Tony Mann. He resented second unit directors and I was going to have difficulties with him. I decided to go along with the setup for a while and see what happened. After all, I had never worked with him before and I thought that we might get along better when we got to know each other.

We continued preparing and I asked the special-effects crew to attach reinforced four-by-fours to the ends of the car at floor level. They then fastened a falling net to strong poles attached securely to the four-by-fours and sticking out from the side of the train a good fifteen feet. This was the first action sequence and I planned to shoot it in a spot I had picked out where there would be no interference on the tracks and I could get a good long run with the train. The snow was deep and the net hung out only a foot or so above it. However, it was safe and had worked out well in rehearsal.

The evening before we were to start, the director told me we would shoot this fight sequence together, and do the fall into the net first. I agreed and the next morning we moved the company out to the location I had picked for the stunt. At my suggestion, we had brought a camera crane from Los Angeles and it was now put on a flatcar for shooting the fight and other shots on top of the train. With the crane, we could go up high while the train was moving and show the top of the train and the ground below.

We set up for the first shot, got the train in motion and the two stunt men did a short fight. After a few punches, they went into a clinch, wrestled into a good position for the fall, and Curtis knocked Brubaker off the car into the off-scene net. Curtis's spinning punch also sent him to the deck and over the side of the car but he caught the safety rod and flipped himself back onto the top. Brubaker did a beautiful fall, but had I been directing I would have changed angles and taken one second fall for safety. However, Gries was not satisfied and shot the same scene all afternoon.

After about the third shot, Brubaker looked at me with one of those "what the hell gives?" expressions, so I walked to him.

"Tony," I said quietly, "when I was doing stunts I loved to work for this kind of director. I did all the falls they wanted and kept track of the exact number."

Brubaker's eyes lit up and a slow grin crossed his face.

"Yeah," he replied understandingly, "when you do a stunt over and over, you get paid for all of them if they're good. Right?"

"Right," I nodded. "If *I* did a stunt and messed it up, I was the first to say, let's do it again, but if it was good, I charged for the next one."

Tony made a lot of money that day.

The next morning the director decided to do some rewriting on the story, and turned the fight over to me. I made one shot that was particularly interesting. Tony Brubaker threw a haymaker that flipped Curtis in a complete back somersault. Curtis came to his feet and ran straight at Tony. Leaping in the air, he kicked him in the midsection with both feet, knocking him over backwards. Then he dove onto him and they fought and rolled to the edge of the railroad car top. I hollered "cut" and we swung the crane over and up so that we would be shooting at an angle over a long trestle and could get the full benefit of the height. We overlapped the scene of the two men rolling to the edge of the moving car, the camera held them in a full shot and panned with them as they went over the side. Each got hold of the safety bar, fighting and kicking each other viciously, then finally clawed their way back onto the car top.

By mid-afternoon, I had the fight finished up to the point of making close shots with the principals, which the first unit director shot. An out-of-sight step was nailed to the side of the car so that they could stand on it. Each man had a strong belt under his shirt and a small, flexible airplane cable tied him off with enough slack so that he could put up a good fight. This was a very spectacular action sequence when edited.

Another week passed and I sat around and suggested certain gags to Gries. In my own mind, I was certain that he was preventing me from getting a full unit so that I couldn't work on my own. I finally had a talk with Jerry Gershwin, the producer on location, and told him the situation. If the director wasn't going to let me have a unit to shoot the action I had scheduled, I might as well pack and go home. Late that evening, I was in my room when I got a call from Gershwin to come down to the lobby. He and Tom Gries were together and Gries was mad.

"Did you tell Jerry I said you couldn't shoot?" he asked angrily as I walked up to them.

"No, I didn't," I replied evenly. "You're too damn smart for that. What I told him was that you keep saying we will shoot the action together, which means you will shoot the scenes and I'll be the ramrod or stand around like a dummy! I don't mind telling you I have had it. Either I get a unit to shoot the scenes as I was hired to do, or I leave. I've had enough of this nonsense!"

Jerry saw to it that I got a crew to work with and from then on, Gries and I got along much better. When he saw the rushes, he even complimented me on the train fight.

The first unit had filmed scenes in the engine cab in which one of the heavies had his clothes saturated with kerosene, stumbled past the open firebox, and out of the scene toward the door. I took over the filming and had special effects fasten a platform on the side of the first car back of the fuel car. The camera crew set the camera up on it and the operator tried it for panning. He had plenty of room to make a smooth pan. My son, Joe, who was by now a top stunt man, got into his fire suit and put the double's costume over it. I picked a good open bank that was around forty feet high and steep enough to make a fast roll. At the bottom, about where he would stop rolling, was a small thicket which could hide a special-effects man who would be ready to put the fire out at the end of the roll.

When all was ready, we started the train. It got under way fast and the operator rolled the camera. On a signal, a special-effects man set Joe on fire, and he leaped out of the cab looking like a human torch. He hit the snow, which was three or four feet deep, and rolled end over end down the slope. When he stopped the snow had put the fire out. The camera got it all in one take.

I spent a couple of days shooting straight travel shots on mountain sides, through tunnels, and across high trestles. In one sequence, as we neared the end of the long climb, the caboose and one car, which was loaded with horse soldiers, is mysteriously cut loose from the train and starts backwards down the tracks. The troop car's doors are locked and the frantic men are trapped inside. A stunt man, doubling the brakeman, climbs to the top of the caboose and tries the brakes, which have been disconnected. He then goes down between the two cars to try the brakes on the troop car. As he gives the brake wheel a hard pull, it spins loose and he loses his footing and falls, but manages to grab hold of the lower platform rail with one hand. Keeping his legs doubled up to avoid hitting the railroad ties, he gradually pulls himself back to the platform, where he works in vain to open the rear door of the troop car.

I made set shots of the two cars going faster and faster down grades and across trestles, filming scenes from the top of the caboose shooting down as the rails and ties passed under the car in a blur. I had to wreck these two cars, but this was our last scene on the location.

In the meantime, we had to film an Indian attack on the train. This was a joint operation—the first and second units working together. Our location was near the village of Reubens, adjacent to the Nez Percé reservation. As I mentioned earlier, these Indians are known for their horsemanship. Jackson Sundown, a nephew of the famous Chief Joseph, won the world's saddle-bronc riding championship at the Pendleton Roundup in 1916. A champion at age fifty, he rode in competition on the rodeo circuit well into the 1920's. I knew him quite well during my own rodeo days.

Like all train and Indian fights, we made use of dynamite as bombs. The Indians chased the train, which was finally stopped—explosions went off among the Indians and many were knocked off their mounts in spectacular falls. Two or three were shot off the top of the car after transferring from their running ponies. We did a full shot as the ammunition car blew up and the cavalry arrived. A big man, by the name of Doug Atkins, who had been a pro football player, was playing one of the heavies. He was on foot and had a huge balsa wood club. My son, Joe, was riding with the cavalry and swinging a saber when this big villain slammed him across the chest, shattering the club. Joe turned a back somersault over the rear end of his running horse. It was a really rugged gag. Of course, we did the usual mop up and the Indians were chased away.

After the main scenes were shot, the first unit went back to Los Angeles and left a number of pickup shots for me to shoot. The wreck of the two runaway cars was the big one. I looked over the railway carefully and found an ideal place for the wreck. Here, the tracks came out of a cut about fifty feet or so from a high trestle that crossed a canyonlike cove. I checked the light and found that to get good results, we would have to shoot between three-thirty and four-thirty in the afternoon.

I then talked with the head man of the railway company in that area, and he sent the foreman and crew up to the site to look it over. The foreman made it clear that we would have to shoot the scene on Saturday or Sunday, that being the only days that the track was idle. I explained how I intended to film the wreck and that in order to be sure that the stunt worked, the track would have to be cut and swung over to the side of the main line to a point even with the near end of the trestle. The foreman agreed and said that he and his crew could start right away and get everything set so that the rails could be moved out from the main tracks Friday afternoon.

I cleaned up all the pickup shots Friday and went up to check on their work. I found that the rails ended about fifteen feet short of my mark. I was certain that the wreck would have been a flop had I used the track in that condition so I drove back to Lewiston and called the head railroad man and told him what had happened. I explained that I couldn't gamble. The company had bought the cars and there could be no second take.

"If you can get the crew up there by daylight," I said, "I'll be there to show them what I want. We can't shoot until the sun is right, which is about three-thirty in the afternoon."

I was there at daylight and so was the railroad crew. They

thought that the gag would work okay the way the tracks were. I explained that if it didn't work, the cars would be broken up and we would have to buy two more cars and spend another week before we could shoot again.

"Gentlemen," I said, "I have a reputation to maintain and I can't gamble the company's money unless I'm reasonably sure of the outcome."

"I don't know if we can get the work finished in time," the foreman said dubiously.

"We can't if we spend too much time talking," I answered flatly.

The foreman grinned, motioned to his crew and they went to work.

A little before three P.M. they had the tracks extended. I used six cameras, which were all placed and ready. My main setup was covered with two cameras, one shooting normal speed and the other slow motion. Earlier in the week, I had worked out all the details with my assistant and had made a mile run which was timed. This was so that we wouldn't waste film and would give each operator time to be sure all cameras were rolling before the cars ran onto the last stretch of track to the wrecking point.

When all was set, the cameraman and operators watched for the signal, a white flag which was to be raised off scene where all could see it. The action started—the cars were on the way and all was quiet. Then the white flag waved and all the cameras were turned on. It seemed to take a long time but in scenes of this kind, there is always that tension. The cars loomed up and came off the track through bushes and out into a long dive, hitting the canyon wall and rolling down to the bottom.

Jerry Gershwin was standing back of me watching. . . . He looked at me and said, "Beautiful!"

Three British stunt men perch perilously on top of a moving cable
car in *Where Eagles Dare*, the World War II spy film with
action directed by Yakima Canutt. (From the
MGM release *Where Eagles Dare* © 1968)

With Joel McCrea and Walter Brennan at the presentation
of the Western Heritage Award, 1971.

Joel McCrea and his wife, Frances Dee, Yakima Canutt
and his wife, Audrea, after Yak's induction into
the National Rodeo Hall of Fame, 1976.

TWELVE

Careers

Looking back over three careers—as rodeo contestant, stunt man actor, and action director of motion pictures—I am very proud of the accomplishments that placed me in the National Cowboy Hall of Fame, and that in 1966, earned me an Oscar from my peers in the movie industry. In 1978 it was my privilege to be honored by the Academy of Motion Picture Arts and Sciences with a dinner billed as "A Tribute to Yakima Canutt." I think I can say that my head size is the same as it's always been, but I can't deny a real thrill when, in front of about nine hundred people, Chuck Heston introduced me as "simply the best that ever was at what he does."

Things have changed a lot during the course of those three careers. I saw changes even during my own rodeo years. At first we rode with two reins and there was no timing in the bronc riding. We rode until the horse stopped bucking and either started running or stood still. In 1914 we began riding with one rein.

My first ride with timing was in 1920 or 1921 at El Paso, Texas, in a Tex Austin show, which I won. As I remember, the timing was ten seconds, starting when the horse cleared the chute.

In the early days some shows used snubbing horses. However, in the last of the teen years all were using chutes, and many shows had their own rules. The rules in saddle-bronc riding are still the same as they were when I left the rodeo field for motion pictures.

The majority of top bronc riders today are much better than when I was competing. Although there has always been a large number of bronc riders, in my day you did not have so many good ones to worry about. After watching the championship ride-off at Oklahoma City in December, 1976, during the time of my induction into the National Cowboy Hall of Fame, I had to admire the young contestants. In my day, when you went into the finals you were actually competing against a much smaller number of riders. Today there is a corral-full of top men, many of them college students who are paying their way through school by becoming rodeo stars. Many have never worked on a ranch.

I was really impressed by the way they rode. One after another came out of the chutes, spurring and raking from the horses' shoulders back to the saddle skirts. I tried to picture myself as a judge, deciding how I would mark their rides. It seemed to me that the judges would have to judge the horse, not the rider. The majority of contestants spurred all the way, right to the gun, and of course the way a horse bucks is certainly a big factor in the contest. As in all competitive events, rodeo records will continue to be shattered—which is really the name of the game.

I was not the only rodeo man who went on to Hollywood. There was Cliff Lyons, for instance, who came into pictures about the same time I did. Cliff was a man who stood about five feet eleven and weighed a hundred and eighty-five, give or take a bit. I used him in most of my silent movies and we did many stunts together.

Cliff was a bit on the awkward side, but he had a lot of guts. He was featured in a couple of silent films, and like most cowboys, he liked to rib. His work was mostly horse and wagon stuff. He was a lousy swimmer, yet he did quite a lot of water stuff, wearing a life belt. He also became a second unit director, although he didn't do a lot of pictures. Cliff was one of my very close friends, and I let him copy all my stunt equipment.

My career as an actor was really bad. I was featured in about twenty silent films, did all my own stunts, and even doubled some of the actors who worked with me. In those days, in the 1920's, stunts were done haphazardly. In bulldogging a man off a horse, you would ride alongside him, grab him and pull him off. He would usually fall between the horses and never fail to get stepped on by one or both of them.

It didn't take long for me to figure out that there were better and safer ways to do stunts, so I started creating good stunt equipment and having it made. It really paid off—both for me and the companies for whom I worked.

When the talkies came, I knew my voice would stop me as an actor, so I decided to settle for stunt work, and hung my shingle out as an all-around stunt man. Most of the stunt men in those days were classified as high men, water men, horse men, etc. However, they all did fight scenes and scenes where they drove cars. There were also two or three motorcycle men.

One of the casualties of the dangerous work that the earlier stunt men did was Jean Perkins. He was killed just at the time I came to Los Angeles in October, 1923, so I never met him, but he had a reputation as a very good stunt man.

He was doubling William Desmond starring in a Universal serial, and was supposed to do a transfer from a ladder hanging beneath an airplane to a train. Paulie Malvern, who was on the train at the time, told me how it happened—it's a sad story.

Jean was climbing down the ladder as the train came on and he slipped down and grabbed a lower rung. The pilot of the airplane approached the train at an angle, and Jean was slammed against the car and was hurt. He couldn't climb the ladder, so he turned loose and fell about forty feet. He hit the ground in a standing position—his leg bones ran through his shoes and several inches into the ground.

Paulie left the train and ran to him—he told me that the bone was sticking out of the flesh three-quarters of the way to his knees. The poor fellow was taken to the hospital and died on Christmas Day.

Some of the stunt men—like Chick Collins, Allen Pomeroy, Jack Stoney and a few others—seemed to resent cowboy stunters taking fight jobs. They felt that they should stick with horses. I ran into this problem when I got a call from Fox Studios to double Henry Fonda in his first motion picture, *The Farmer Takes A Wife.* He was to fight Charles Bickford, whom Jack Stoney was to double.

I had never worked with Stoney and when we met, he didn't seem very anxious to talk with me. I learned why, when another cowboy I knew came to me and said that Stoney was real upset that the company had hired a cowboy to do a fight scene with him. This fellow warned me to watch out for Jack.

I replied that I was in good condition, and if Stoney wanted to play rough, I'd play rough too.

When we began to fight he *was* pretty rough, so I started to throw punches on a par with his. After a couple of takes my shoulders and chest were a bit sore, but I was convinced that he was also a bit ouchy. He finally turned loose with a haymaker that I stopped with my left shoulder. It nearly put that arm out of commission.

I decided that it was Stoney or me. I threw a punch that really hurt him. We went into a clinch and rolled on the ground, really fighting. The director hollered "cut!" and glared warningly at us.

"What's the matter with you fellows?" he demanded. "It doesn't have to be that rough."

"I thought we were going pretty nice," I replied with a grin.

Stoney didn't say anything, and we did the rest of the fight the way stunt men should.

At the finish of the fight, I congratulated Stoney. "I like the way you fight, nice and easy," I said, straight-faced.

"Get away from me," he growled, and walked away.

However, in a short time we became good friends.

At that time, there were a number of stunt men in pictures who were a bit clannish, and tried to keep new men out of the business. I felt just the opposite way. I was always on the lookout for promising new stunting cowboys, and by working hard to get good equipment—like the open "L" stirrup for falls from horses, or jumps to runaway wagons, or over a running horse to take the rider off—we soon had a number of good stunting cowboys. We were able to break the clannish group and start an organization.

As in any line of work, you are bound to have a bit of trouble at first, but it wasn't too many years before the stunt men were a congenial group, and if a new man showed up wanting to get into stunt work there was always someone to give him a hand. In my day I took a number of men on a job—if they had what it took they were in, and that's the way it should be.

Some of the stunt men of today have a big organization. It also seems that some of them have a stunt school. A few weeks ago, I answered my doorbell and a young, athletic-looking man said that he was a stunt man who had done quite a few stunts in New York, and that he was wondering if I could help him get into the stunt organization.

I gave him the names of some people that I thought could help him. I wasn't working on any pictures at the time, or I would have at least tried him out.

He came back a few days later and said that he had met several stunt men, but that they had a stunt school, and they told him he would have to go through their school before he could get into movie stunt work. The fee would be five thousand dollars!

I had never heard of such a deal, but in talking to some of my friends I found out that his story was true. A few of the stunt men were actually setting up schools. To me it sounded disgraceful. During my stunting and directing in England, Spain, and Egypt I had set up schools and trained men and horses for stunt work, but they were being paid while they were learning. I have also trained new stunt men during the shooting of a picture and had no trouble getting good work out of them.

The Hollywood stunt men of today are a different breed from what we were. I understand that some of them do a bit of drinking while working. But different or not, most of them are tops. Some of their car and motorcycle stunts are terrific. There is a lad who is a real champ in high falls. His name is Dar Roberson and without a doubt, he is the greatest. He started working in 1973.

One of Roberson's high falls was off the top of a ten-story building, in Los Angeles, onto a huge airbag. A couple of years ago he did a fall from the top of the Astrodome in Houston—200 feet. His highest fall was from a helicopter to his air bag three hundred and eleven feet below.

Another fine high man, A.J. Boakunas, from New Jersey, came out to California to break Dar's high-fall record. He fell three hundred and twenty-one feet. His air bag practically exploded, and he was killed in the fall. Not too long ago, a stunt man drove a sedan off a dock into the Pacific Ocean. He never got out of the car. The same stunt could have been done without any danger.

When I received the Academy Award Oscar in 1966, the citation said, in part, that the award was for "achievements as a stunt man and for developing safety devices to protect stunt men everywhere."

I think that my safety record is what I am most proud of. I would like to close this account of my life with my best wishes to all stunt men.

The Films of Yakima Canutt

Editor's note: Yakima Canutt's long and varied film career, as silent-film actor/star, stunt man, and action director, encompassed hundreds of films, both silent and sound. Many of them were "blood-and-thunder" quickies produced by small studios long out of existence. In addition, this dean of Hollywood stunt men doubled in many short scenes in more important pictures and for these appearances, again, no record exists except that of the memory. This filmography, therefore, cannot be complete, although it includes all of the memorable pictures in which, in one capacity or another, Yakima Canutt played so important a part.

Silent films include the serials:
1920s   Branded a Bandit (Arrow)
        Ridin' Mad (Arrow)
        Romance and Rustlers (Arrow)
        Scar Hanan (FBO)
        Riding Contest (FBO)
        King of the Rodeo (FBO)
        White Thunder (FBO)
        Hell Hound of the Plains (Goodwill)
        The Iron Riders (Goodwill)
        Bad Men's Money (Bell)
        The Cactus Cure (FBO)
        Wild Horse Canyon (FBO)

Three Outcasts (Bell)
Captain Cowboy (Bell)
Riders of the Storm Ranch (Bell)
The Vanishing West (Mascot)
Fighting Stallion (Goodwill)
The Devil Horse (Roach)

1930 Canyon Hawks (BF)
Firebrand Jordan (BF)
Ridin' Law (BF)
Lonesome Trail (Bell)
Bar-Z Ranch (BF)

1931 Westward Bound (Bell)
The Pueblo Terror (Cosm.)
Hurricane Horseman (Artc.)
Lightning Warrior (Mascot)

1932 Two-Fisted Justice (Monogram)
The Devil Horse (Mascot)
Cheyenne Cyclone (Columbia)
Wyoming Whirlwind (Capitol)
Telegraph Trail (Warner Brothers)
Hurricane Express (Mascot)
Shadow of the Eagle (Mascot)

1933 Scarlet River
Fighting Texans (Monogram)
Sagebrush Trail (Monogram)
Law and the Lawless (Majestic)
Via Pony Express (Majestic)
The Three Mesquiteers (Republic)

1934 Lucky Texan (Monogram)
Texas Tornado (Monogram)
West of the Divide (Monogram)
Blue Steel (Monogram)
The Man from Utah (Monogram)
Randy Rides Alone (Monogram)
The Star Packer (Monogram)
Fighting Through (Monogram)
'Neath Arizona Skies (Monogram)

1935　The Last Days of Pompeii (RKO)
　　　　Lawless Frontier (Monogram)
　　　　Circle of Death (Monogram)
　　　　Paradise Canyon (Monogram)
　　　　Dawn Rider (Monogram)
　　　　Westward Ho! (Lawless Range) (Republic)

1936　King of the Pecos (Republic)
　　　　The Vigilantes Are Coming (Republic)
　　　　Darkest Africa (Republic)
　　　　San Francisco (MGM)
　　　　Rose Marie (MGM)
　　　　The Oregon Trail (Republic)
　　　　Winds of the Wasteland (Republic)
　　　　Wildcat Trooper (Amb.)
　　　　The Lonely Trail (Republic)

1937　Trouble in Texas (GN)
　　　　Ghost Town Gold (Republic)
　　　　Riders of the Dawn (Monogram)
　　　　Roarin' Lead (Conn.)
　　　　Come On, Cowboys (Republic)
　　　　Riders of the Whistling Skull (Republic)
　　　　Range Defenders (Republic)
　　　　Gunsmoke Ranch (Republic)
　　　　Riders of the Rockies (GN)

1938　Mysterious Pilot (serial) (Republic)
　　　　Army Girl (Republic)

1939　Stagecoach (UA)
　　　　Wyoming Outlaw (Republic)
　　　　The Kansas Terrors (Republic)
　　　　Cowboys from Texas (Republic)
　　　　Gone with the Wind (MGM)
　　　　Man of Conquest (Republic)
　　　　Jesse James (20th Century Fox)
　　　　The Light That Failed

1940　Pioneers of the West (Republic)
　　　　Ghost Valley Riders (Republic)
　　　　The Ranger and the Lady (Republic)

Under Texas Skies (Republic)
Frontier Vengeance (Republic)
Young Bill Hickock
Virginia City (Warner Brothers)
Dark Command (Republic)

1941   Prairie Schooners (Columbia)
The Great Train Robbery (Republic)
Gauchos of Eldorado (Republic)
They Died with Their Boots on (Warner Brothers)
Idaho (Republic)

1942   Gentleman Jim (Warner Brothers)

1943   Shadows on the Sage (Republic)
In Old Oklahoma (Republic)

1944   Pride of the Plains (Republic)
Hidden Valley Outlaws (Republic)

1945   Sheriff of Cimarron (Republic)
Dakota
Sunset in El Dorado
The Untamed Breed

1948   G-Men Never Forget
Red Stallion of the Rockies (Eagle Lion)

1950   The Showdown (Republic)
The Devil's Doorway (MGM)
Rocky Mountain (Warners)
The Great Missouri Raid

1951   Only the Valiant (Warner Brothers)

1953   Ivanhoe (MGM)
Mogambo (MGM)
The Naked Spur (MGM)
Battle Circus (MGM)
Knights of the Round Table

1954   The Lawless Rider (Republic)

1955 The Far Horizons (Paramount)
   Westward Ho, the Wagons (Walt Disney)

1956 Helen of Troy (Warner Brothers)

1957 Old Yeller (Walt Disney)

1958 In Love and War (20th Century Fox)

1959 Ben Hur (MGM)

1960 Spartacus (Universal)

1961 El Cid (Allied Artists)

1962 Son of Captain Blood (Paramount)

1964 Fall of the Roman Empire (Paramount)
   Swiss Family Robinson (Walt Disney)

1965 Cat Ballou (Columbia)

1966 Khartoum (United Artists)

1967 Where Eagles Dare (MGM)
   The Flim-Flam Man (20th Century Fox)

1968 Blue (Paramount)

1969 A Man Called Horse (National General)
   Song of Norway (ABC Pictures)

1970 Rio Lobo (National General)

1973 Breakheart Pass (United Artists)

1976 Equus (United Artists)

Afterword

Dear Yak:

If you capture a mite of the printable experiences
that we went through during the Wayne period of
your life, the feeling of our industry in the '30's and
'40's will come to life for the generations since.

[signature: John Wayne]

John Wayne

Index